Praise for *He Talk Like A White Boy*

"In *He Talk Like a White Boy*, Phillips addresses issues of race, identity, and cultural values with humor, passion, and a great deal of insight. It is a page-turner that teaches, inspires, and motivates us to look deep into the better part of our American selves. Phillips is a new and refreshing voice that I think has broad appeal across the political spectrum."

—*J.C. Watts*
Congressman

"*He Talk Like a White Boy* is the latest entry in an emerging literature of dissent from black writers who have grown tired of seeing themselves through the prism of an exhausted civil rights ideology. This book is part of a historical correction, but what makes it a good read is the story—an American story—of Joseph C. Phillips. Here is a life that meets the great challenge for blacks today: not to go out and win freedom, but simply to accept the freedom that is already here. Here is a man in full protest against a black identity that has become afraid of freedom. And, in the end, he talks only like himself."

—*Shelby Steele*
Senior Fellow, Hoover Institute and award-winning author of
The Content of Our Character

"Unless you're describing your divorce, addictions, or terrible childhood, it's no mean feat to put yourself out there the way Joseph Phillips does and create a book so hard to put down. *He Talk Like a White Boy* is heart and soul in high style."

—*John McWhorter*
Senior Fellow, The Manhattan Institute

"This book makes the case—through study, reflection, experience, and personal observation—that success results from hard work, deferring gratification, and refusing to play the roll of 'victicrat.'"

—*Larry Elder*
Syndicated Radio talk show host and New York Times *best-selling author of*
The Ten Things You Can't Say in America

"If you haven't heard of Joseph Phillips yet, you soon will. He's a young writer who appreciates the solid values of family, faith, community, and self-reliance that provide the most effective engines for long-term success. In an era of excessively partisan commentators, Joseph cares less about what's right or left than what works! Welcome to the pantheon of punditry, Joe."

—*Clarence Page*
Syndicated columnist for the Chicago Tribune

"Joseph Phillips is a true renaissance man. We all know of his skills as an actor, but few of us knew of his tremendous writing ability. From page one, I was completely engaged with his essays. Joseph Phillips' ability to seamlessly transfer his most heart-felt emotions to paper is remarkable. I recommend this book to all of us trying to understand the many and varied relationships of our lives. Not only will you recognize yourself within these pages, but you will learn so much in the process."

—*Hope Sullivan, Esq.*
President of The Sullivan Foundation

"Yes, Joseph C. Phillips is a conservative, but *He Talk Like a White Boy* is ultimately an uplifting story about the potency of dreams. Phillips begins with a tragic tale of loss and survival and ends with an affirmation of the power of dreamers to transform society."

—*Binyamin L. Jolkovsky*
Editor in Chief, JewishWorldReview.com

"Don't buy this book. Don't borrow it from somebody else. And for heaven's sake don't read it! Unless, of course, you enjoy having all of your precious notions about life altered for the better. Now that I've read *He Talk Like a White Boy*, I'm having a very tough time getting all these new ideas out of my head. SAVE YOURSELF!"

—*Robb Armstrong*
Nationally Syndicated Cartoonist and creator of the comic strip, "JumpStart"

"*He Talk Like a White Boy* is an enthralling piece of work! In many ways, Joseph C. Phillips challenges his readers to consider thinking original thoughts with honesty. This book is definitely a page-turner!"

—*Tony Magee, MS, MBA*
Author of Can't Shove a Great Life into a Small Dream:
12 Life-Essentials to Grow Your Dreams to Match the Life You Want

"Phillips provides an insightful and poignant analysis of the socio-political issues affecting African American men. His wide-ranging commentary vividly tackles the principles of raising young children amidst the myriad of societal influences, maintaining a successful relationship, and the importance of family generally. His perspectives expressed throughout the book are simultaneously refreshing, thought provoking and inspirational. America has a new voice in the social commentary arena and his name is Joseph C. Phillips!"

—*Alvin Williams*
President and CEO of Black America's Political Action Committee

he talk like a
white boy

he talk like a white boy

by Joseph C. Phillips

RUNNING PRESS
PHILADELPHIA • LONDON

9 8 7 6 5 4 3 2 1
Digit on the right indicates the number of this printing

Library of Congress Control Number: 2005929974

ISBN-13: 978-0-7624-2399-6
ISBN-10: 0-7624-2399-4

Cover design by Whitney Cookman
Interior design by Bill Jones
Edited by Diana C. von Glahn
Typography: Adobe Garamond

This book may be ordered by mail from the publisher. Please include $2.50
for postage and handling.
But try your bookstore first!

Running Press Book Publishers
125 South Twenty-Second Street
Philadelphia, Pennsylvania 19103-4399

Visit us on the web!
www.runningpress.com

For my family:

My beautiful Monkey,
Stinky Molloy,
Crusty Flannigan,
&
Lumpy Sandoval

All that I have.
All that I am.

CONTENTS

Faith

Idealism

Identity

ACKNOWLEDGMENTS

Thanks be to God from Whom all blessings flow.

I am simply not smart enough, talented enough, or pretty enough to have completed this book by myself. I was blessed with family, friends, and associates who gave their time, talent, and encouragement in order to see this endeavor came to successful fruition.

Thanks first to my brother Tavis Smiley, who pulled away the underbrush and showed me the road. There is no question that this book would never have been written had Tavis not challenged me. Though we disagree on a great many things, he believed I had something important to say and threw down the gauntlet.

Thanks also to John McWhorter who reassured me over and over again. To Orville Lynch, who gave me space in his paper without ever having read a word, and the editors of the other publications in which my column runs for saying, "Why not?" I would be remiss without also offering heartfelt thanks to the staff at NPR for providing me a forum, my sister Lisa for being a good sport, Wheaton James for his incredible imagination and vision, and my best buddy Leonard for telling me to walk the road with more confidence.

I would have been lost without Pamela Thornton at the Columbus Post who edited my column for three years; Kim Tolley, who now enjoys that task; and Diana von Glahn of Running Press who provided editorial guidance. Special thanks and a big hug to Elyse Dinh-McCrillis who has been with me from day one, editing countless rough drafts of the book, organizing essays, and offering an incredible amount of encouragement all without ever having met me face to face. I may never have been in the presence of her person, but I have been in the presence of her beautiful spirit. Thank you.

I am also grateful to Denise Pines for all her assistance, Vanesse Lloyd Sgambati for making a phone call, Carlo DeVito for returning her call and to Sam Caggiula for seeing the potential (and introducing me to "the Palm, baby!") Thanks also to the rest of the staff at Running Press for their enthusiasm. Let's do it again!

Most of all, I must thank my family: My beautiful wife Nicole, My sons Connor, Ellis, and Samuel. I never realized writing a book would take so much time away from them. I thank them for their patience and for not playing on daddy's computer.

There are, no doubt, many others who contributed kind words, advice, encouragement or who, through heated conversations, provided me with information and perspective. Though space does not allow me to mention you all by name, please know that you have not been forgotten and your support was appreciated.

FOREWORD

I often think that the *C.* in Joseph C. Phillips' name stands for *courage*. It takes a lot of courage these days to be black and Republican-especially in Hollywood. It takes a lot of courage to write and say things that aren't politically correct, or to challenge black leaders and the beliefs held by many black folk in this country. It takes a lot of courage to share the personal pain and joy of marriage and fatherhood. It takes a lot of courage to simply broach the subject of race or racism, even among people who look like you. And perhaps most of all, given our differences on so many issues, I would have to say it takes a lot of courage to ask ME to write the foreword to this book.

I met Joseph years ago when he was starring on NBC's *The Cosby Show*. I am still a die-hard Cosby show fan, and I've always been amused by his role as Denise Huxtable's husband, Lt. Martin Kendell. It was funny to see how often his character illustrated the contractions and stereotypes that exist in the black community regarding patriotism, gender roles, and family values. It wasn't until he became a regular commentator on my National Public Radio show that I came to understand and appreciate that he actually champions many of these same issues in real life.

Joseph's thoughts on politics reinforce the fact that being African American and a conservative Republican are not mutually exclusive. Whether he's talking about R & B or reparations, his regular commentaries, many of which are contained in this book, offer a fresh, unflinching approach to the tough questions and answers regarding love, leadership, responsibility, and authority often debated in Black America and beyond. Political ideology aside, Joseph eloquently expresses the idea that in an era of corporate scandals and general moral decline, basic principles matter. I couldn't agree more.

Joseph's writing is perhaps most passionate when it comes to the issue of fatherhood. The father is often perceived as someone absent from the African American family, but this book shows another side to that image—one depicting a black man as a supportive and nurturing parent. Using his own childhood as an example, Joseph explores the relationship between fathers and sons in all its diversity and complexity. And he doesn't just "talk the talk." I've seen him in action with Connor, Ellis, and Samuel—his three beautiful boys. Whether it's his stoic approach to discipline or his longing to upstage his wife in managing the household, his experiences will either make you laugh out loud or shake your head in disbelief.

He Talk Like A White Boy is a poignant portrait of Joseph's life as an actor, activist, writer, husband, and father. This book provides considerable insight into American culture and delivers valuable messages to everyone-black, white, young, old, Republican, Democrat-about character, relationships, family and the daily struggle each of us face to make a difference.

Whether the essays in *He Talk Like A White Boy* make you feel at home or heated, you will find them provocative, inspiring, and at times even entertaining. I don't share Joseph's love affair with cowboys, but I do share his appreciation for what it means to be a hero-someone who strives to lead by example.

—*Tavis Smiley*

INTRODUCTION

Writing helped me do a couple of things. First, it motivated me to finally clean my office. I had papers everywhere-books, CDs, computer discs, and junk stacked a foot high on my desk. I found it difficult to think with all that clutter. I sifted through the mess and gave myself a clear space in which to work.

Second, it helped me clear the clutter from my mind. For years these stories and thoughts have been piling up inside me and, quite frankly, my wife told me she was tired of hearing them. "Why don't you write some of that stuff down?" she asked. I began putting pen to paper. Before I knew it, I had a weekly column that was appearing in newspapers across the country and one of the best roles of my life: a regular political and cultural commentator on "The Tavis Smiley Show" (and later on "News and Notes with Ed Gordon") on National Public Radio.

As I wrote, a pattern began to emerge. I realized there were a handful of themes I continued to revisit again and again. The essays that follow are drawn from my weekly column and commentary. Some have been rewritten and some are new, but all of them reflect those recurring themes: my love for America, my belief that the values that make the black community strong also make America strong, and my life as a husband and father who is also black in America.

I have grown tired of hearing people badmouth America. I love my country and claim it as my own because I believe America is good. And to those who would question my allegiance to a nation that once enslaved folk who looked like me, I answer that I proclaim my Americanness precisely because my people are in the soil. Our roots extend deeply into the mud of Mississippi, the dust of Texas and Arizona, the red clay of Colorado, the black earth of Virginia and North Carolina, and the sand of New England. This nation is mine! I claim it boldly and without hesitation, and I dare anyone to try and deny me my full inheritance.

I originally called this book *Cowboys and Colored People* from an old joke told by the late great comedian Flip Wilson. Wilson tells the story of an encounter he had with an Indian named Henry. While at a party, Wilson pulls Henry aside and advises him that it's time the Indians got their act together. Wilson points out all of the progress black people have made over the years, noting the prominence of African Americans in sports and entertainment and their emerging political clout. Wilson even suggests to Henry that black people would be willing to change the name of the NAACP to the "National Association for the Advancement of Colored People Immediately and the Indians on a Gradual Basis." After a time, Henry is fed up and responds, "Yeah, you may be right, but I never heard of anyone playing 'Cowboys and Colored People.'"

(I admit my retelling does not do the joke justice. A joke fails to remain funny after some knucklehead has explained and analyzed it to death. I urge you to either hunt down the original album recording on Atlantic Records or check it out of your local library.)

It's a tribute to Flip, a master of his craft who, in 1967, was so deftly and humorously able to point out that, in spite of the great social and economic strides made by black people, we had yet to weave ourselves into the fabric of Americana. We had not received our full inheritance. We had Ralph Bunche, Willie Mays, and Sidney Poitier in the mid- to late sixties, but we remained stepchildren in America.

Needless to say, the publishers didn't like my title. In fact, they hated it. But the soul of that idea is still a part of what this book is about. The forward progress of this nation and of black people in asserting their citizenship cannot be turned aside. We are stepchildren no more, even if at times we seem unwilling to accept that reality. The doors of opportunity are flying open at an obscene pace. No, we are not quite at the mountaintop but we are within view. To paraphrase John McWhorter in his book *Authentically Black*, life is not perfect but certainly we can make our way up the last few steps to the mountaintop by pulling in our stomachs and forging ahead.

Of course black folk are not supposed to say that, at least not in public.

The day after my high school graduation I was at my friend Jerald's house. His older sister was commenting on the previous day's ceremony and complimented me on my commencement address. "You gave a good speech," she said. "You sounded really smart," to which she added, "You sounded white." I looked at her cross-eyed and asked, "Did you hear what you just said?"

Of course this was not the first time I had heard this, nor would it be my last. The charge of sounding white had haunted me all through school and would haunt me well into my professional acting career. "Joseph, do it again and this time try to sound more black." I have been black all my life. How can I be *more* black? I told this story to the publisher and wham! There was the title of the book. As I shared it with friends and family, it seemed to resonate. A great many people, it seems, shared my experience and agreed that to assert a belief in black self-sufficiency is not a betrayal of the race. Here is another important theme of this book. The essays between these covers explore the attributes that I believe to be the core strength of the black community, namely: faith, character, idealism, and family values. Oddly enough, these attributes also represent the core strength of America.

Writing about America's strength, French philosopher Alexis de Tocqueville said: "I sought for the greatness and genius of America in her commodious harbors and her ample rivers, and it was not there; in her fertile fields and boundless prairies, and it was not there; in her rich mines and her vast world commerce, and it was not there. Not until I went to the churches of America and heard her pulpits aflame with righteousness did I understand the secret of her genius and power. America is great because America is good. And if America ever ceases to be good, America will cease to be great."

The apostle James said: "I will show you my faith by my works."

The goodness of America begins with faith and so too the goodness of men. Faith is the beginning because faith inspires behavior, which is character manifest. In other words, faith is the bedrock on which notions of charity, justice, and morality are built. The conviction that character counts-that principles and values are important-is the definition of idealism. And in no place is our idealism, the modeling of character, more important than in our families. The family is really the incubator of the next generation of citizens and citizen leaders. Family values really mean the disciplining of our children in standards of behavior in order that they grow to be adults who humble themselves before God and infuse their lives with a greater sense of purpose.

It is my heartfelt belief that children raised in faith grow to be men and women with a true sense of morality and justice. Children raised in faith grow to be leaders of men, instruments of change and healing; because of their faith, character, and idealism, they grow to be lovers of and guardians of liberty. Moving away from these values weakens our families, which weakens our communities, thereby weakening our nation.

Finally, this book is about me. Like most of us good folk here in Hollywood, I love to talk about myself. However, on these pages I am not merely shamelessly self-promoting; I am telling *my* story.

Years ago, when the John Singleton film *Boyz N the Hood* opened to critical acclaim, I remember hearing Singleton say during an interview, "Finally the truth of what it is like growing up black in America is being told." I thought, *whose* truth? That may be *your* truth but it is certainly not *my* truth. In my 'hood the nights were filled not with the sound of helicopters hovering overhead but the sound of water sprinklers and crickets, and snow falling during the winter. Not only was my 'hood integrated, we somehow managed to get through the day without gang fights and drive-by shootings. Sure there were fights and drinking and dope. I imagine Denver during the seventies was like most other metropolitan cities with its share of drugs, sex, and rock 'n' roll, as they say. But there was also hope. We talked about doing great things with our lives—starting families, going to college, and changing the world. Our dreams were not constrained by race or hindered by pessimism. The realities of the world were not lost on us. We were just a generation that believed all things were possible.

I've grown tired of the one-dimensional portrayal of black life in our cultural discourse—the pessimism, nihilism, and hedonism. I have grown frustrated by the limits imposed on black individuality by white liberals and I have grown impatient with the limits that are just as often imposed by the black community. It seems an obvious notion then that if you don't tell your own story, someone else will tell it for you and you may not be happy with what they have to say.

Quiet as it's kept, black people like me exist and I grow more convinced every day that more and more black people share my thoughts on a great many subjects. They share my belief in the dynamism and vitality of the black community and my belief that this is a great nation not because of the good things we have, but because of the good things we believe. They feel betrayed by the progressive leadership that has led us away from the principles of faith, character, and idealism and they are waking up to the need to rededicate ourselves to the traditional values on which this nation was founded. The old paradigm is shifting and a new black thinking is emerging that will carry us well into the twenty-first century and finally the last few steps up to the mountaintop.

Although I like to make speeches, I am not a politician. Nor am I an academic. I am a husband and father of three boys, a man who loves to cook and watch western movies. I am an actor who has had a whiff of celebrity and liked the way it smelled, and I am a black man whose politics tend toward the conservative and who, much to my wife's dismay, happens to have an opinion on just about everything.

Welcome to my world.

—JCP

CHARACTER

Membership Card

Let me take you back-September 1974. A little Seals & Croft playing on the AM transistor radio, maybe some Three Dog Night. Denver, Colorado. This is where my story begins. Like so many autumn afternoons in Denver, the brightness of the sun belies the crisp chill in the air. Place Junior High school, eighth grade English class—not just regular English, mind you, but *accelerated* English class. My teacher was Miss Smith. Her class stands in my mind as a monument, a shrine to all that is cold and cruel about this world.

I don't remember what the class discussion was about, but after an undoubtedly brilliant and insightful observation on my part, a black girl from across the room raised her hand and announced to the class, "He talk like a white boy!"

I don't know what this had to do with the discussion or why she felt the need to share that little observation with the rest of the class. But one thing I do know is that in an accelerated English class, the teacher should have corrected her immediately.

"No, LaQueesha. Joseph *speaks* like a white boy! Class, repeat after me. 'Joseph speaks like a white boy.' Now, LaQueesha, you try."

"Miss Smith, Joseph speaks like a white boy!"

"Very good."

Bam! I was thrust into the spotlight. (And me not even knowin' how to tap dance!)

What did LaQueesha mean? That I spoke clearly? Intelligently? That some timbre was missing from my voice? At twelve, should one *have* timbre? I didn't know then and still don't know now. But that moment was not only the beginning of junior high school, it was the beginning of my life.

The man I am today has its genesis in that moment. In that instant I became acutely aware that I was different. Until that moment, I never realized there was something wrong with the way I spoke, that answering questions in class was acting "white."

I never knew how ugly, or hurtful, the words "Uncle Tom" were. In that moment, the tyranny of opinion—the notion that there are some people empowered to stand at the doors of a culture and determine who and who is not welcome—was made painfully clear to me. *My* definition of blackness-more accurately, my black self-was unimportant. That decision was left to the anointed, and no matter how idiotic, arcane, or nihilistic their definition, any deviation would be dealt with swiftly and decisively.

So there you have it. At the tender age of twelve, with no warning whatsoever, my membership credentials to the brotherhood were confiscated and ripped to shreds. The mere difference in how I spoke—the sound of my voice, my diction—clearly meant that I was trying to be something I wasn't, that I was an infiltrator, and that difference, real or perceived, made me an outsider.

I have been writing a weekly column for more than three years. During that time, I have occasionally received mail from people who disagree with me. The letters are mostly polite, even if they sometimes strain for that politeness. Like other folks who decide to offer their opinions for public scrutiny, I have also received my share of correspondence that is not so polite. The comments range in anger from "you have no idea who you are" and "your thoughts are dangerous to black people" to being called "Stepin Fetchit," a reference to the black film actor, Lincoln Perry, who was known for playing subservient shuffling servants to white masters in the 1920s, 30s, and 40s. I recently received an email from a group called Conscious Black Citizens for Negro Reform informing me that I had been nominated for the Sambo/Uncle Tom of the Year Award. According to the group's email, their objective is to "out" politicians, entertainers, and other public figures who are betraying the race.

It would appear that things have not changed all that much since eighth grade. These charges are quite frequently leveled anonymously and rarely, if ever, do they address the substance of whatever I allegedly said that makes me a traitor. Like the little girl in my eighth grade English class, they are content to simply comment on my lack of adherence to their definition of blackness. In their minds, I no longer *speak* like a white boy, I now *think* like a white boy.

The hazard with this type of collectivism is that the bar is always moving. An editor for one of the papers that publishes my column took offense at an essay I wrote in defense of a local proposition that would have outlawed California's collection of racial data. In the article, I made an appeal to begin taking steps to move beyond the artificial construct of race. For this gatekeeper, my stance was anti-black and unworthy of publication (though she was outvoted by her editorial board and my piece was allowed to run as scheduled in spite of her objections). What does it say when appeals for brotherhood, once a mantra of the Yippie generation, are now deemed traitorous? It is a fool's game, one that honest men cannot win.

The criticism has also come from sources much closer to home. My older sister, Lisa, whom I love dearly, tells me, "I'm ashamed to tell people that my little brother is a Republican!" She doesn't understand how my wife can bear to sleep with me. I have a younger sister who has alternately been a lesbian, a drug addict, in and out of mental hospitals, and on the run from debt collectors most of her adult life. But I have never heard Lisa say to her, "I am ashamed of you," or "I don't know how your husband sleeps with you." (Somewhere between the lesbianism and the drug addiction, baby sister decided she had to get married. It's all very complicated.) But *me* she is ashamed of.

Of course, I am a rather minor player in the cultural scheme of things and I suspect very few people have ever heard of the Conscious Black Citizens for Negro Reform, nor are they likely to. I am also fairly certain that if push came to shove, my older sister would prefer me to be a Republican than a drug addict. At any rate, this is a microcosm of what happens in larger society.

Witness the treatment of Ward Connerly, the University of California regent who authored and pushed through Proposition 209, the initiative that outlawed affirmative action in California. For daring to question the morality of affirmative action quotas and insisting that black children are capable of competing with white children, Connerly was called everything but a child of God. During a debate with then California State Senator Dianne Watson (now congresswoman), the senator accused Connerly of being ashamed of his heritage, proof of which could be found in his marriage to a white woman. I had a discussion with another editor about a piece in which I only mentioned Connerly's name. The editor said that Connerly wakes up in the morning looking for ways to deny opportunities to black people. This editor added, "I hope he burns in hell." Pretty strong stuff.

John McWhorter, a former linguistics professor at Berkeley and a black man, wrote a book entitled *Losing the Race: Self Sabotage in Black America*. The *New York Times* review of his book concluded he really hadn't been exposed to African-American culture and was therefore not black enough to write about black people with authority. A fellow professor denounced him as a "rent-a-Negro." Shelby Steele, who had the temerity to suggest that current black leadership had grown rich on the currency of race, is sneered at. Walter Williams and Thomas Sowell, the economists who, among other things, have argued that the black middle class did not spring from affirmative action or the welfare state, are routinely ignored by the mainstream press and were miraculously not included in a list of public intellectuals compiled by "race expert" Michael Eric Dyson in his book *Race Rules*. During a debate sponsored by the Maryland chapter of the NAACP, Republican candidate for Lieutenant Governor, Mike Steele, was pelted with Oreo cookies, referencing the Cabinet choices made by George W. Bush. Liberal attorney and talk-show host Gloria Allred referred to Colin Powell and Condoleezza Rice as "Uncle Tom types." And need we even begin to address the black community's complete ostracizing of Clarence Thomas, an associate Justice on the United States Supreme Court?

The black monthly magazine *Ebony* refuses to include Justice Thomas on their list of "100 Most Influential Black Americans." One could easily make the argument that he is perhaps the *most* influential black person in America. The decisions he makes every day affect black Americans far more than the rather mundane edicts handed down by the heads of the black fraternities and sororities that are regularly included on the list. In an episode that displayed the utter absurdity of this thinking, an elementary school in Washington D.C. asked that Justice Thomas not appear at the school to speak to the children. Apparently a number of parents complained that he was not a proper role model. The schools had no such complaints, however, when they invited the crack-addicted, philandering former mayor of D.C., Marion Barry. Yep. Much better that the children should hear from a real black hero like Marion Barry than from a tyrant like Clarence Thomas—*Uncle* Thomas, as he is routinely referred to by black "leaders" like Al Sharpton.

The substance of the ideas put forth by these men is rarely argued. Their characters however, are routinely attacked and maligned. They are threatened with death! They aren't black. They are Toms, one and all! They are traitors to the race because they have chosen to think outside of the accepted black liberal dogma. They are— hide the women and children—CONSERVATIVES!

What remains unclear is who anointed these folks the right to stand at the door checking ideological credentials and confiscating the cultural membership cards of those who refuse to hoe rows on the liberal plantation? From whom do they get their authority? Quite simply, they have no authority except that which we grant to them.

In his book *Fatheralong*, John Edgar Wideman points out that *race* is part of *racism* and *racist*. The very notion of race grew out of an effort to distinguish that which was not white. In playing race we play a game in which "the fix is in. . . . The inventor of race always holds the winning cards because he can choose when to play them and name their value." This too is the source of the racial guardians' power: Using the same tool used by those they call oppressors, these gatekeepers define those who view the world with different eyes as "less than" and the accusation is evidence enough of its veracity. The attempt to *defend* oneself from the scurrilous charge that one is a race traitor means that one is *defensive* and only confirms for them (and those that listen to them) that they are correct. They argue, "He wouldn't be defensive unless he felt guilty for the subversive thoughts in his head."

During a break between shooting segments of the syndicated talk program *America's Black Forum*, I was verbally attacked by liberal journalist Deborah Mathis. Interrupting a conversation I was having with another panelist, she spat out, "I just want to know one thing: Why are you conservatives so fucking defensive?"

Without missing a beat I responded, "Perhaps it is because people we barely know curse at us."

"Well I don't like you," she shot back.

"Good. I guess that means you don't have to speak to me, right?"

More ugliness ensued with her cursing like a sailor until I finally had to call the producers. Mind you, she never once took issue with any of the arguments I had made during the course of the program. Her attack was personal!

You see, as guardians, the anointed have the power to define what is traitorous and what is not and to put value on certain behavior when it serves them. Imagine if I had cursed at Deborah Mathis in front of a studio audience. My inappropriate behavior would have signaled the bankruptcy of my arguments. To the guardians however, Deborah's inappropriate and unprofessional behavior is seen as a righteous defense of the race.

Better yet, imagine the debate between Ward Connerly and Dianne Watson over a matter of policy. Watson leaps outside the substance of the issue to attack Connerly's racial pride. If Connerly responds in defense of his choice (indeed, freedom) to marry a white woman or any woman he pleases, he proves Watson correct. If he protests that he is in fact proud of his race, he proves Watson correct: why is he being defensive? No matter that renowned black figures like Frederick Douglas, Jack Johnson, Johnny Cochran, and, yes, even Deborah Mathis had interracial marriages. For the purposes of *this* debate on affirmative action policy, interracial marriage explains Connerly's traitorous views. The crowd applauds its approval.

The threat of banishment or being "put on silence" cannot be underestimated. I think all people search for a sense of belonging and the menace of being on the outside is often much more frightening than being deemed "that which is not."

This black and "not black enough" stuff is to me like that old vaudeville routine, "Slowly I turned." Two actors are on stage. There is a thought or a word that just sets one of the actors off. The straight man, while trying to carry on a conversation, can't help but say that word and every time he does, the other guy gets crazed and starts a rant with: "Slowly I turned. Step by step inch by inch . . . . It makes me angry." All the old tapes in my head begin to play. The email I received from the CBCNR took me back to those days in the eighth grade. Here I am, a 40-year-old man letting silliness like this get under my skin. It made me want to fight—not argue, but hand out a good old-fashioned butt-whooping like they do on the street corner! The irony is that I am fairly certain this cat would never approach me on the street in such a disrespectful manner. Chances are he would see me as a celebrity and smile, want to pose for a picture, shake my hand and ask what it was like to kiss Halle Berry in *Strictly Business*.

Unfortunately, black students who are harassed and teased if they do well in school or "talk white" do not have the benefit of semi-celebrity status. If they read books, if they get good grades, if they involve themselves in school activities like debate and Key Club or any organization outside of those deemed acceptable by the junior anointed, they are subjected to the threat of being cast aside and ignored. For every student who refuses to buckle under the tyranny of opinion, there are those who cannot withstand the harassment and fold under pressure. If anecdotal evidence means anything, I can testify to the reality of the pressure placed on youngsters to conform.

In my youth, I wanted so badly to fit in. I wanted to be a regular black kid like the other black kids. And I tried.

My best friend, who also lived in a white neighborhood, left private school and started eighth grade in a public school a few miles away from mine. Like me, after that first week, he felt like an outsider and wanted to fit in. So the first weekend after school, we tried. We spent the entire weekend calling each other niggers. You know, like "Nigga, please!" Or, "Nigga, whatchu talkin' 'bout." Except our proper English kept getting in the way. So for us it was, "Nigger, please!" And "Nigger, what are you talking about?" All weekend it was "nigger this" and "nigger that." By Sunday night I was exhausted! My head was spinning. I just couldn't do it anymore. It felt unnatural, as if I was putting something on. It felt as if I were denying who I really was. My buddy, on the other hand, continued working on his dialect and I imagine it has been thirty years or more since he has hit the "r" in nigger.

Maybe I should have followed my buddy's lead. I have often wondered if my life would be different today had I continued trying. The only thing I am certain of is that I would have had greater success with women. Let's be honest. I am a healthy heterosexual male and more than anything else, talking like a white boy has hit me most often where it counts—my ability to get nookie! I discovered much to my chagrin that black women in particular suffer from something called the Not Black Enough Syndrome.

Black women like the jive talk. I wish I were joking but I am not making this up. It is an actual syndrome! Not only have I lived it, but it is also documented in the book *Black Rage*, written by two black psychiatrists, William H. Grier and Price M. Cobbs. Experts! Page 127! Check it out for yourselves. (I've got it memorized!) And I quote: "A group of black men was asked to describe their techniques of seduction. Without exception each said that at a crucial point he reverted to the patois." But they went further. "Black women said they experienced an intensification of excitement when their lovers reverted to the 'old language.'" I remember reading that and saying to myself, "Do you mean to tell me that the only thing standing between me and unlimited romance is patois?" I couldn't help but get a little giddy at the prospects. Of course then it occurred to me—as was pointed out in the eighth grade—that I don't have the patois!! I fell to my knees and pleaded with God, "WHY? WHY DON'T I HAVE THE PATOIS?"

The book goes on to say, "Finally, Shakespeare demonstrates in *Henry V* and *Othello* that a man who is confident of his strength and powers may enter the arena of love disavowing verbal facility. That his passion, directness and virility convey an eloquence unattainable by ordinary men." (Sure, if you have the patois, you don't even have to ask; women just throw it at you!) "For the black man in the United States, the boudoir is a field of combat in which rightfully or not he is deemed by his society pre-eminent. His use of the patois, like Shakespeare's hero's, may dramatically highlight an already heroic presence." No comment.

I will offer as proof the crush I had on Robin Givens. I dated Robin Givens *years* before she was *Robin Givens*. I was really laying down my best stuff. I wore my good cologne and was so clever, telling my best little jokes, trying to sound sophisticated, discussing art and politics. I even got in good with her mother. But nothing! Don't get me wrong, she was friendly enough, but I was getting nowhere. Of course, later she married Mike Tyson. Yes, Tyson had fame and fortune. However, later on, I met a couple of white guys who dated her—white guys who, as my grandfather would say, "didn't have a pot to piss in or a window to throw it out of" and who frankly just weren't as cute as me. Then I heard her on a radio interview with Howard Stern talking about how she loves really thuggish black guys. She also said she liked corny white guys, but not corny black guys. (Yes, I took this just a bit personally.) What a gyp! I go to school, stay out of trouble, really try to make something of myself, but the street thug gets to make love to Robin Givens? What the hell is that about?

Well, I refuse to fake the funk for anyone, including Robin Givens! I feel quite comfortable with who I am and am urging all corny black guys to embrace the sentiment. In fact, we should form a group. We can call it the NAACCP—the National Association for the Advancement of *Corny* Colored People. We'll petition black women to give us equal access to the booty! Are you with me?

Fortunately, there was a happy ending. Years after rebounding from my Givens snub, I met and fell in love with a pretty young black woman with red hair and freckles who would eventually become my wife. Oddly enough, while we were dating I would speak to her on the phone and find myself thinking, "She talk like a white girl!" It was a match made in heaven.

I have been having an interesting discussion with a friend about gradations in culture, specifically that there are some traits unique to a people that define them and that the degree to which a member embodies those traits gives him more cultural caché. That is to say, it is possible some black people *are* blacker than others (and I suppose, conversely, some white folks are more white than others). My friend argues that these gradations have always been present; what changes is which traits we choose to emphasize at any given time.

I am curious how I might fare on my friend's current blackness scale:

Black English—The sound and syntax, the turn of phrase, the inflection. As an actor I can do this, but it is not my normal way of speaking. In fact, hardly a week goes by without someone commenting on my "proper" speech. An actor I worked with years ago nicknamed me Professor Lombooza Lomboo. He swore that the professor was an actual character from his Trinidadian youth who one day waded too far out into the ocean. Instead of hollering, "Help! Help!" Story has it that he called out, "Excuse me, may I have some assistance please?" ("LaQueesha, repeat after me. . . .")

Food—A taste for and appreciation of home cooking or soul food. Bonus points are given if one has a propensity to add hot sauce to just about everything. I get high marks on this one. Much to the surprise of those who have always seen me as near black, I grew up eating chitlins, pigs' feet, greens, and cornbread. To this day, my wife cannot believe that I actually ate something called a pig-ear sandwich or tasted head cheese and *liked* it. I also have three or four different brands of hot sauce in my pantry.

Dancing—A sense that one's style is an expression of whatever is in the soul. There is a kind of suave looseness on the dance floor that women find sexy in men. It makes them think that the guy will move like that in bed. A note to the ladies: he doesn't! And you wouldn't want him to. Not with these new dances, anyway. One of y'all would need traction! I do get some credit in this area. I am a great chair dancer! So long as I am sitting down, I can rock my head and snap my fingers and look like I can really get down. It is only when I stand up that my feet and hips refuse to move in coordination.

Christianity—Not just growing up in the Christian church, but growing up immersed in a particular style of worship. Gospel music, black preachers, call and response, 3-hour worship services, and dinner prayers that can last as long as twenty minutes. I am a Christian. However, I was raised in the Episcopal Church—not AME, just regular Episcopal. We sang hymns, no one spoke back to the pastor, and like most protestant services we were in and out in an hour—less when my mother attended. She always left promptly after taking communion, shaving about five or six minutes from the service. Of course, so much of this is style over substance. Witness the many musical performers who record lyrics featuring misogyny, murder, and sex, who accept awards wearing barely any clothing and announce: "First and foremost, I would like to thank my Lord and savior Jesus Christ. . . ." I guess I split on this one.

Facial expressions—The ability to "read" people with a look or a purse of the lips. Black people are very expressive and black women especially. Women roll their necks when they get angry, roll their eyes when they are incredulous, and suck their teeth when they are annoyed. Black men too cut their eyes and are famous for the look that, in the words of Grandmaster Flash and the Furious Five, says: "Don't push me cause I'm close to the edge." Alas, according to some less-than-kind reviews of my acting work, I *have* no facial expressions so I will pass on this one.

Walk—The way some black men walk with that cool, that confidence, that rhythm. I walk normally without the pimp in my step. I have found that walking with that little hitch takes too much time and throws my back out of whack.

Sense of style and high fashion—Dressing fancier than whites would on the same occasion and a love of bright colors and fanciful patterns. Anyone attending a Baptist church on Easter Sunday can attest to the truth in this. Black women love to parade their new Easter hats looking as if they are preparing to take flight and blocking the view of everyone sitting behind them. I do like the sense of occasion that accompanies getting dressed up. It shows respect for the occasion. Though I am developing an affinity for more colorful garments and taking risks with style, I am not quite ready for purple suits or blue shoes. A simple tux or dark suit and a nice tie still does me quite nicely, thank you very much.

Music—This one requires a knowledge of or affinity for soul, R & B, or gospel music. I love 70's R & B, but my collection of Gene Autry albums, alas, does not qualify.

Black names—A person with roots in the culture will be able to sniff out a black name. I must admit I do have a nose for that. I am not talking about the obvious names like "Tameeka" or "Shaundell". I can often sniff out the more subtle names. I can not count the number of times I see a name on a document or hear that I am supposed to see Mrs. Frieda something or other, or a Mercedes and know instantly this is a black woman. An Asian friend of mine asked me how I would know this, is Frieda a black name? I just replied that it is a black thang and she wouldn't understand.

Open style of courting—I am skeptical of this one. My buddy defines this category as being more open to overt advances during courtship. He contends that black women are more likely than a white woman to take as a compliment a group of construction workers whistling at her. I have a sneaking suspicion that women, no matter their color, don't appreciate this. I know that when I walk past a construction site and the men whistle at me, it gives me the creeps. At any rate, as evidenced by my Robin Givens story, my courting style has always left much to be desired. The fact that I am married and have three children is purely an accident of nature. I fail this one.

Loud talking—The big laugh. He calls it "turning it out and mixing it up." I might add to this the annoying habit of talking back to the movie screen. I score very high on this. I love to get loud and at home I talk to the television screen all the time. It drives my wife crazy.

Love of basketball—On this one I fail completely. I watch about as much basketball as I do golf, which is to say hardly any. Football is my game and as far as I am concerned, autumn is the only time of year real sport is played.

And finally,

A sense of rebelliousness—From Nat Turner on up to Malcolm, there is a tradition of struggle against the Man—of fighting the power, as the rap group Public Enemy might say. Of all the aforementioned traits, this one is perhaps the most important. It *is* possible to not play basketball and remain "authentically black." However, as another friend put it, "there remains the idea that unless you are professionally angry, you are missing some crucial element." I would like to think that I score rather high in this area. Though my experience tells me that when one is as vocal about the perils of white guilt and black victimhood as they are about the evil of racism, it somehow doesn't count.

So there you have it. I didn't do too badly. I lost some crucial points with the Gene Autry music, but I think I was able to rebound with the pig-ear sandwich.

Noticeably absent from my friend's list are academic excellence, intellectual pursuits, and entrepreneurial skill—all of which I believe black people have—and that is one of the bothersome aspects of discussions such as this: The cultural traits so often ascribed to us seem so superficial. Unlike other peoples who would be described as literate, business-minded, or ambitious, we are relegated to the back of the cultural bus where there is loud talking, lively dance, and bright clothes. Worse, lists such as this tend to become more than just innocent fun, they become currency on which our culture is traded. Fearful of being labeled "less than," we rush to become authentic and in so doing we begin to define our culture downward. We embrace a music genre that celebrates violence and disrespect towards women. Doing well in school and reading books become anti-black, joining the debate club instead of the basketball team is anti-black as well, speaking correctly becomes "talking white" and thinking outside the accepted dogma is thinking white.

I recall reading an article not too long ago featuring a well-known celebrity discussing his children. The article quotes the father as saying he is most proud of the fact his teenage son is one of the better junior basketball players in the country. A few sentences later, the writer (not the father) mentions that the boy is also on the honor roll. It struck me as odd. Certainly any parent would be proud that his son is a terrific athlete. I must admit that I would be likely to boast a bit if my son were one of the better ball players in the country. To be *most* proud of this fact, however, strikes me as having one's priorities misplaced. We can be happy that our children are active and enjoy athletic prowess, but it better serves us to describe ourselves culturally by our intellectual prowess.

It certainly wouldn't be outrageous to describe black culture as being one of accomplishment and industriousness. At the close of the Civil War, black Americans were almost ninety-nine percent illiterate. One generation later we had created colleges and universities, had thriving business centers and an entrepreneurial class that was growing. We were practicing law and medicine; we were architects and craftsmen. Today, just 130 years removed from bondage, we sit on the heads of major corporations, run city and state bureaucracies, are leading experts in the fields of medicine and law, and set trends in music, fashion, and pop culture. There was a time in this country when men of letters were celebrated. It would not be unusual to find photographs of intellectuals like W.E.B. Dubois, Paul Robeson, Langston Hughes, or Zora Neal Hurston hanging in black homes. Today, we brag about our sons' field-goal percentage.

Even accepting my buddy's list as incomplete, the very fact that there are so many areas of crossover—white kids who can rap, white girls who can shake their groove thang as well as or better than any sista, white boys who can charm the pants off any woman, and white families who get loud in public—suggests either that black culture covers a broad spectrum and that some of us live in different places along the spectrum, or that there is really is no such thing as a black culture *per se*. Perhaps there is only an American culture that includes many races and covers a broad spectrum of behavior and many of us live in different places along that spectrum.

For what it's worth, I have in my lifetime felt "that which is not." But more often than not I have felt myself less southern, less citified, more privileged, smarter than, not as smart as, less talented, more talented, and better looking than a whole lot of folks both black and white. Maybe that is why I prefer the latter implication, if only because it moves us beyond discussions of cultural and/or racial authenticity, cultural purity and racial prejudice. If the notion of what is black is a carryover of the racist efforts to distinguish that which is not white, don't our attempts to be defined by those very characteristics permanently exclude us from the mainstream culture? The effort then should be to move beyond race in search of some higher, common ground. We liberate ourselves from the tyranny of opinion through realizing a personal definition that draws on all things—all ideas—which can live in all houses on the human spectrum.

What Are We Teaching?

The history of this millennium will be determined by today's teens. Recent experience has made me a bit nervous.

In an era dominated by the Internet, video games, and latchkey kids, who takes responsibility for our youth? Our teachers have the charter to provide an academic education, but what about the role of parents and the charge of society?

Not long ago, a friend invited me to speak at her school about my life as an actor. While I have made presentations to kids in every corner of this country, I have never been treated as rudely as I was by these seventh and eighth grade students. Students talked amongst themselves, read magazines, pulled out headphones and hand-held computer devices, and walked around the classroom while I was speaking. Mind you, this was not some inner-city jungle falling down around the student's ears. This school was a magnet attached to the University of Southern California, specifically for kids interested in the arts. Here was someone they recognized from television and movies speaking to them and they could not have cared less. It did occur to me that they found me uninteresting. Unlikely, but I suppose not out of the question. But boredom is one thing; disrespect is another.

One of the classes only asked questions about whether the love scene in the film *Monster's Ball* was real. You may recall that *Monster's Ball* is the film for which Halle Berry won an Oscar. The film was controversial in part because of a couple rather explicit love scenes. Actually, the expression "love scene" may be a little misleading. As they say on the street, "Love ain't had nuttin' to do wid it." The scene was softly pornographic. We may disagree on the worth of that film, but I am certain all reasonable adults will agree that the film is inappropriate for young teenagers. Yet, according to these kids, they had seen the film with their parents' permission.

Children who sneak lollipops into class and find it difficult to sit still for a guest speaker are not responsible enough to handle discussions of an explicit sexual nature.

Those who agree with me are not provincials or old sticks in the mud. We simply believe that we respect our children when we make the conscious decision not to pollute their minds with concepts they are not emotionally prepared to handle.

As often happens with my own children, I found myself raising my voice. It soon dawned on me, however, that I was not morally or legally responsible for those knuckleheads and I had better things to do with my time than take their abuse. I quietly explained to the kids that I had pulled myself out of bed very early in order to be there and I was sad they were so lacking in manners. Some of the kids seemed a bit remorseful, but most just smirked as I gathered my things.

As I wished them luck in the future, one student, with typical adolescent audacity, asked me for an autograph. Needless to say, I politely declined.

I remember well the silliness with which my junior high classes often greeted guests, but understand that I am distinguishing between general childhood precociousness and out right rude and disrespectful behavior. I cannot ever recall having a speaker walk out on a class I attended, and if one had, we would have been horrified. Not these kids.

As I discovered not too long afterwards at my son Connor's school picnic, the disrespect I encountered at the junior high school begins developing from an early age.

There was a small pond at the park where the picnic was held and most of the kids wanted to ride in the paddleboats. There was quite a line and as little kids are wont to do when faced with a long wait they began to grow skittish. Some of the children began throwing rocks into the water. The lifeguard asked them to stop. My son threw rocks and I asked him to stop. Not too long afterwards another boy began throwing rocks in to the water. Again the lifeguard asked him to stop throwing rocks. The little boy replied, "Are you the boss of me?" My jaw dropped. If there is one thing I hate it is smart-mouthed children. Always one to stick my nose in to things I replied, "Yes, he is your boss. Don't throw rocks." The boy spat back at me, "Are you his sidekick?"

Now I was really stunned. "Is that the way you were taught to speak to adults?"

"Yes."

"Little boy, where is your mother?"

Much to my amazement, the boys' mother was standing right behind him listening to every word.

There is no question that I indulged in my share of brazen behavior as a boy. I didn't just start to share my opinions the other day. Like all children, I pressed for limits. The difference is when I was a child, insolence carried a price. More than once I received a tongue lashing from an adult or a phone call to my parents that resulted in some heat being applied to my backside. Back-talking an adult in front of my mother or father would have been to take my life into my hands.

I looked to the boy's mother as if to ask, "Are you going to allow this?" His mother's response? A smile and a rather weak, "Josh, what is wrong with you?"

There are two things I know with certainty: this is not the first time Josh has been disrespectful of an adult and if he is disrespectful of adults in general he is more than likely disrespectful of his parents. And disrespectful little boys grow into disrespectful men. If I had to offer a guess, I suspect there is little chance he respects other children and no reason to believe when he grows up he will respect his peers.

What is wrong with Josh is he has not learned to respect his elders and mind his manners. His parents are failing to build this boy's character. I don't profess to have any solutions, but I suspect a quick smack to the back of that boy's head might do wonders for his disposition. It certainly would have lifted mine.

It may be unfair to single this mother out. There were a number of ill-behaved children at the picnic and she was one of many befuddled parents I witnessed. I have never heard so much back-talking to parents in my life! Little girls and boys telling their parents what they would and wouldn't do, others were disregarding instructions from volunteers and their parents simply accepted this as if it were the natural order of things.

Episodes like this and the debacle at the junior high school are not isolated events. They happen every day all over this country and I believe it is a direct result of the casual attitude with which we approach the interaction with and discipline of our children.

One of our neighbor's children insists on calling me by my first name. I am a bit old school when it comes to how one addresses an elder. I am over forty and if a man is older than I am, I will still refer to him as "Mister." I still find it difficult to address my mother-in-law by her first name. This little boy is eight years old and can't understand why I can call him by his first name but I ask him (repeatedly) to address me as "Mister Phillips." And he is not the only one. I find myself correcting children all the time. It's "Mister Phillips." They look at me as if they have never heard of anything so absurd. When my son ventured down that road and was corrected by me, he demanded to know why. "You are a little boy and they are adults," I replied. "It is disrespectful to call an adult by their first names. It implies that they are on the same level as a 7-year-old boy."

The casualness with which we approach discipline is also to blame. When children are taught that values are without purpose, that morality is subject to opinion and honor is a commodity to be bought and sold on a whim, it is no wonder they smirk and disrespect their elders.

Okay, so Josh's mother should have disciplined him, but what about my friend? Why didn't she or one of the other teachers step in to admonish the students at her school? In all fairness, she did and was largely successful. The instructor for the other classes had a tougher time of it. The children didn't listen to him any more than they were listening to me, and quite frankly, it becomes impossible to try and give a presentation when you are being interrupted every minute and a half with, "Sit down! Put that away! Pay attention! Stop it!" And honestly, I am not certain what more teachers can do. If they act too severely to enforce order and discipline they risk invoking the wrath of parents.

Recently in California, a school vice principal came under intense fire for lifting girls' skirts in order to check for G-string panties before they could gain entrance to the school dance. Parents protested the violation of their children's privacy and called for her resignation. The vice principal was placed on administrative leave. While I do not advocate panty monitors in our schools, it does seem a bit curious that parents would raise such a stink. Many of these same parents are seemingly unconcerned with issues of privacy during school hours. The teenage girls I see walking to the schools in my neighborhood are dressed provocatively, oftentimes with their G-string panties prominently displayed for the world to see. They didn't buy all those clothes themselves and they didn't leave the house with their parents unaware of how they were dressed. Isn't it worse for their daughters to regularly display their wares to little boys with raging hormones?

I am not so old that I do not remember being in junior high and high school. We saw a lot less skin in those days and it was still difficult to concentrate on algebra. It's a wonder that some boy has not sued for sexual harassment. I think that rather than complaining about their little angels' hurt feelings, the parents might have considered thanking the vice principal for having the courage to teach their daughters that modesty is of value and that class and character walk hand in hand. Whatever happened to taking pride in being considered a lady?

My friend called me to apologize for her students' behavior. Apparently, when the school's principal got wind of what happened, she gave the students a rather stern lecture and insisted they write me letters of apology. A nice gesture, but a lesson I fear will be lost on the kids. How many other guests have been treated as rudely? Were they too offered letters of apology (which, by the way, have yet to arrive)?

I often hear that children are growing up too fast nowadays, but maybe they are just growing in direct proportion to the amount of responsibility parents are abdicating. As parents, we are the vanguard, the lions at the gate. Nothing should enter or leave our homes lest it pass by us first. As guardians of the next generation our moral messages must be clear. The respect we demand from and give to our children is the same respect they will in turn give to others.

Macy

Macy is a friend of mine who lives up the street. Macy is seventeen years old and spent the last year battling bone cancer. While her classmates spent their senior year in high school planning for college, dating, and buying Prom gowns, Macy was in and out of the hospital and watching her hair fall out from the chemotherapy treatments.

Macy confided in me that when she found out she had cancer, she called her friends to let them know. Only five returned her call. Perhaps her friends were uncomfortable with her bald head and the weight she gained. Girls her age tend to be preoccupied with such superficialities. However, I suspect it was because mortality is not a word in the teenage lexicon. At seventeen, the world is bright, responsibilities few, and the future an empty canvas waiting to be filled. The notion that you might not be around to celebrate your eighteenth birthday just doesn't occur to someone so young. No doubt her friends were confused—even frightened—when confronted with this reality.

I can recall the death of a classmate of mine soon after her twenty-first birthday. She had contracted Leukemia but was determined to graduate from college. The summer before our senior year, she passed away. At her funeral, amidst the tears of her family and friends, sat row after row of her classmates stunned into silence that someone so young could simply die. Mortality slapped us in the face. We woke to the realization that no one promised us tomorrow.

This past spring, Macy attended her graduation and I understand that many of her old friends didn't recognize her. "What was your name again," they asked. Had it really been that long? Had her appearance changed that much? Or is it that life simply moves on; not only theirs, but hers as well. Macy had outgrown her classmates during the year. If they didn't recognize her, perhaps it was because Macy is no longer a little girl with the petty concerns of adolescence—who's dating whom, whether she is wearing the latest fashion, or there is a pimple on her face. The struggle of this past year gave her maturity and an appreciation for what is truly important in life—a perspective that has not been grasped by those other teens.

This preoccupation with trivial matters is not only unique to young people. How many of us spend far too much time on equally petty concerns? Here in Hollywood, we dash about seeking fame and fortune, forming relationships with people who don't care about us any more than they can use us to enrich themselves.

My wife and I discovered Macy was ill quite by accident. We were on our way out to dinner. Our regular babysitter failed to show up and after exhausting the list of friends with children, we remembered Macy. I ran up the street and happened to catch her father in the driveway. "We're desperate," I told him. "Our babysitter hasn't shown up and we are already an hour late for our reservation."

"I'll check with Macy," he said. I followed him inside and found Macy wrapping her bald head in a scarf. "Interesting look," I quipped. "Yeah, well I have cancer," she said shyly. "Great," I said, "You want to get going? I'm really late."

It took a while for the news of Macy's illness to sink in. When it did, it hit us like a ton of bricks. Here was a seventeen-year-old girl certain to lose part of her leg and unsure if she would live out her teen years. We were worried about being late for a dinner reservation and angry that our babysitter had failed to show. On the way to the restaurant, we pulled the car over and said a prayer for Macy and for ourselves. Please, Lord, help us get our priorities straight!

I know in her moments of solitude, Macy struggled with fear and resentment, but I never heard her complain. I do not know if I would have carried myself with as much dignity and grace. Something tells me I would have stayed indoors, cursing God for cheating me of my precious life. Not Macy! I can't tell you how many times I called the home only to be told, "Macy's not here now. She's out with her friends."

Sunday was Macy's birthday. She turned eighteen and is cancer free. As I left her birthday party, she was showing off her new silver mustang convertible replete with leopard skin seat covers and vanity plates. She was celebrating the eighteenth year of her life surrounded by what really matters—a family that loves her and friends who support and pray for her. It was good to see her laugh.

People Are Worth More Than the Money They Hold

I was five years old when I met cousin Jimmy. He was on his way to Viet Nam and, not knowing if he would return, he stopped through Denver to spend a few days with my family. I remember following Jimmy around. He taught me how to tie my shoes really tight so they wouldn't fly off my feet when I ran fast. Dressed in his uniform, he seemed a giant to my small eyes.

I met him again fifteen years later when I moved to New York to finish college. He wasn't so big to me then. I had grown to four or five inches taller than him, but he continued to teach me things. His last lesson might be the most enduring.

Almost four years ago, we had a bit of a falling out. My grandmother (his aunt), who had been living with me, had died. Jimmy promised to send a check to help defray some of the cost of her funeral. The check never came and I didn't hear from him for two years. When I finally received a voice mail message from him, I was angry at being left in the lurch financially, so I chose not to return his call. I figured he should have to work to get back in my good graces. The odds were, he would call back and we would speak at that time. He never did. Recently, I received a call in the early hours of the morning, informing me that Jimmy had died.

The first order of business was to locate a will or any insurance policies. The search left my family sifting through the pieces of Jimmy's life and what we found gave us pause. These last few years had not been kind to my cousin. The small business he had been trying to nurture had gone belly up, he had accumulated massive amounts of debt, and had been suffering from one of the great unseen killers of black men: depression. It became clear that I never received the financial help Jimmy promised because he was flat, busted—broke! I didn't hear from him for two years because he had been too proud to admit it.

Damn foolish pride! Why couldn't he just embrace me and say, "Brother, I ain't got it." I would have understood. After all, my wife and I were also struggling at the time. The more significant question, however, is: Why was I so self-indulgent? Pride be damned twice! I was so intent on dramatizing my displeasure with him, I behaved like a child. How I wish I had humbled myself. I let valuable time slip by—time I will never get back. What's worse is that in my self-righteousness over what I perceived to be his lack of interest in taking care of family business, I forgot all the truly good and selfless things he did for me over the years.

Upon my arrival in New York, he took me under his wing. He carted me around in his Lincoln, took me out to dinner, came to every play I was in, and was a regular racquetball partner. Didn't this count for something? In hindsight, I realize its true value.

We all have moments of frustration, anger, pride, and self-indulgence. The struggle we face is in not allowing these passions to dictate our lives.

I learned a lot from Jimmy. After he died I learned a tough lesson about love and forgiveness, about moving beyond petty disagreements, about the importance of reaching beyond pride and embracing family and friends in the immediacy of today.

You never know what tomorrow will bring.

All That Glitters

My son Connor was a big, solid baby. We nicknamed him "Moose." When we took him out with us, people would see him and wink at me saying, "Future NBA star, huh?" or "Going straight to the NFL!" The automatic assumption of athletic prowess made me grit my teeth. I wondered whether these strangers would be making similar predictions if my son were white. It got so bad, I began responding with a few acronyms of my own: "Try PHD, DDS, or MD," I would say.

I am very sensitive to charges of anti-intellectualism in the black community, where there tends to be an over emphasis on excellence in athletics over academics. Truthfully, it is a topic that has been discussed to death and I struggled with writing this essay, feeling we have 'been there and done that.' But the other day, I had an interesting exchange with my son on this subject.

As we arrived late to his baseball practice, he whined, "Daddy, I'm late." I told him it was because he had to finish his schoolwork first. He's only in the first grade. I believe you must plant these seeds in kids' minds while they are young so they will bear fruit later on. "Sports are fun," I continued, "but books come first." My son looked up at me with big, brown, innocent eyes and asked, "Why?"

Soon after this conversation, it seemed I couldn't escape the smiling face of Lebron James. In anticipation of his professional debut, all the major news and sporting magazines began writing stories about Lebron and he began popping up on television commercials. Basketball is not a sport I follow, so the only thing I really know about Lebron is that he graduated from high school and chose to forego a college education to become an insanely wealthy professional basketball player. My son's question about the importance of his homework rang in my ears.

As parents, we want the best for our children. We lecture, discipline, and encourage in order to provide them with the means to go further and live better than we did. Part of our hope is that they achieve financial security. There are those who will quickly say that money does not buy happiness. These are people who obviously do not have any money. There's a reason wealthy people are described as "living the good life." Money makes life good. No, it doesn't chase away personal demons, but if one must visit the therapist's office, driving a Lexus sure beats taking the bus.

And let's face it, college isn't for everyone. With the amount of money at stake, the notion that any young person who's blessed with great athleticism should forego the opportunity to set himself up for life in order to pursue a college degree strains credulity. At nineteen, Lebron is earning more than $100 million in salary and endorsements. Very few college graduates will see anywhere near that kind of scratch.

So, why shouldn't my son and other black kids want to be like Lebron? (Hey, I want to be like him!) The answer is that Lebron James is the exception that proves the rule. Most children are not so athletically gifted. Of the handful of young black men and women who do excel in athletics and go on to play Division 1 college ball, two thirds of them will fail to graduate within six years. Of those who do manage to get to the professional ranks, their careers will last in the neighborhood of three years. No matter the ability, few will see the kind of professional or financial success realized by the likes of Lebron James.

One need only look to the trials of one of James' close friends, Maurice Clarett.

In 2002, as a freshman running back for the Ohio State Buckeyes, Maurice Clarett led the Buckeyes to a National Championship, breaking the team's single-season rushing record, and was named Big Ten Freshman of the Year. The following year, he was suspended for breaking about fourteen NCAA rules of conduct. Rather than swallowing his medicine like a man, Clarett pouted and threatened to leave the OSU program for the NFL. In the fall of 2003, Clarett's lawyers challenged the NFL league rule that requires players be out of high school for at least three years before joining the league. Clarett hoped to force a supplemental draft so he could make the leap to the fame and fortune of professional football. However, because he spent so much time with lawyers and advisors, Clarett was distracted from his education.

This is what my friend's mother would refer to as "missing a blessing." Because of their athletic ability, young men like Clarett are able to attend fine universities for FREE! How many students at OSU are working part-time jobs just to pay tuition? How many more were unable to attend due to finances or low grades? Yet, Clarett threw that blessing away for a possible seven figure NFL signing bonus. At the time of Clarett's suit, he was without a doubt a gifted football player, but the history of the NFL is littered with the names of gifted college running backs who failed to achieve success in the professional ranks. Running backs who—for my money anyway—were better ball players than Clarett.

Does the name Marcus Dupree ring any bells? At 6'2" and 225 pounds, Dupree was bigger, faster, and stronger than Clarett. After a brilliant freshman year with the Oklahoma Sooners, he had a falling out with then-coach Barry Switzer and left school. A year later, at age nineteen, he was playing pro ball for the New Orleans Breakers of the United States Football League. Dupree blew out his knee and, two years later, the career of one of the most exciting backs to play college ball was over. But Clarett and his advisors suffered from such a lack of humility, they believed that after just one year of college ball, Clarett would be a high first-round draft pick worth millions of dollars. However, there was also the very real probability that a running back who was not able to finish one full Big Ten season without injury and who demonstrated a severe lack of judgment and maturity would, at best, be a long shot for professional success.

Periods of great trial can often provide us with an opportunity for tremendous growth and even greater success if we only take the time to learn the lessons such trials present. How I wish Clarett had thanked his advisors, placed his lawyer's phone number safely away in a footlocker, and knuckled down on his schoolwork. Clarett could have used the year off as an opportunity to heal his body. Taking time to recuperate and train hard would have only benefited him. Further, accepting his punishment with grace and silence would have exhibited maturity and demonstrated to his teammates that he was a true Buckeye and not simply out for personal glory. Upon returning to the starting position the following season, he would have earned the respect of his teammates and would truly have been a team leader. But most importantly, a year without the pressure of playing football would have given him an opportunity to catch up on his studies and pick up a few more college credits so he could actually GRADUATE.

Clarett was three times blessed. I wish he had been thankful for the opportunity to eat his humble pie and spent the remainder of his time at OSU doing more than dreaming of dollar signs and taking up space. But as they say, if wishes were horses. . . . Clarett spent the following year at OSU doing nothing. He was so pitiful, he even failed black studies (for a black student, failing black studies is like failing gym class!)

After dropping out of college, Clarett showed up at the NFL recruiting combine in 2005 and ran a 40-yard-dash in a time more befitting an offensive lineman. Gone was the degree from a premiere university and gone were his dreams of first round draft riches. Clarett was drafted by the Denver Broncos in the third round of the 2005 draft and was eventually cut from the team never having played a down. I hope he didn't rush out and spend that big signing bonus.

The tragedy is that many young black men and women ignore the morality tales of the Claretts of the world and focus on the fairy tales of the Jameses. Many still see athletics as the lone and best path to success. *Sports Illustrated* recently published a disturbing story about 10-year-old boys playing football in Florida. Most of the boys were from single parent homes, raised in neighborhoods best described as "undesirable," with drugs and gangs infecting their communities. Of the boys featured in the story, none were doing well in school, but both they and their parents dreamed of their professional athletic success. Yes, sports can be a road out. However, a lot more time with academics and a little less time on the ball field/court is a more realistic avenue to success.

I should pause here. It occurs to me that one can't really talk about the importance of academics in our communities without also addressing public education. The fact is my son is not attending the same schools as the boys featured in the *Sports Illustrated* article. Chances are that their schools do not have a brand-spanking-new computer center, or a library stacked full of books, or a PTA that is actively involved in supporting the school. It is difficult to talk about this phenomenon and not also talk about the deplorable state of our public education system.

During a recent trip to Nigeria, I had the opportunity to visit a primary school in the heart of the capital city, Abuja. I was there with a delegation from Zion Baptist Church in Philadelphia to donate a computer to the school. Other members of the delegation donated pencils, schoolbooks, and periodicals. The welcome ceremony took place in the school's library, which consisted of a dirt floor, bare brick walls, no bookshelves, and no books.

My reaction was similar to one I had thirteen years ago when I visited a high school in Newark, New Jersey. I was there as part of their annual career day and while I waited to be assigned to a classroom, I was asked to wait in the library. The bare shelves and the lack of periodicals dumbfounded me. Later in the day, I sat in on a class and thumbed through the history book the teacher was using for the lessons. The most recent President mentioned in the book was Lyndon Johnson. There I was, in a major U.S. city, and the students did not have a functional library and were studying history out of twenty-year-old textbooks.

Sadly, in those thirteen years, not much has changed. In remarks delivered to the Manhattan Institute in September 2000, Cory Booker, a Democratic city councilman from Newark, told the story of a penny drive local school children had in order to purchase basic school supplies. Booker recounted tales of teachers begging him to help them get books for their classrooms.

This story is not unique to Newark. Similar tales are playing out in cities like Cleveland, Washington D.C., Milwaukee, Memphis, and Los Angeles. When my son started attending public school, parents received a notice asking us to provide teachers with reams of paper, boxes of pencils, glue, and other basic supplies. Imagine my chagrin when *The Los Angeles Daily News* recently reported that officials of the Los Angeles Unified School District (LAUSD) spent $16 million on conference centers and lavish hotels. There is a budget crisis in California. School programs for children are being cut, parents are being asked to make up the difference, and meanwhile bureaucrats are spending money on themselves as if it were Christmas.

Our children are lucky that we live in an area where parents can afford to pick up the slack. My wife and I are also blessed with the finances to send our children to private school if the public schools are unsatisfactory. But what about parents who have not been blessed with choices? They must look on helplessly while their children are forced to slog their way through substandard schools. And if these students *do* graduate, they are often unable to pass basic skills' tests and are under-prepared for college-level work. In the meantime, politicians continue to write checks and bureaucrats keep spending.

Is it any wonder parents in many less affluent neighborhoods look to athletics as the primary "ticket to ride"? Education is vitally important for later economic success, but when education fails, something must fill the void.

Waste and mismanagement impairs the effectiveness of our public schools and the failure of the school system wreaks havoc on our community. According to a report prepared for *The Black Alliance for Educational Options*, only fifty-six percent of black students graduate from high school. The numbers are slightly less for Hispanic students. Without a diploma, their prospects are dim. As the report states: "The median income for those who left school without a high school diploma or GED is $15,334 dollars compared to $29,294 dollars for people with at least a high school degree or GED."

The report goes on to say, "Students who fail to graduate high school are also significantly more likely to become single parents and have children at young ages. And students who do not graduate high school are significantly more likely to rely upon public assistance or be in prison." In short, education is the keystone. We cannot seriously address issues in our community like unemployment, poverty, or the integration of our nation's institutions without first drastically improving every child's chances of graduating with a quality education. Nor can we who value education compete with the lure of riches unless we find a way to energize our children to seek education for education's sake.

More money is not the solution. The city of Newark spends over $10,000 per student and yet children still do not have school supplies and teachers do not have books. It is time for us to begin thinking outside the box and that may mean we must redefine just what a public education means.

Is public schooling simply the brick and mortar buildings filled with children from a specific zip code? Or, is it more accurately, as Councilman Booker describes, "The use of public dollars to educate our children at the schools that are best equipped to do so."

The issue is not about the virtue of vouchers. It's about a real commitment to educate our children and how to give our children the skills necessary to compete in an increasingly demanding labor market. It's about expanding opportunity for our children and empowering parents with choices. Public dollars should go to those institutions that achieve results. Whether they are public or private, religious or secular should not matter. Regrettably, as long as the checkbooks are in the hands of politicians, schools will not be accountable to parents, and spendthrifts, like those in the LAUSD, will not be held responsible!

When schools in the world's most powerful and innovative nation resemble those in Third World countries, we should all bow our heads in shame. I'm not saying anything that has not been said many times before. But, it bears repeating until the message sinks in. Every day, there are millions of little boys and girls, just like my son, who ask why schoolwork must come before sports. We had better have an answer.

Children must understand that the more time and energy they invest into education, the greater the odds are that they will achieve success. Just as importantly, we must provide parents with the support that will deliver on the promise of public education because at the end of the day, school offers far better odds than the Russian Roulette Lotto that is the pursuit of athletic stardom.

I have been watching my son during his little league baseball games and, let us just say, he is not the next Derek Jeter. Having to face the question of him leaving school for the lure and riches of professional sports is not one I foresee. I do, however, anticipate having to coach him through a far more daunting life decision: Harvard or Princeton?

It's About Character, Dahling!

The first time I met Rosalind Cash, I fell in love with her. Roz (as I called her) was part of a panel discussing black images in the media. During the discussion, there was a lot of grumbling about "Coon shows" when I stood up and suggested we were perhaps being a little too hard on actors who took roles in debatably offensive programs when people had to put food on their tables. Roz said to me, "I have never been that hungry! And if you are ever that hungry, you come to my house and I will feed you." I tucked my tail between my legs and sat down.

Another beautiful, no-nonsense woman I adore is Angela Bassett. I fell in love with Angela more than twenty years ago when I was a contract player on the soap opera *Search For Tomorrow* and Angela was hired to play my older sister. We became fast friends and have remained so ever since.

As young actors in New York, we spent a lot of time together discussing the intricacies of the unemployment system, finding love in the Big Apple, and maintaining our sanity while waiting for the phone to ring. I can testify that she is a woman filled with grace and blessed with a terrific sense of humor and drama. Sit in the room with her for ten minutes and you know she was born for the stage. She may not have coined the phrase, "God don't like ugly. And he ain't too fond of cute," but she delivers it with more panache than anyone I know.

In 2002, not long after Halle Berry became the first black woman to win the Academy Award for Best Actress for her role in *Monster's Ball, Newsweek* magazine did an interview with Angela and asked her about the film and about Halle's award. Industry insiders had known for some time that Bassett had been offered the role and turned it down. While an actor turning down a role is commonplace in Hollywood, stories like this provide an endless source of intrigue for those outside.

Released in 2001, *Monster's Ball* is the story of a white, racist, prison execu-tioner who falls in love with the African American wife of the last man he put to death. Two people who are awash in death find a pathway to life through their unlikely love affair. The final image in the film is perhaps the most moving—while rummaging in the attic, Leticia Musgrove (Halle Berry) discovers Hank Growtowski's (Billy Bob Thornton) secret: he put her husband to death. Shaken, she goes downstairs and the two sit silently on the porch together. The film is about life and the need for human connections. The film also contains very graphic scenes of a sexual nature. Scenes that, frankly, I found to be gratuitous.

Apparently, so did Angela. After reading the script, she expressed reservations about the nudity. The producers informed her that they would not or could not cut the scenes out of the film, so she politely passed. History will of course record that Halle Berry did not pass, performed admirably, and won the Academy Award for her performance.

The interviewer asked Angela if, in light of Berry's award, she now regretted turning down the role. The weekly quoted her as saying not at all. "It's about character darling!" Unfortunately, her comment was seen as cattiness and sour grapes.

A handful of years later, the roar has faded away to a few whispers at parties. Mainstream moviegoers have largely forgotten the controversy, but her words—like Roz's words—and the manner in which she was attacked has stayed with me. This may be as a result of my personal relationship with Angela. I prefer to think it is because I know that she was absolutely right: it *is* about character.

I am not surprised really. An excess of principles inspires only ridicule, because trivialities become bloated, but when something important is at issue, principles have to come first.

I wonder what Roz would have thought of the *Newsweek* interview. Something tells me Roz would have given Angela a high five and kept stepping.

What Bassett and Cash have in common is that when they talk about character, they are not talking about just choosing acting roles; they are talking about making choices in every aspect of their lives consistent with their belief and value system. There is nothing trivial about that. Both women speak to the need for each of us to define who we are, what we stand for, draw our line in the sand, and then—most importantly—have the courage to follow through. They are telling us that the strength of our character is demonstrated by how often and how far we are willing to move that line. The fact that Angela was forced to do damage control, and believe it or not continues to this day to defend her words, is evidence of our fundamental misunderstanding about the importance of character and our misguided emphasis on feelings—what some call self-esteem.

When the interviewer asked Angela if she had regretted turning down the role, he was implicitly asking: Doesn't personal glory change the equation? Do those things we claim to be immoral or uncouth suddenly become acceptable once there are riches or accolades to be had? Put another way: Shouldn't our choices change if we are really hungry? What if we are really, *really* hungry?

Character often requires making difficult choices, which is why character and comfort are often at odds with each other.

I have had more than one discussion on this point with my sister, Lisa. Not too long ago, she and my nephews were visiting from Virginia. For some reason, we began debating the morality of stealing bread when one is hungry (go figure). I took the concrete position that stealing was wrong no matter what, while my sister reasoned that if her children were starving she would do what was necessary in order to feed them. I posited that digging through garbage was an alternative to theft, but my sister would have none of it. In her view, if a starving man steals bread, he has not committed a crime. She failed to see that the morality of theft is most at issue precisely because one is in need. Not stealing bread is easy when one has a full belly. The decision to scavenge or beg rather than steal is the principled decision and alas one that will not likely deliver fresh baked bread. My sister's position bespeaks the dilemma most of us have with making principled decisions: character most often goes un-rewarded. There are no parades, no awards, and no bands, just the sound of hunger pangs accompanying the quiet knowledge of having made a righteous choice. We are forever trying to figure out how to eat our cake and have it too.

My best friend told me it was more important that his daughter have self-esteem than be of good character. Character, to him, was simply the ability to follow rules. His view—moral principles are merely arbitrary rules imposed upon us by society—is cut from the same corrupt fabric that allows famous actresses to speed from the scene of an accident, leaving the injured to fend for themselves. Or to expose their breasts during halftime at the Super Bowl and blame others for the mess that follows.

My buddy, alas, does not love Western films like I do. There are several I would recommend that might illustrate the fallacy in his thinking in a more entertaining way than any conversation he might have with me.

Fade in:

In the distance, a steam whistle blows announcing the arrival of the noon train—right on schedule. Marshal Will Kane stands alone on the town's dirt street with the sun beating his brow. His eyes nervously search the deserted town. He wipes the sweat from his brow, straightens his gun belt and begins walking toward the edge of town resolved to meet his fate. . . .

Recognize the scene? It's the beginning of the climactic third act of the classic Western, *High Noon*. This film is why I love Westerns! The story is simple: On the morning of his wedding, the hero, Kane (Gary Cooper), discovers that the killer he sent to prison five years ago is headed back to town for revenge. Three of the killer's cronies are in town and waiting for the killer, who is on the noon train.

Rather than run, as he is urged to do by the town elders, Kane chooses to stay. The law, the politicians, his friends, and even his new wife abandon him. Yet, he is resolved to do what is right. (Storytelling just doesn't get any better than this!) For the most part, Westerns play on similar themes—loyalty, bravery in the face of overwhelming odds, and rugged individualism. *High Noon* weaves these traditional themes into a complex study of human nature. In the end, it is much more than a simple morality tale. The film hits on an essential truth of manhood: Once a man abandons his principles, he ceases to be a man.

In trying to get him to leave town, Kane's wife argues that the killer is no longer his problem. Marshal Kane replies that he is the same man, with or without the badge. Later, (in one of the great lines in the history of Western Film) Kane's former lover tells the Young Deputy Harvey Pell (Lloyd Bridges) that "It takes more than broad shoulders to make a man." In other words, principles do matter! Men of responsibility are expected to behave with character, regardless of the circumstances.

What my buddy is missing, and what Bassett and Cash make clear, is that self-esteem is the *result of* good character. CEOs of major corporations do not take huge bonuses while their companies flounder because they have low self-esteem. It is a lack of character that informs this behavior. Gold is nice, but doing what is right no matter the cost is what builds self-esteem. I have heard that *High Noon* is on the list of the 10 best films for young boys to watch. Every corporate CEO, at least one former president I can name and my best friend should rush out and rent this film!

The gentle admonishment I received from Rosalind Cash that day held special resonance. Roz was the first woman in Hollywood to wear dreadlocks in her hair and her career suffered because of it. While her friends worked on television series and lived the high Hollywood lifestyle, she grew her food in a garden and lived in a garage in Venice Beach. Rosalind Cash wore those dreadlocks until she died, having resigned herself many years before to waiting until Hollywood caught up. In the end, her reward was greater. Rosalind was loved. I loved her! When she died, I cried like a baby. Her memorial service was packed with her peers who loved and respected her strength. Her physical beauty was remarkable, but her spirit was what filled the church with mourners. In the end, that kind of esteem is more valuable than a fleet of Mercedes.

The same is true of Angela. After bursting onto the scene as Tina Turner in *What's Love Got To Do With It* and leaving women cheering as she flicked her cigarette onto her cheating husband's burning sports car in *Waiting to Exhale*, her career stalled. It wasn't for lack of offers. Those beautiful cheekbones could have appeared in any number of films, but she chose not to be seduced by fame and material gain or intimidated by professional repercussions. This is called walking the walk.

People like Rosalind Cash and Angela Bassett understand that character is meaning what you say. We should feel good about ourselves not based on the number of trophies on our mantels but because we make decisions that are true to our nature as strong, principled people. If the cost of a gold statuette is Angela's soul, I, for one, pray she is never that hungry.

My agent recently sent me a script for a film being produced by Danny DeVito. The film was a vehicle for two rap stars I had never heard of, but if DeVito was involved, I wanted to be part of the project. To my utter horror, the first twenty pages were filled with more racist stereotypes than I could count. I thought, "Why don't I just put on blackface, grab a piece of watermelon, and start tap dancing?" Just to be safe, I gave the script to my wife to read. I offered no introduction other than, "read this and tell me what you think." Fifteen minutes later, she returned with a long face. As she handed me the script she said, "Honey, no one wants you to get a job more than I do, but you can't do this." For a moment I wondered if I could bear my sons seeing me shuck and jive as the script required. Roz's words rang in my ears. I called my agent the next morning and passed. Of course, the film went on to be produced with actors I know personally in the roles—actors whose work in other films I admire. Like Angela, my decision was not a comment on the choices made by other actors but an affirmation of the kind of actor I want to be and, by extension, the kind of man I am struggling to become. When the dust settles we are only left with ourselves. The eyes looking back in the mirror don't belong to anyone else.

Success is Opportunity in Disguise

My best friend likes to tell a story from his high school football days. During one game, the coach called him off the bench to field a punt from the opposing team. My buddy knew his team's punt return squad was poor so hoping to avoid being crushed, he pointed to his supposedly sore ankle and begged off. The coach sent another player into the game, who promptly fumbled the ball away.

My friend thought, "Well, I could have done *that*!" This was the moment he realized for the first time that opportunities often arrive in plain, brown paper packages, that success often depends on recognizing opportunity when it presents itself, being prepared to take advantage of every opportunity and maximizing every effort.

Years ago, while I was working on *The Cosby Show*, we were shooting an episode that centered on Rudy, the youngest daughter, and tap dancing. While we were preparing for the dress rehearsal, a young 10- or 11-year-old boy found his way backstage, walked up to Bill Cosby with the boldness that is only present in youth, and demanded, "Put me in your show. I can tap dance!" Bill didn't miss a beat. He cleared some space in the room and gave him the floor. "Show me what you got." The boy danced a few simple steps. Bill asked if he could do any tricks. "Sure, I can do tricks," the boy responded. Again, Bill stepped back giving him the floor. The boy stared up at Bill with wide, innocent eyes. "I can't do them now. I have to go home and practice." My heart sank. He had come so close. He had created an opportunity but would not get on television that day because he was not fully prepared.

Success is not always a matter of raw talent. This boy's disappointment was not due to any lack of talent. If he had just done something—anything—Bill probably would have written him into the show simply because he had shown courage and spunk.

My childhood dentist used to be a star running back at the University of Kansas. He loved to regale us with tales of his glory days. The one thing he emphasized to us kids over and over again was that in his hometown, there were half a dozen guys standing on every street corner who were bigger and faster than he was. The world of sports and entertainment is not so different from any other endeavor. To be sure, talent is important but more often than not, the difference is hard work and preparedness. As my best friend's story illustrates, sometimes all you have to do is show up.

My role as Mayor Morgan Douglas on the CBS series *The District* was purely a result of divine benevolence. I did everything I could to get out of "showing up" to the audition. I feigned illness and complained about the travel time. I even took the absurd position with my agent that the producers had not really meant to call me. Surely, they must mean another actor named Joseph C. Phillips. It was not until my agent told me the producers were looking for a Blair Underwood type that I was at all motivated to go. My wife assured me that I am much better looking than Blair, so showing up suddenly seemed less of a hassle.

Fortunately for me, this story had a happy ending. However, the sad truth is that in my career, I have begged out of many auditions, more than I care to count—sometimes with a good excuse and sometimes not. If the worst thing one can say at the end of this short life is "what if . . ." then upon my death, my list of "what ifs" will be as long as my arm. I may not have been hired for all of those jobs, however one thing is for sure, by not showing up I was ensured I wouldn't be hired for any of them.

This may be odd for an actor to admit, but I suffer from severe auditioning anxiety. In my entire career calls from my agent, rather than eliciting excitement and anticipation, routinely result in stomachaches and depression. There have been times when the prospect of reading before a producer or director has literally made me physically ill. (Yes, I know. Considering that most of what actors do is audition, perhaps another line of work might be in order.) It was once suggested to me that I had a fear of failure. Fear of rejection is a possibility. But I am not afraid of failure. Failure is easy. Just ask my friend who begged off the punt return team. Failure only requires that you sit on the bench. Success requires that you show up, and once you show up people demand excellence, they demand that you be prepared, that you show something—do some tricks.

It has taken me forty years, but I now use these stories to motivate myself. As you can plainly see, sometimes I need a lot of motivating. I am not so naïve as to believe that every opportunity will go my way. Life certainly throws us curve balls. Things don't always work out as we planned and often when our wishes are granted, they turn out to be nothing like we imagined. Anxiety is a fact of life, but fear can't be allowed to deprive us of whatever blessings God might bestow upon us.

Disappointments do happen and sometimes we fumble the ball. But there are also triumphs. If we are lucky—if we are prepared to seek opportunity and take advantage of it when we find it—our triumphs should outnumber our disappointments.

Old School

Rap music gives me a headache. The repetitive backbeat makes me anxious and tense. For the most part, I find the videos one long boring and monotonous montage of rump shaking, scantily clad women fawning over guys with unusual hairstyles and clothes that are too big for them. The lyrics—when I can understand them—don't often make sense. They seem angry, sexist, and rather like bad high school poetry—they rhyme but their substance is ankle deep. In fact, the entire enterprise seems orchestrated to give entertainment careers to a generation of young men who are marginally talented. Were it not for rap, I suspect many of these guys would be working menial jobs or serving time in prison. What am I saying? Many of them *are* serving time. And if there is any justice in this world, the rest will soon be washing dishes at the local IHOP.

If that sounds elitist of me I apologize. Truly, I am just venting. It is difficult for me, however, to take seriously young men who call themselves musicians but who can't read music and make money from sampling (stealing) other people's music; who call themselves artists and yet only seem capable of expressing themselves with imagery that is vulgar and language that is profane.

My wife says I sound like an old fuddy-duddy. She's right, of course. But I just tell her I'm old school.

Actually, not all rap music gives me a headache. Ninety-nine percent of rap music gives me a headache. The other one percent—the more mainstream or novelty stuff—is stuff that I find myself tapping my foot to. True rap aficionados shake their heads and laugh when I talk about MC Hammer or Will Smith. Hip-hoppers refer to that type of rap as "soft." I don't want to be soft! I have been musically soft for too long!

It could very well be that my aversion to hip-hop is generational. After all, I don't exactly fit the demographic. Hip-hop is for young people, just as funk and rock and roll were for young people. I can recall my father not really digging the music I liked as a teenager. He tended to shut the door to my room when I turned up the volume on my stereo. So, it may be that I don't get rap music because I am not supposed to get it. On the other hand, I have heard too many people claim that there is something prophetic about hip-hop. Everyone from presidential candidates to my nephews has talked about the complexity of the music, the cultural significance of rap. Some of these rappers are supposedly the great poets of our time. "The music is a reflection of what is happening on the streets and in the lives of young people," they say. "We had better listen." Some of these folks are older than I am so it can't all be a matter of age. Maybe I just don't understand the music. I want to know what it is I am missing. I may be over forty, but it is never too late to develop new tastes in music.

I have, therefore, decided to immerse myself in rap music. I am going to quit listening to talk radio and old-school rhythm and blues—cold turkey! For the next week, I am going to listen to the hip-hop radio station and watch the rump-shaking videos on BET (Black Entertainment Television). I am going to buy copies of *Source* and *Vibe* magazines and read them cover-to-cover. If my wife lets me, I may even start wearing my pants baggy, letting them rest low on my hips so my boxers show, turn my hat around backwards, and plug in some gold teeth. I want the whole experience.

I realize a week is not very long, but I know my limitations. My track record with this type of experimentation is not good. Years ago, I attempted something similar. I was determined that if I couldn't learn to like rap, I would at least develop a working knowledge of the music so I could discuss it intelligently. I dashed out to the music store and bought CDs by Public Enemy, Big Daddy Kane, and a list of other artists who were hot at the time. The only ground rule I set was that I had to play each album all the way through at least once. As an illustration of my lack of commitment, I soon decided that playing an album all the way through didn't necessarily mean I had to be in the same room while it played. Strictly speaking, so long as the album played all the way through, I didn't even have to be in the apartment. I will never forget putting NWA (Niggaz with Attitude) on the stereo. I almost broke my neck sprinting across my apartment to turn the volume down when "Fuck the Police" began blasting through the building.

Clearly, I just didn't have the conviction necessary to pull it off. Or it may have been that I was/am just a square. L7! The embodiment of the funk group Parliament Funkadelic's character Sir Nose, genetically programmed to resist the power of the backbeat. Sadly, I have come to accept that it may be the latter, and for that I blame my father. In elementary school, while other black kids were listening to James Brown and the Temptations, my father had light radio playing every morning. You know, the Carpenters, Lesley Gore, the Seekers. "Hey there, Georgy girl/ swingin' down the street so fancy-free/nobody you meet could ever see the loneliness there inside you." Of course I remember the lyrics! This was the stuff I ate breakfast to every morning. As I got older it seemed to just get worse. Black kids in my school were listening to the Ohio Players and Kool and the Gang while Don Mclean's "American Pie" and Helen Reddy's "I am Woman" wafted throughout my home. Thank God for my older sister. If it were not for Lisa introducing me to War, Isaac Hayes, the Isley Brothers, Sly and the Family Stone and Rufus, I would never have discovered R & B music.

But I suppose once a square, always a square. The corniness has never left me. Just for fun, I rifled through my music collection looking for the four albums in my collection that identify me as a square:

Tom Leher; *That Was the Year That Was*—Oh, what the heck. I have all of Tom Leher's albums. Hint: If you are black and you know who Tom Leher is, well now, you got a bit of the old L7 in you as well!

The original Broadway recordings of *Finnian's Rainbow* and *The Magic Show*—What can I say? I like show tunes. My wife thinks there is something weird in a straight man loving old Broadway show tunes. Actually, it is the fact that I like to cook, garden, and know how to sew in combination with enjoying show tunes that worries her.

The Essential Gene Autry—I grew up in Denver, Colorado. I love cowboy music. I love cowboy movies. I loved Gene Autry, Hopalong Cassidy, and Rex Allen. Unfortunately for my eldest son, I am dooming him to a similar fate. The other day he confided to me that his two favorite singers were Gene Autry and Li'l Romeo.

The Best of Johnny Mathis—No explanation should be necessary. I don't care what anyone says, Johnny is as right as rain. Mellow as a shower on a summer's day!

I was going to say five albums and include the Spice Girls' *Spice*, but in all fairness I didn't buy it, my wife did.

My struggle with being square was particularly difficult once I got to high school. Living in a white neighborhood and speaking "proper" had rendered me a social outcast while in junior high school. I was banished to a vast desert wasteland of "in-betweeness"—not really black and obviously not white. It was territory I detested but in time grew to take ownership of. The problem was that once I reached high school, musical tastes began to get all mixed up in the socioracial politics of the day and in many ways my predicament not only intensified but also became more convoluted.

In my school there was white music and black music. Funk and R & B were black. Rock 'n' roll and most pop music were white. That is not to say that there was *no* crossover, just that there was very *very* little.

On the musical spectrum, Parliament was on one side and Led Zeppelin was on the other. I identified Parliament with the black kids—specifically, the black kids who had been making my life miserable since the eighth grade. I identified

Led Zeppelin with the white kids (not just white kids, but *really* white kids). Let me make clear that I like music. It may be that all those mornings listening to Andy Williams influenced me so that when I hear a song and like it, I don't care what kind of music it is or who is playing it. But in high school, in order to defend my individualist middle ground, I suddenly had to be very careful about the music I liked. Or at least, the music I admitted to liking. The result? I was a closet Parliament Funkadelic fan. "If you hear any noise it's just me and the boys . . . ." I loved "Mothership Connection"! I loved most of the stuff that P-Funk and other funk bands were doing back then but I had to listen in secret. There I was, with my transistor radio, the little white earplug hanging from my head, jamming to P-Funk in the privacy of my room.

There was some safe music—that narrow crossover I spoke of earlier. I could listen to Earth Wind & Fire or Heatwave, for instance. Even the Commodores were safe. Rufus and Chaka Khan were just avant-garde enough to be acceptable. I loved Chaka! Still do. On the other side, there was Steely Dan. Everybody liked the album "Aja!" That was *cool* white-boy music. There were also Chicago and Average White Band, of course. Disco was popular, so stuff by KC & the Sunshine Band was safe. But Zeppelin? No way! And I loved "Stairway to Heaven"—one of the greatest songs of all time! Not that I would ever admit it. I refused to give it up for Zeppelin, Aerosmith, or Billy Joel for fear of sounding too white. "Ugh! I can't listen to that. That's lame! No soul." And lest I sound too black: "Dr. Funkenstein? 'Baby, I am the big pill?' What does that mean? Come on!"

At one point, I decided it would sound so much more refined and intellectual (not to mention safe) to say that I preferred jazz. "Yeah, I'm into jazz. No, thank you, I prefer jazz." Jazz, meaning George Benson. Talk about ankle deep. No one else. Just George.

So, here I was, kind of tenuously negotiating this middle ground—black but not too black and white but not too white—and doing okay when suddenly rap hit. Aaargh! I was f***ed! Sugar Hill Gang had to go and release "Rapper's Delight," a fourteen-minute song about . . . what the hell *was* that song about?! My freshman year in college that song was *huge!* Everybody was listening to Sugar Hill Gang. And not only listening, but memorizing and repeating the lyrics. I couldn't bring myself to admit that I thought the tune was kind of catchy (too black) so I didn't memorize any lyrics. I could sing "Georgy Girl" by the Seekers, but couldn't—and *still* can't—rap "Rapper's Delight." One night, I confessed this to my wife. She rolled over in bed, smiled, and said, "The hippie the hippie to the hip hip hop, a you don't stop the rock it to the bang bang boogie, say up jumped the boogie to the rhythm of the boogie, the beat." How embarrassing!

I did eventually give it up for Kurtis Blow and the Breaks, but I was late because I was standing on the outside unable to cede the middle ground for fear that I might lose some part of myself in the transaction. It would get worse before it got better. I came home from college finally ready to embrace rap and my black friends were listening to John Cougar Mellencamp!

Today, when I am driving down the street and some fool has the music in his car turned all the way up, making my eardrums bleed from the heavy bass, there is every likelihood that the driver will be white. My barber (who is also an aspiring hip-hop music producer) tells me that of the last three rap concerts he has been to, only ten percent of the audience has been black. If there is any one good thing I can say about hip-hop, it is that all kids—black, white, yellow, and brown—have embraced the culture. There seems less of a divide. Nowadays, I imagine you would be hard pressed to find the kind of tightrope walking I was attempting twenty-five years ago.

There are, of course, other things that are good about hip hop. The beats and the melodies (when I could find them) are infectious. Too much bass still makes my head begin to throb but several times I have caught myself bobbing my head (or "bangin' my head" as we hip-hoppers like to say) and snapping my fingers to the music. Square or not, I can recognize a good beat when I hear it. Infectious beats and a nice melody are why I loved so much of the music I listened to when I was growing up. I found rap a bit unsettling early in the morning, but I discovered that some of it is good music to exercise to. I have to admit that I even began to appreciate some of the wit in the lyrics. I remain unconvinced that these are great poets, but I did begin to appreciate the difference between artists who told good stories and offered interesting plays on words versus those who simply rambled on about booties shaking and living ghetto fabulous.

Unfortunately, the interesting stuff was in the minority. The majority of what I heard was a celebration of nihilism: gangster life, pimping, smoking dope, and promiscuity. Then with a nod to being politically conscious, they blamed all of this pathology on the white man. This, I believe, is called "keeping it real."

It was a long week. The entire time, an old Earth Wind & Fire song was playing on a continuous loop inside my head: "Would you mind\ if I touched\ if I kissed\ if I held you tight\ in the morning light?" As soon as my week of experimentation was up, I pulled out the vinyl and the seventies soul flowed so deep in my home that I had my sons singing "Float On" by the Floaters. I know—soft. But what is wrong with soft?

Senior year in high school, I took Margaret Wilson to see the Commodores perform at McNichols Arena in Denver. I will never forget how she melted into my arms as Lionel Ritchie crooned "Three Times a Lady." I kissed Margaret for the first time that night. If I ever meet Lionel Ritchie, I am going to shake his hand. That night, soft was okay by me!

The lack of softness is perhaps my biggest problem with hip-hop. There is anger—constant rage, with people yelling into the microphone, looking and sounding hard—but there is no love in this music. And where there is a lack of love, there is lack of hope.

It's not just rap music. New-school rhythm & blues have become as homogenized as whole milk. Everyone sounds the same. Singers play second fiddle to producers. And the slow jam, once a staple of courtship, is now a shadow of its former self. I challenge you to name one song written in the last twenty years that will elicit the kind of squeals from women as will the first few bars of Earth Wind & Fire's "Reasons."

I blame the men. The slow jam used to be the gentleman's domain. Think back to the Isley Brothers: "Drifting on a memory/ain't no place I'd rather be than with you/loving you." Along with EW&F and the Commodores, we had the O'Jays, Harold Melvin, Smokey Robinson, Al Green, Barry White . . . I could go on and on! Not only were all of them distinct stylistically, these guys used to be able to wrap a lyric around a woman and make her swoon. What happened to the men? They've decided that they are gangsters and not lovers! Today, Shaggy is "bangin' on the bathroom floor." (Perhaps the charm of this ditty is lost on me because after potty training three boys, I don't want to walk on the bathroom floor much less romance my wife on it.) P. Diddy and Usher dance together on a video while rapping a sophomoric tune about wanting a girl who is "like a brother." I have never described a lover as being "like my brother." And what is up with these guys constantly taking their shirts off? Stevie Wonder and Ronnie Isley never whined off-key while showing their six packs. Since when have women been interested in six packs? Women sighed over Barry White! Guys are the ones obsessed with rippled abdominal muscles. One has to wonder for whom, then, these young men are preening.

After listening to a weeks' worth of rap music and watching dozens of rap videos, I am left asking: Are men no longer required to woo women? I was not blessed with a smooth rap for the ladies. Thank God for the Commodores, the Isley Brothers, and Frankie Beverly! While dating my wife, I kept Maze's *Live in New Orleans* playing on my turntable around the clock. To this day, she still gets frisky when she hears Frankie Beverly's voice. Is love so cheap today that girls just give it away? (Don't answer that!) Or was my generation the last to really understand romance? I am not talking about sex. Young people understand sex. Listen to their music and they describe the act of sex in excruciating detail.

Folks have been singing about sex since the beginning of time. There was plenty of sexual content in the music of my day, but it was infused with romance. Marvin Gaye sang "Let's get it on." The difference was that Marvin also said, "If you believe in *love*/let's get it on." Marvin and the other male singers of that era understood the art of seduction. For the life of me, I cannot imagine what young men today put on the stereo when trying to set just the right mood for a lady. Oh, wait, I can: old-school R & B! Al Green, the Whispers, the Stylistics, the Dramatics, the Chi Lites, the Intruders.

There is a reason the music of my generation was called Soul. The music comes from the gut. Soul music of the seventies was rooted in the blues tradition—personal lyrics that conveyed honest longing, pain of loss, and, most importantly, hope. Beyond the broken hearts and unrequited love there was the hope of a better world. Artists of that era not only sang of good times, they sang of a world filled with brotherhood and peace, where a lover's embrace could shield you from the cold winds of an unforgiving world. This dearth of romance is really a dearth of hope. If music is a reflection of each generation, what does it say about this generation that their music is so lacking in optimism?

With two teenage boys, my sister is on the front lines. She is convinced that today's youth is reacting to "too much exposure to situations and life experiences that they are too immature to handle." No doubt she is referring to AIDS, terrorism, gang violence, and drugs. But doesn't every generation have its crosses to bear? My sister and I grew up with the Viet Nam War on television; the assassinations of Martin, Malcolm, and Bobby; the struggle for civil rights; drug culture; and the sexual revolution. Still Harold Melvin and the Blue Notes sang, "I can remember planning/building my whole world around you./I can remember hoping/that you and I would make it on through." Today, Jay-Z raps: "If you got women problems I feel sorry for you, son/I got ninety-nine problems but a bitch ain't one!"

Kids talk about keeping it real, but there is more to "real" than what they sing about. Their music is all about profiling and bling bling. Sex before love, skepticism before faith, style over substance. If there is disillusionment, it is because after all is said and done—after all of the "thug life" and "thug appeal"—they still find themselves empty and longing for hope.

True, these kids did not invent the world they live in; they inherited it. But I would argue that they are lacking in faith and hope because, in spite of sampling yesterday's music, they have failed to digest the lessons of the "old school." Life is best seen through the prism of love, togetherness, and devotion.

If men have largely abandoned their role as guardians of the "woo woo" in order to strike gangsta poses, it is the young women who will save the day. Women are increasingly taking up the mantel and moving music in a positive direction.

Hip-hop has not marginalized women, it has objectified them. They are called out of their names in lyrics and in videos; they are portrayed as sex-crazed freaks who are quick to get their groove on for a shot of Cristal champagne and a ride in an SUV with rims that spin. The women of Spelman College (an all-female, historically black college) finally got fed up with this degradation and shut down a charitable event being sponsored by rap artist Nelly. They were motivated by a recent video, which featured Nelly using his credit card on a woman's butt as if it were an ATM machine. The black women's magazine *Essence* has stepped into the fray by running articles by columnist and vocal hip-hop critic Stanley Crouch. If you are like me, you are asking: What took so long?

I like to think of the joy of Jill Scott's "The Way." Scott takes the listener through the mundane chores of her day but you can't help but feel the excitement and anticipation of her lover's return. She asks rhetorically, "Is it the way you love me, baby?" She then answers, "Yeah." Scott and artists like Vivian Green, Alicia Keyes, Deborah Cox, and Mary J. Blige are proving that real talent can be very sexy. This group of young women is taking the best of hip-hop and old-school and making beautiful music that, while grounded in the blues tradition, is new and exciting. All without removing a stitch of clothing.

Alas some women, like their male counterparts, are not as interested in making great music as they are in exposing their six packs and indulging their egos.

Who can forget the 2004 Super Bowl during which Justin Timberlake tore Janet Jackson's costume and exposed her breast to an international audience? It was no accident that Jackson came on stage singing a song more than a decade old and dancing steps last seen in 1991! Jackson had an album due to hit the stores soon after the event. Her protestations notwithstanding, you will be hard pressed to convince me she wasn't trying to hype her record release.

There is a line from the Broadway musical *Dreamgirls* that tells us, "Only a desperate man would drop his pants in show biz." Jackson's "artistic" choice to reveal her breast merely reflects the desperate state of popular music today. Her behavior was no more extreme than that of Madonna, Britney Spears, L'il Kim, Christina Aguilera and the rest of the pop divas competing to see who can redefine the meaning of "uncouth." Breasts don't impress an audience and neither do girl-on-girl kisses. You want to show me something, hit the E above High C; take music in a new and exciting direction; perform a concert without lip-synching!

Shock, however, is easier than writing good music and that's the point. Aretha never took her top off. Marvin Gaye never ripped Tammy Terrell's clothes from her body. The Supremes were the epitome of beauty and class and Patty Labelle never lip synched to a strip tease in her entire forty-year career. These artists and others never had to shock because they had three things: too much integrity, too much talent, and too much charisma. Today's artists' need for shock is sad evidence that they have reached the limit of all three of these attributes. Happily, there are a handful of women who don't need gimmicks and don't need to bare their breasts. They listened to the lessons of the old school and are making beautiful music.

In 1964, The Temptations were a hit with "My Girl". They sang: "I don't need no money/ fortune or fame/ I got all the riches, baby, one man can claim." Today Alicia Keyes belts out: "Some people want diamond rings/ some just want everything/ but everything means nothing if I ain't got you./ If I ain't got you with me baby!"

Now, that's old school made young again!

Maybe there is hope for us yet.

God Give Us Men

God, Give Us Men
". . . A time like this demands
Strong minds, great hearts, true faith and ready hands;
Men whom the lust of office does not kill;
Men whom the spoils of office cannot buy;
Men who possess opinions and a will;
Men who have honor; men who will not lie. . . ."
—Josiah Gilbert Holland

I watched the film *Patton* recently. What a wonderful film! The film paints a moving portrait of a brilliant and complex man. As portrayed by George C. Scott, Patton was a self-described prima donna and son of a b**ch! By most accounts, Scott's portrayal was not too far from the authentic animal. Patton was a flamboyant, charismatic, military genius who captured the public's imagination and commanded the respect and dedication of his troops. He possessed the heart of a poet, cursed a blue streak, and saw his life and battlefield heroics as a fulfill-ment of his destiny. Patton's intemperate manner landed him in quite a bit of hot water throughout his career, but he is regarded by most historians as one of the most successful American field commanders of any war. During the campaign to liberate Europe in World War II, Patton's third army traveled faster and further, killed, wounded or captured more enemy soldiers, and conquered more territory than any other army in the recorded history of warfare. Supreme Commander of the Allied Forces General Dwight Eisenhower told one of his senior officers, "Patton is indispensable to the war effort, one of the guarantors of our victory." Respected by his men and feared by the enemy, he was known as "America's fight-ingest general." He was truly an extraordinary man made for an extraordinary time.

I am not old enough to remember those days of world war but I would suggest the times in which we are currently living are as extraordinary as any: The United Nations has yet to decide whether or not it will be an organization of significance; the French and the Germans seem determined to challenge America's leadership at every turn; Europe is poised to become one big Socialist super state; Israelis and Palestinians continue to saturate the sand with blood; Muslim terrorists seek to destroy Western culture by blowing up innocent men, women, and children; madmen in North Korea and Iran are determined to build nuclear warheads; and all the while China sits quietly planning the annihilation of the United States.

In the center of this international storm stands the United States, which must grapple with her own domestic problems: secularism versus open recognition and celebration of our Judeo/Christian heritage, gay marriage, socialized medicine, and illegal immigration. Extraordinary times indeed, in need of extraordinary leadership. The times call for a bigger-than-life character who can capture the imagination of the American public, avoid the traps of political life and earn the dedication of a partisan Congress here at home while commanding the respect and awe of America's friends and enemies abroad.

It is a tall order and one that forces us to ask: From where and when will the "extraordinary" leaders for these extraordinary times emerge? Do great men define their times as the poet Holland suggests, or is it the times that define great men?

Patton once said, "Moral courage is the most valuable and usually the most absent characteristic in men." A man must posses an underpinning of character and philosophy that will support him when faced with great trial. Without that foundation, he withers in the face of fire when his leadership is needed most. But it is also true that a single man's base is simply too narrow. Great leaders must have men to follow them. People are more willing to follow a man of vision, conviction, and faith. Churchill, for example, could have chosen to negotiate with Hitler. On the other hand, without the support of the British people, his choice not to would have meant little. As great a general as Patton was, without the brave soldiers of the third army, he was little more than a military fancy full of spit and polish.

During the past several years, we have been witness to a couple of hotly contested presidential elections, elections I believe raise the question: Are we producing political leaders who fit the bill?

I campaigned for George W. Bush during the 2004 election. I traveled the country and appeared on radio and television as a surrogate for him. As an aside, I understand differences in political vision. What I do not understand are liberals whose opposition seems primarily based on the hope that his presidency fails miserably. As his administration goes, so goes the nation and as this nation goes, so goes the world. For the record, I would say the same thing during a Democratic administration. Conservatives who would work to hinder the forward march of democracy for all Americans deserve rebuke. Rooting for the failure of any presidential administration is to root against American success. It would, therefore, behoove all of us to give Bush, or whoever is in the White House, all the support we can. That said, is he really destined to write the kind of legend that the age demands? Time will tell.

This much, however, is true: if Bush is going to realize greatness, it will certainly be in part due to the strength and confidence he has demonstrated during our war on terror. His leadership has been steady and his moral courage cannot be questioned. Unlike his predecessor, who didn't move without first lifting his finger to test the political winds, George Bush was willing to risk himself politically in order to do what he believed was right. There is little question George Bush is a man of vision, conviction, and faith. For me, the Bush vision of a democratic and free Middle East is luminous. The determination to transform America into a society of owners and investors in the American dream is righteous. His faith in a higher moral power than himself brings me comfort. The left calls his vision myopic and interprets his conviction as foolhardiness. His faith has earned derision from portions of the left who do not trust a leader who seeks council with God before he acts. Time will ultimately tell, but when his story is written, no honest man could say that he was indecisive or that his leadership lacked sincerity.

This is perhaps one of the things that angered me most about Bill Clinton: his unfulfilled promise. Clinton was capable of being a good, if not great, president. There can be no question that he was a brilliant politician. He outmaneuvered Newt Gingrich and the Republican Party at every turn and somehow managed to receive credit for the success of policies he initially opposed—welfare reform, for example. He succeeded in exiting the Oval Office with a huge popularity rating even while leaving the nation in recession and after being impeached for lying while under oath and obstruction of justice. I have got to give him some credit. But can a man really distinguish himself beyond what the times may dictate if he has no conviction?

Bill Clinton believed in nothing but himself. He was too afraid of being unpopular to be decisive and too insincere to inspire true affection. (He never received a majority of the popular vote.) Had he not been a lying snake who harbored genuine contempt for the people he was sworn to serve, he may very well have distinguished himself as a leader. Democrats like to play the game that he was a truly great president. The fact that they can't really identify any great accomplishments (save the dishonor of his office to say nothing of his wife) suggests to me they are responding not to what *was*, but to what *might have been*. It also suggests to me that I am not alone in my hunger for heroic leadership.

In fairness to Clinton, he had some rather large shoes to fill. Following on the heels of Ronald Reagan could not have been easy. George H. Bush found it a "hard row to hoe," as my father used to say. I imagine Clinton felt much the same as former heavyweight boxing champ Larry Holmes did after taking the stage upon Muhammad Ali's exit. No matter what he did, fans still longed for the days of "The Greatest."

Upon Reagan's death in June 2004, syndicated columnist George Will wrote, "One measure of a leader's greatness is this: By the time he dies the dangers that summoned him to greatness have been so thoroughly defeated, in no small measure by what he did, it is difficult to recall the magnitude of those dangers, or of his achievements. So if you seek Ronald Reagan's monument, look around, and consider what you do *not* see."

What we no longer see is the Soviet Union. What we do not hear is the drumbeat of America's failure. Reagan's vision and strength led to a renewed national spirit, the collapse of the Soviet empire, and a loving embrace by the American people.

I am old enough to remember the pessimism of the late seventies. Under Jimmy Carter, the morale of the nation was low, unemployment and inflation were high, and thugs all over the world were pushing America—the leader of the free world—around. There was a belief among those who study these things that the United States could not win the Cold War and that the best we could hope for was a draw. But to this, Reagan said, "No!" He took office and immediately began the task of restoring the morale of the nation. He articulated a belief in the superiority of the free world, of the righteousness of liberty. Reagan "shook up the world" by declaring the Soviet Union an "evil empire." He confidently announced, "The march of freedom and democracy will leave Marxism-Leninism on the ash heap of history as it has left other tyrannies that stifle the freedom and muzzle the self-expression of the people." He asked this nation to stand tall and to resolve that there would be no peaceful coexistence with the Soviets. There would only be resounding victory. Standing at the Brandenburg Gate in Berlin, Reagan delivered what may have been the rhetorical knockout punch when he demanded of the Soviet dictator: "Mr. Gorbachev, tear down this wall!"

Rising to meet the demands of one's time—demonstrating moral courage—is not without cost. For facing down the Soviets, Reagan was castigated and vilified. On one chilly morning in March 1981, an attempt was made on his life. All men are not willing to pay the price.

Colin Powell, I believe, is a man for whom the times have been calling. Alas, he has chosen not to answer. Least ways not in the manner *I* would wish. Powell's refusal to run for our nation's highest office represents one of the greatest political tragedies in my lifetime. Make no mistake—I admire General Powell a great deal. (Clearly, that is why I would like to see him become president.) When his book, *My American Journey,* was released in 1995, I rushed out to purchase it. When Powell came to Los Angeles for a book signing, I dragged my best buddy Leonard to Brentano's in Century City to have my book autographed. General Powell is one of perhaps two or three men in the world I would wait in line for. When we arrived, the line stretched for a mile. It looked very doubtful that we would get our books signed that day. As we began the slow walk to the end of the line, a woman at the front of the line recognized me and asked for an autograph. I traded my worthless signature for a very valuable piece of real estate: the place behind her in line. Hey, what good is being a celebrity if you can't cut in line every once in a while?

Colin Powell is no George Patton and thankfully so. The times do not call for the flamboyance and bluster of a Patton, but the moderation and strength of a man like General Powell. I believe he, perhaps more than any currently on the scene, is capable of delivering the redeeming level of leadership our times demand.

Powell's reputation is impeccable. He carries none of the moral baggage of Clinton or Bush. He is pragmatic but sure. More importantly, he commands respect from the international community but is not afraid to pull the trigger, with or without their support. He is not part of the privileged class so he can't be accused of buying influence. He is also a moderate, which should nip any legislative logjam in the bud. And if, as some say, race still dominates our domestic discourse, who better to bridge our nation's racial gap than Colin Powell? All other potential candidates pale in comparison and offer nothing but the same old stale, uninspiring leadership we have had for the last fourteen years. Stories have circulated that his wife Alma is particularly resistant to a Powell candidacy for fear of attacks on his life. I can respect his family's choice not to bear the cost of leadership, but I can still dream, can't I? With respect to Josiah Holland, God give us Colin Powell!

Powell aside, there *are* men who hear the call of their time and choose to answer with a booming, "Where do I sign up?" One such man who heeded the call and along the way discovered the brutal cost of moral courage is Paul Robeson. An admitted socialist and communist sympathizer, Robeson stood tall and courageously demanded that America overcome racism. For his outspoken efforts, he was virtually erased from America's cultural history.

I must admit that I have struggled with Robeson's politics. I do not, however, require that my heroes be paragons. Such narrow scrutiny would eliminate most men from consideration. I have struggled with Robeson in the same manner I have wrestled with the fact that another man I admire, Thomas Jefferson, was a slave owner even while writing extensively about the immorality of slavery. Certainly, writing about the natural rights of man while holding men in bondage is no less morally repugnant than being a socialist, and Jefferson is a revered historical figure. I only ask that men (and women) I admire face extraordinary circumstances in their ordinary lives with extraordinary effort. In this way, Robeson stood tall.

In fact, Robeson towered above his contemporaries. He was an intellectual—Phi Beta Kappa at Rutgers College (now university) and valedictorian of his senior class. He was a phenomenal athlete earning letters in four different college sports and was Rutgers' first All-American football player. He later put himself through Columbia University School of Law while playing professional football on the weekends. He spoke twenty languages, thirteen fluently. In addition, Robeson was an international star of stage, screen, and the concert hall.

Robeson was perhaps one of the first truly global artists. Dr. Mark Naison of Fordham University writes eloquently of Robeson: "If the purpose of great art is to allow us to feel a higher sense of our own possibility as human beings, then Paul Robeson was perhaps the greatest artist of his time. . . ."

At the height of his fame, he was more widely known than Joe Louis and earning more money than Joe DiMaggio. But most importantly, Robeson, a staunch advocate for human rights, refused to perform before segregated audiences and was one of the first international artists to publicly oppose apartheid in South Africa.

Robeson was a huge celebrity at a time in American history when, as a black man, he was barred from being served in many major restaurants or hotels in a northern metropolis like New York and would be subject to the humiliation of Jim Crow in the south. Robeson was a passionate man committed to ridding this nation of racial prejudice. In the America of the 1930s and '40s, communists and progressives were the only ones talking about civil rights for black people and human rights for the world's oppressed. (In this light, Robeson's communist sympathies are put into their proper context.)

The end of the Second World War brought on America's Cold War with the Soviet Union, and it was Robeson's embrace of Soviet communism that led to his confrontation with the United States federal government and his eventual downfall. His passport was confiscated, promoters cancelled his concert performances, his trophies were removed from display at Rutgers, his recordings disappeared from shelves, he was removed from the college football hall of fame, and ignored by the mainstream press.

It is to Robeson's detriment and my great sorrow that even after the murderous regime of Josef Stalin was exposed he did not disavow communist ideals. But in spite of Robeson's blindness to the evils of communism, he was at heart an idealist. Robeson didn't believe in the communism of Josef Stalin and had no desire to live as a citizen of the Soviet Union. Robeson *loved America* and wanted above all else to live in a nation that celebrated its diversity and embraced all of its citizens regardless of race or economic class. Robeson was dreaming two decades before Martin weaved the dream into poetry. The unforgiving minute offers no quarter and Robeson asked for none. That dream and the determination to make it come true cost Robeson his fame, his fortune, and his place in history. And until the end, Robeson continued to sing the refrain of human rights and human dignity. Few men have possessed the heart, mind or dignity of Paul Robeson.

Another man who answered the call was the Reverend Dr. Martin Luther King, Jr. My youth was shaped by the great courage of Dr. King. He is a man who embodies that same spirit of heroism exhibited by Robeson, but who paid the ultimate sacrifice: A true example of courage and selflessness, he has been a shining light in my life.

April 4, 1968. I was in the first grade. Time has dimmed my memory, but I can still see my mother entering my classroom, taking me by the hand, and whisking me home. Later, I discovered Martin Luther King, Jr. had been assassinated. Riots had broken out at many of the schools in town and rumors swirled that violence was going to overtake the entire city, as had happened in other parts of the country. The frustration, rage, and grief of a people lit the country on fire.

The following year, as I readied myself for school, my mother thrust a black turtleneck at me announcing that I would be wearing the shirt to school. I hated turtlenecks and protested. My older sister Lisa, ever the diplomat, explained that it was "Wear Black Day" at school and if I didn't wear the shirt, I'd be beaten by my classmates. Needless to say, I wore the shirt. I wish my mother had told me that I was wearing the shirt to honor Dr. King. Perhaps then the gesture would have had meaning. As it was, I spent the entire day tugging at the shirt, scratching my neck and wondering why I was one of the only kids wearing black on "Wear Black Day."

Throughout my college years, I adopted the wearing of a black armband on King's birthday as my own personal tribute. I like to say I wore it as a symbol of remembrance and solidarity with The Cause. I did. But it is also true that it was a political statement as fashion. I was never one to be part of the "in" crowd but on January 15th, with my black armband, I was so "in" I was out the other side. When my classmates asked me about my attire, I would casually respond that this was my way of paying tribute to an American hero. Their eyes would grow wide and for a brief moment I was hip and oh-so-politically conscious. I was also pretentious as hell, but thankfully, such pretensions in our youth are forgiven.

I have grown out of my armband stage and now simply offer a prayer to God for blessing this nation with a man such as King. Dr. King dedicated his life to the uplifting of people and in so doing, he made this nation a better place. He spoke of himself as an extremist for love. He committed his body to laying the case for human dignity and his sacrifice is a testament to one man's ability to alter his times through strength of will and moral righteousness.

As these men demonstrate, it isn't pretty speeches, but conviction and action that make for great leadership. People will follow a man who possesses the courage to stand up and articulate his beliefs and demonstrate a willingness to follow through to the end no matter the personal cost. That is the trait that distinguishes men like Patton, Powell, King, Robeson, and Reagan from also-rans like Clinton. I hunger for that kind of leadership! I am eager for a hero to step forward and put an end to political cynicism and partisan sniping. I want a leader who will build bridges and harness the talent and creativity of a unified America so that this nation may stand proudly with her friends and face her enemies with assurance.

I am tempted to put my pen down and leave my thoughts at this. However, it occurs to me that there is an element to heroic manhood that needs addressing. Leaders such as the men I mentioned (and so many more that I didn't) will not simply fall from the sky as in Greek tragedy. They must be nurtured and grown. Distinguishing oneself in battle or leading a movement that changes the world are not the only paths to heroism. There is another type of heroism—a quiet heroism that garners no headlines, no monuments, and no parades. The foundation of character, moral courage, and the idealism that is the underpinning of heroism is the stuff instilled in men as children; it is the stuff—the right stuff, as it is said—that is the result of the quiet courage of men who lead through the example of their lives. I am talking of course about parents and teachers.

My father gave me a copy of Rudyard Kipling's poem "If" when I graduated high school. The last stanza of the poem reads:

". . . If you can fill the unforgiving minute with 60 seconds worth of distance run, yours is the earth and all that's in it, and what is more, you will be a man my son."

At the time, I believed my father was trying to teach me something about the transition from boyhood to manhood. As I have read and reread the poem over the years, however, I am convinced that I was wrong. My father was not talking to me about the transition from boyhood to manhood; Kipling's poem is about the transition from manhood to heroic manhood.

My father, for instance, didn't blaze any new trails in medicine. He didn't put his life on the line for mankind. He did however, raise four children and put them all through college, which was no small accomplishment.

My father was born the illegitimate son of a twenty-year-old unemployed laborer in the heart of depression-era Brunswick, Georgia. If you go any farther south in Georgia than Brunswick, you are in Florida! When he was still an infant, his mother moved to New York in search of work, leaving him to be raised by his aunt and grandmother. He was a good student who also excelled in athletics. After graduating high school he attended Hampton Institute (now university) and made extra money working in the tobacco fields during the summer. He served two years in the army as a second lieutenant and then went on to Howard

Medical School. He met a young divorced schoolteacher and mother of a little girl. They married and moved to Denver, Colorado where he completed his pediatric residency. A year later, I was born; two other children would follow. Miraculously, he (and my mother) managed to do all of this without the aid of racial preferences.

My father never made a lot of money. His practice never realized the kind of income other doctors were seeing. We never went hungry, though, and we were blessed with the kind of opportunities my father could only have dreamed of as a boy. The striving of his life provided four children with an example of hard work and sacrifice that gave us the chance to dream of becoming anything we wanted to be and going anywhere we wanted to go. He may not have been marching with King, but he did something equally as important—he attended to his responsibilities and gave his children options. In the vast sea of his generation he was indistinguishable from most, just one of many who was determined to achieve in spite of the roadblocks placed in his way and to make a better path for those who would follow—a man who recognized the demands of the times and found nobility in answering the call.

The pastor at my church in Denver taught that recognizing great moments was easy. Much more difficult was recognizing ordinary moments as great. It is easy to recognize the heroism in men like King or Patton. Much more challenging is seeing the sort of heroism displayed by men like my father.

Every man has choices to make within the general framework of things that have perhaps already been decided for us. Only time will tell us if George Bush will be added to the pantheon of America's heroes. The one thing of which we can be sure is the next cultural and political chapters written in this nation will be provided not only by men (and women) who distinguish themselves in war and politics, but also by those that engage in the difficult day-to-day work of disciplining children, and being devoted to family and community. The sacrifices these quiet heroes make ennoble us all by shaping the strong minds, great hearts, true faith, and ready hands that are the foundation of the next generation of great men.

Cowboy Up

Although my wife has never fully understood my love of Western films, she saw no harm in allowing me to indulge my passion. She even agreed to spend our honeymoon at a dude ranch in Montana. We spent our first week as man and wife outfitted in cowboy boots, hats, and bandanas, riding horses and hiking the logging trails that surrounded our little newlywed enclave. Our honeymoon cottage was nestled against the mountains on one side and the corral on the other. To my way of thinking there are few things more romantic than lying in the warmth of your lover's arms, trying to fight the chill of the early morning mountain air while listening to the stamping and whinnying of horses.

Years later when we had a satellite dish installed in our home, she was equally as understanding. I told her I didn't care which premium movie channel she signed up for so long as I was able to get the Starz westerns channel. All cowboys, all the time! It was not until our children began running around the house pretending to shoot guns that her view of horse opera began to darken. Suddenly, my love of cowboy movies became a dangerous and violent influence on our sons.

My wife is like many other women I have met who have an immediate and visceral reaction to boys pretending to play with guns. Some of their nervousness is due to society's increased sensitivity about guns but some of it also has to do with the fact that mothers are still little girls at heart. They didn't understand the way little boys played as children and quite frankly they don't understand them any better now that they are adults.

When I was in the third grade, Donald Yin brought his toy rifle to school because he was going to, in his words, "Kill the Yankees." Our teacher, Miss Heemstraw, just told him to put the rifle on the coat rack in the hallway and to not bring it to school anymore. Simple. Over and done with. I relayed this story to my wife and her jaw dropped in disbelief. "You're kidding!" she exclaimed. Of course in today's climate, Donald would have been suspended, perhaps even expelled. He would have been required to see a therapist before being reinstated in the school, his parents would have come to the school to speak to the principal, and the local law enforcement authorities would have been notified. The recent spate of young people bringing real guns to school for the purposes of killing their schoolmates (as opposed to the Yankees) certainly makes the zero-tolerance policy adapted by schools and my wife's incredulity understandable. At the same time, however, the zero-tolerance policy has led to little boys being suspended merely for making a gun with their fingers and making shooting sounds with their mouths.

Like my wife, the drafters of the policy either ignore or have forgotten that little boys play guns because they are little boys. We have never bought our sons toy guns but that doesn't stop them from making guns out of anything they find: old coat hangers, sticks, you name it. Fine, they watch reruns of *Gunsmoke* on television, but I hear the same stories from parents who never let their boys watch anything but public television (or so they swear). They complain that their sons bite their breakfast toast into the shape of guns and drink their orange juice to the tune of "pachew! pachew!" The fact that they are shooting bad guys suggests to me that they possess a certain understanding of the constructive role violence can play in this world. It can be used to protect one's life or property, for instance, to enforce the law or defend the weak. Oh, that some adults I know would only find their way to a similar understanding. My sons pretend to shoot guns not because they watch westerns, but for the same reason they throw karate kicks at each others heads: They are little boys.

Still my wife claims that the films are a negative influence. I suggested to her that her husband, the man she chose to have children with, grew up playing with toy six-shooters and watching Westerns every Saturday. "I didn't turn out so bad, did I?" I insisted. I didn't think I was going to like her response, so I quickly pointed out that our boys also watch the *Iron Chef* cooking show with me, and so far not one of them has prepared me a meal. My logic fell on deaf ears. What my wife is missing is that westerns contain gunplay but they are not *about* gunplay. As the gunfighter Shane said to a young Joey Starrett: "A gun is as good or bad as the man using it." Western films like *Shane* are, by and large, about character, right and wrong, and what it means to be a man.

The other night, I watched *Ride the High Country*, one of my favorite westerns. Joel McCrea and Randolph Scott star as two aging former federal marshals now reduced to transporting gold for a mining company. They are glorified security guards. Scott spends a good deal of time trying to convince McCrea that they should simply ride off with the gold and keep it for themselves. After all, they have given a lifetime of service and have nothing but bullet wounds to show for it. "Do you know what is on the back of a poor man when he dies?" Scott asks. "The clothes of pride. And they don't keep him any warmer when he is dead than they did when he was alive." But McCrea wants nothing more than to go to his grave "justified." To this poor hero, there is nothing more important than a man's honor and self-respect. In the end, Scott puts friendship and honor above riches and McCrea dies a noble death, not protecting gold but the rights and honor of a young woman. Contrast that with much of the more recent product coming out of Hollywood.

The director of the Turner Broadcasting remake of *High Noon*, in my opinion one of the best Westerns ever made, Rod Hardy, said he adjusted elements of the original story to give it a more contemporary flavor. It was his belief that the modern-day retelling would be more identifiable with today's viewing audience. Let us hope he is wrong.

High Noon is why I love Westerns! The story is simple and in my mind not in need of any adjusting: On the morning of his wedding to Amy Fowler, Marshal Will Kane discovers that Frank Miller, the killer he sent to prison five years ago, is headed back to town for revenge. Three of Millers' cronies are in town and waiting for Miller who is on the noon train. The climactic third act begins with a steam whistle blowing in the distance announcing the arrival of the noon train—right on schedule. Kane stands alone on the town's dirt street with the sun beating his brow. His eyes nervously search the deserted town. He wipes the sweat from his brow, straightens his gun belt and begins walking toward the edge of town resolved to meet his fate.

Where the original tells its story in stark black and white, emphasizing the dry heat of moral struggle, the remake is lush with color and covered in mud. If McCarthyism gave the original its clarity and poignancy, the Bill Clinton era of moral relativism informs this overly sentimental remake. Sadly, where the original film fills me with hope, this contemporary remake left me strangely pessimistic.

The original film, which starred Gary Cooper and Grace Kelly, was unequivocal in its assertion that evil (embodied in the character of Frank Miller) exists. However, in the remake, we are told over and over again that Frank Miller is crazy. It is only in the current climate of moral relativity that a man bent on not only taking the life of an officer of the law, but on destroying a town, cannot be labeled as evil. Today, we search for the root cause of anti-social behavior.

Evil is distinct from insanity in that the insane do not know what they are doing. The destruction they reap is the result of a diseased mind. The evil, on the other hand, know exactly what they are doing. They destroy because it gives them gratification—sexual, moral, or personal. It is worth remembering that the 9/11 murderers did not attempt to build something greater than the World Trade Center Towers. They knocked them down. And their supporters danced in the streets just as the barkeep in *High Noon* buys drinks for the house upon receiving the news of Miller's return. Frank Miller is hell bent on destruction and if left unchecked, he will destroy everything in his path.

The remake also gives us more insight into the roots of Amy Fowlers' pacifism and, in so doing, shifts the focus of the film from the cost of manhood and the price of standing up for what is right, a central theme of the original, to the more general (and muddy) observation that it's important to stand up for one's principles.

Thus, the remake renders every principled stance as moral and suggests that we must all follow our own moral compass. The original film was saying just the opposite! In 1952, the height of the McCarthy era, the filmmakers said in no uncertain terms: There is "right" and there is "wrong" and that "sometimes it is just that simple." All behavior, no matter how well intentioned, is not moral. What a difference fifty years makes.

In the remake, with misty eyes, Amy tells how guns killed both her parents. "I admire the manner of their death." She adds, "They could have picked up guns. They could have killed to save their lives. Instead they chose to show love in the face of hatred. Love is the only way things ever really change." It is worth pausing to remember that Actor Richard Gere exhibited a version of this same naiveté soon after the murders of 9/11/01, while speaking to an audience filled with New York City firefighters, policemen, and their families. Gere encouraged the audience to look upon this time of mourning as an opportunity to reach out and show love to the world. He was appropriately booed off the stage.

Love is not a passive emotion. It is proactive behavior. Embracing one's enemies at the cost of the lives of the innocent is not an act of love, but an act of contempt. Should I embrace those who are bent on destruction? Or is my violent act of taking the life of an evildoer an act of love for the innocent?

Perhaps the most disturbing portion of this contemporary retelling occurs during the climactic shootout when Amy Fowler saves Will Kane's life. In the original, Fowler's act is an independent act of love and loyalty. (I have long held that the original film is ultimately about what it takes to make marriage work. The very first words the audience hears are sung by Tex Ritter, "Do not forsake me, oh my darlin'. On this our wedding day. . . ." In a world that often seems committed to marrying but ambivalent to marriage, this film makes it clear and drives it home that all things are possible when a couple is committed to standing together through the toughest of times. When you get right down to it, that is what making a marriage work is all about—fighting against temptation, ego, and the hundred other evils that come riding into town on the noon train. But I digress.) In the remake, however, Fowler does not pick up a gun until *after* she has been roughed up by one of the assassins and her husband is on his knees before Miller. It is a sad commentary on contemporary society when we demand that our heroes bow before evil as Tom Skerrit's Will Kane does. Gary Cooper would never have gone to his knees!

They truly "don't make 'em like that anymore." The Western of my youth has been replaced with fare that is morally ambiguous and, as a result, much more violent.

The movie theatres and my living room are not the only places the cowboy has been forsaken. In greater culture, "cowboy," once a term of endearment, has now become one of contempt. Detractors labeled presidents Ronald Reagan and George W. Bush as cowboys. The epithet was a comment on their plain language and what some describe as a proclivity to shoot first and ask questions later. What they're missing is that cowboys are heroes. Cowboys never looked for trouble but when it came, they faced it with courage. Cowboys are self-sufficient, independent, and honorable. Cowboys persevere in the face of overwhelming odds and they respect women, children, and horses. They may often be men of few words, but more importantly, they are men of action.

Theodore Roosevelt, our nation's first cowboy president, said, "[The cowboy] possesses, in fact, few of the emasculated, milk-and-water moralities admired by pseudo-philanthropists, but he does possess, to a very high degree, the stern, manly qualities that are invaluable to a nation." What my wife doesn't understand, what Hollywood has forgotten, and what the current culture is overlooking is that the cowboy is the embodiment of all the values we hope to instill in our sons and the totality of what our times demand.

The cynics in our culture ask, "What place does an idealistic cow punch have in today's world? We need heroes made for the digital age. What do the likes of John Wayne and Randolph Scott have to offer in the war against corporate scandal and Islamic fanaticism?" It is through the celebration of heroism that society moves toward its ideal. The celebration of heroism inspires future generations to achieve great things! Cowboys offer me hope. I say the cowboy is not an anachronism, but a man built for this age. In a world where men fly airplanes into buildings, what better ideal than that of men who don't start fights but are not afraid to finish them, men like Glenn Ford in the film *The Violent Men* who look tyrants in the eye and say, "Don't force me to fight 'cause you won't like my way of fighting."

In the 1958 film *The Law and Jake Wade*, Richard Widmark remarks to a young Deforest Kelly, "Sonny, I can see we ain't going to have you 'round long enough to get tired of your company." What better response to the greed of corporate leaders whose shenanigans undermine the trust necessary for free markets to work? The code of the West may be more relevant today than ever before. Let's not forget that riding tall in the saddle is the description of pride, of a sense of righteousness, and dignity. Riding tall is riding with confidence, purpose, strength, and virtue.

I bought a new cowboy hat the other day. It's a white hat with a tall crown and a wide brim. It reminds me of the kind of hat William "Hopalong Cassidy" Boyd wore in so many films. While I was in the store, my son Connor decided that he also needed a new cowboy hat. We found a nice, inexpensive hat and he proudly wore it out of the store. The next morning when I returned from the gym, he was seated at the table dressed for school in jeans, plaid flannel shirt, cowboy boots, bandanna, and his brand-new cowboy hat. I looked at my wife who just shrugged and said, "He wants to wear it to school and I am too tired to argue." I looked back to Connor and, fearing that he might be teased by his classmates, prepared to try and persuade him to tone the look down a bit. Then I changed my mind and thought, Why not? I went upstairs and dressed in *my* jeans, flannel shirt, bandanna, boots, and new hat. My son clearly understands what I have been trying to explain to his mother: These are precisely the times for a new sheriff to ride into town, with gun belt slung low on his hips, making the town safe for God-fearing men, women, and children.

FAMILY

The Death of Dreams[*]

I was born inside of her. I was nurtured by her flesh and literally cut from her body. I was part of her. The life she choked out of herself one cold February morning was part of my life; it was part of the lives of my three sisters. Her death was the death of my childhood; it seemed then the death of my dreams. It was as if my mother gathered her family and hacked her life out of our flesh. We were left standing, eyes agape, staring at a huge bloody wound—emptiness where dreams should have been. We averted our eyes from those watching. We built walls around us, afraid the world might see that we were no longer whole.

It has been more than twenty years since my mother's suicide, and in that time I have been haunted by a recurring dream: I am standing alone, surrounded by mountains of granite. The sun is pouring down on me, perspiration running in rivers over my muscles. But I am tireless in my work, a latter-day John Henry, I turn the mountains to dust with each angry swing of my hammer. Over the years, I have accepted this as my legacy: a lifetime at hard labor, breaking rocks as punishment for the sin of not loving my mother enough to keep her from leaving and for the lesser sin of being too young to understand that even my unconditional love could not ease the pain she felt. I wake every morning with a hundred unanswered questions.

I realize now that I never really knew my mother. Though I inherited more of her personality than my three sisters did, I am not sure my mother and I ever understood each other. Or perhaps we understood each other all too well. How will I ever know? This is the true tragedy: I was never my mother's friend and, more importantly, she was never mine.

I never bought my mother lunch or just sat with her, sipping a glass of wine. We never talked politics or argued religion. She never had the opportunity to meet any of my girlfriends, and I was never able to hear that "original feminine voice"—the standard by which all others are measured—tell me that the second

*This essay was originally published in a January 1991 issue of *Essence* magazine.

feminine voice simply was not good enough for her only son. What is more important is that I will never be able to shield her from the elements or comfort and nurse her when she is sick. All those experiences are gone, but they never were. They were sealed and buried with my mother.

In the decades since her death, I have missed her terribly. I have yearned for her and, like a small boy, dreamed of experiences I can never have. At times, I have cursed my mother for denying me the opportunity to be her friend—the one thing I view as my birthright—and hated her for leaving me a lifetime of penance.

It has taken time and more than a few prayers, but I have finally come to realize that my dreams did not die with her. I see now that the mountains I smash every night are the pathways to wholeness. These mountains are anger, they are guilt and mourning. They are perceptions of myself as incomplete. If I am to be free to move forward, free to dream, the mountains must come down.

Healing means realizing my mother has missed out on a friendship with a great guy, and wholeness is recognizing that my relationship with my mother is ongoing. The man I have become is due to the relationship I've had with her since her death, and that relationship will play an important role in determining the man I am yet to be.

It has taken me a few years, but now I understand that my recurring dream is not a nightmare at all. The hard labor is not punishment, but healing. The rocks I break with every heavy swing of my hammer represent the inadequacy and failure, hurt and rejection I initially accepted as my legacy. I also understand that I will break these rocks for a long time. Each swing brings me a little closer to healing, and healing, like growth, is a lifelong process. The pain dulls but if we are to remain whole, we must continue to explore. Our eyes must stay open and if we are to continue growing, we must never stop dreaming.

My Father's Hair

As I stood at my father's bedside watching the life slowly leave his body, I stroked his hair. I was surprised at how soft it was. In the midst of this incredibly intimate moment, perhaps the most intimate moment I had ever had with my father, I became a child again. Children are fond of asking "why;" it's their favorite question. I have three sons and no morning is complete without a "why" chorus. Why is the sky blue? Why do you shave? Why is your belly so big? Those are the easy ones. The questions I asked my father that day were the hard ones. Why this moment? Why now? Why are you being cheated of your life and why am I being cheated from having you in mine?

The day after my father died, I received a phone call. Through tears, the feminine voice on the other end of the line explained, "You don't know me, but I want to tell you who your father was." She went on to tell me she had been one of my father's patients during her childhood. When she had the misfortune of becoming a young, unmarried mother, my father became her child's doctor. "Your father never charged me once," she told me. "Long after most doctors stopped making house calls, your father came to my home and not only attended to my son, but wrote out a prescription, picked up the medication and paid for it himself."

I hung up the phone with tears streaming down my face. The sadness I felt at the loss of my father was now mixed with a deep sense of pride. It was also a moment of revelation: sometimes "why" is not as important as "how." My father had answered my "how" in the way he lived his life, his adherence to principal, and his sense of humor. He was a humble man with a strong faith in God. My father told me "how" in the way he treated his fellow man, his fidelity to family, and his work ethic. These are the "how's" of manhood. These were the answers he gave me and more importantly, these are the answers I will give to my sons.

I have three sets of eyes watching me. I show them how to be a man every day in everything I do. Each day I wonder why this enormous responsibility was entrusted to me—I can't even keep track of my car keys. No doubt my father wondered the same thing about fatherhood. While playing catch with me in the backyard, watching me perform in school plays, and spanking my behind, he probably wondered, "Why, Lord?" but continued teaching by example.

It is a shame that as social currency, fatherhood has been so drastically devalued. A man's honor is cheap. Starlets grace the cover of magazines celebrating the birth of their fatherless children. Actors, politicians and any number of professional athletes are seldom taken to task for fathering children out of wedlock. Oh sure, it makes grist for the gossip mill, but there is little, if any, social cost. I guess we have only ourselves to blame. A seventy-percent illegitimacy rate means the first lesson seventy percent of our children learn is: Fatherhood means having the government garnish child support from your paycheck.

It is a long and winding path that leads to manhood and I guess along the way boys will never stop asking questions—and no offense, ladies—it is up to men to answer them. Boys must see the pride in their father's smile, feel the firm hand of a father's discipline, and hear the bite of correction in his voice. Boys will not grow into men unless men lead them. And I am not talking about role models. Boys do not need male role models and they don't need father *figures*; they need fathers *in the home*. Prisons are overflowing with men who had loving mothers and great father figures.

I confess I am still figuring out this manhood thing, this husband thing, this father thing. It is during these moments of feeling my way through the darkness that I miss my father's guidance and friendship most. But I think back to that phone call and the grieving voice on the other end and I remember the challenge I made to myself. I offer that same challenge to every other father. We don't always know the answers to "why"—they're sometimes best left to one who's wiser and omnipotent—but we can show our sons "how."

Frozen Wedding Memories

Often, I wish my wife and I had videotaped our wedding ceremony. The fact that we did not was a bit of arrogance on our part. We couldn't imagine that we would ever want to sit down and watch ourselves on tape. People who videotape their ceremonies are just a bit full of themselves we intoned. As a record of the event, we felt traditional photographs would suffice. While we do have a wonderful wedding album, I wish we had put our puffed-up arrogance aside and videotaped our ceremony. The wedding day was such a blur of ritual and salutations that afterwards, we couldn't remember very much about it. Friends told us it was wonderfully romantic and brought tears to their eyes. Videotape would have allowed us to witness it for ourselves. More importantly, during those moments when my wife and I have struggled, when we held our noses and wondered what in the world we ever saw in each other, the video would have served as a real-time reminder of how deeply in love we were.

I woke up on my wedding day too nervous to concentrate. A good run would have helped me to work off the excess energy that was twisting my stomach into knots. I just wanted to run. I wasn't looking to run away. I just needed to pound out three or four good miles. My best man—my bodyguard for the day—didn't want to let me out of his sight so I didn't get a chance to jog along the shore of Lake Michigan and contemplate the enormity of what I was about to do. I suspect that the ideal time for contemplating the significance of marriage is before one proposes and not the morning of the wedding day. I have also learned that there are moments after marriage that lend themselves to pondering the wisdom of matrimony. Besides, in my anxiety over getting married, I had forgotten to bring black dress socks with me to Chicago. There was no time for exercise. I had to go downtown to shop for socks.

My wife, on the other hand, was the picture of calmness. Before heading downtown, I called her at her mother's house. "Hello!" she answered. "Happy day!" My anxiety doubled. "What in the world is she so happy about?" I wondered. Sure, it was easy for her to be relaxed. She had used up all of her angst in the six months leading up to our nuptials. While she worried about losing her identity, I was the picture of cool composure. While she was tortured by the fear of losing her friends, I remained unruffled. While she struggled with cold feet, I couldn't wait to become her husband. Now, I was sitting in my hotel room, feeling sick in my stomach, trying to figure out how to ditch my best man so I could run around Lake Michigan.

We were adamant that our ceremony begin on time. Ours was not going to be like so many weddings we had attended that kept guests waiting. The wedding planner walked into the room promptly at ten after 5:00. "It's time," she said. As the gentle strains of Erik Saties' "Tois Gymnopedies" began to play, my best man and I made our entrance. The only thing I could think of as we proceeded down the aisle was the climatic scene in the Sean Penn film *Dead Man Walking*.

The late afternoon sun poured into the front windows. I was sweating like a pig when the musicians struck the first few chords of the Pachelbel's Canon. I turned to receive my bride and lost my breath. I suddenly forgot how hot I was. She was beautiful! I have always thought my wife was a beautiful woman, but as she walked down the aisle with a huge smile on her face, in that moment, she was the loveliest I had ever seen her. My nervousness was instantly replaced by the familiar thumping in my chest that I felt the first time I laid eyes on her. I was in love and I was indescribably happy.

That's the moment I'd like to see. That moment, along with a thousand other subtle and emotional moments, are ones none of our photographs captured. As beautiful as wedding stills can be, a photograph will always miss a groom's voice cracking when he is overcome by emotion during the exchange of vows. A photographer might fail to catch a mother's tear as she reads from First Corinthians. A wedding still could never repeat the band striking up Fats Waller's "This Joint is Jumpin'" as the pastor pronounces the couple man and wife.

Marriage has not proven to be a cakewalk for my wife and me. I imagine it has also presented challenges for others as well. Juggling needs, personalities, and moods is tough work. Over the years, our efforts have yielded more tight jaws, pursed lips, and scratched throats than I care to count. There have also been times when, under the guise of meditation, I have withdrawn to my closet wondering what happened. I imagine that I am not alone here either. I suspect there are plenty of men and women who have at sometime retreated to the comfort of the clothes closet, the garage, or the gym to meditate. These are the periods I think it might help to be reminded of a time when love was fresh and strong, when we danced with our lover to sweet music while the champagne flowed.

The Rewards of Marriage

I have two very good friends who are on opposite ends of the marriage spectrum. One is preparing for marriage and the other feels he is an authority on it. Neither wanted their names used so let's call the first one "Ralph" and the second one "Stan." Ralph will be walking down the aisle in November and Stan (the expert) has become so disenchanted with his marriage that he is on the golf course seven days a week trying to avoid the situation.

After years of playing the field, Ralph decided to get married. I get a kick out of talking to him. He has always been an intellectual and is convinced he has the marriage puzzle figured out. He has found the key to unlock a lifetime of fun. Poor sap! He has no idea what he's getting himself into. I'm sure that a year from now, I will find Ralph glassy-eyed, wandering in the women's section at Macy's, carrying a purse, and mumbling to himself.

Stan, on the other hand, has been married sixteen years and summed up his philosophy of marriage thusly: "Love has nothing to do with feeling good!" To say he is unhappy is an understatement. Stan has no plans to divorce. If he were having a beer with Ralph, he would lecture him about marriage being a duty—a right of passage a man must suffer in order to earn Brownie points with God. I know better than to believe the love-struck ramblings of a "soon-to-be-married," but neither am I convinced that marriage is akin to ritual circumcision. I think both my buddies have got it wrong.

When I was a teenager, a family friend told me, "Marriage is the best life." Notice that she didn't say, "Marriage is the most fun life." In fact, marriage has little to do with fun. Matrimony is about enriching and ennobling our lives through the discovery of some greater humanity within ourselves. For men, marriage is another step in the transition from boyhood into manhood. That is not to say that one cannot have fun while married, but marriage in and of itself does not provide a lot of yuks!

The world tends to revolve around us as singles. There are those things of significance—*my* happiness, *my* needs and *my* opinions—and there is everything else. When we marry, we are forced to give up this very narrow, self-centered view of the world. The capacity to turn on a dime so that someone else's concerns become primary in our lives is the revelation marriage seeks to unfold. This is no easy feat and invariably leads to resentment. Yet that is exactly what we take a vow to do—put aside our interests in favor of someone else's with no guarantee that our efforts will be reciprocated. Let the fun begin!

I can't be certain, but I have an inkling that a great deal of marital discord arises from one or both spouses reverting to and relying on this old notion of "I, not I." Seeking momentary pleasure without concern about its impact on one's spouse or children leads to infidelity. The seeking of self-fulfillment without regard to its impact on family leads to abandonment. How many of Stan's golfing buddies have driven similar stakes into the hearts of their own marriages?

I suppose there is always the single life—plenty of time for golf and pretty young things who demand nothing and only have pleasure in mind. Nice work if you can get it! Regrettably, my days as a bachelor were never like that. In spite of my occasional dreamy walk down memory lane, the Dallas Cowboy Cheerleaders never stopped their bus in front of my apartment. I spent many a lonely night wishing I had someone with whom to share my life.

I will never forget the premiere of *Strictly Business*. Lights, news cameras, limousines, movie stars, red carpet. . . . It should have been one of the happiest nights of my life. Instead it was a lonely, dreadful evening. I was by myself. Sure, I could have taken a date. There were several women hinting that they wanted to attend. At the time, I subscribed to the bachelors' credo that one doesn't take sand to the beach. And let's face it, asking one girlfriend would mean making the others angry, which would have seriously cramped my style for months. Such are the machinations of the single life. Some guys don't mind living like that. They clearly have more game than I did. But I much prefer sharing life's special moments with someone special over calculating how to keep the revolving door to my bedroom from jamming shut.

Thankfully, I now have someone who laughs when I dance, falls asleep in the middle of every video we rent, and, more importantly, holds me up when I no longer have the strength. But all my years of marriage have also taught me there is something greater than myself. I discover every day that submission to the needs of others not only gives our lives greater purpose, but is also what separates us from the apes. This is why Ralph should walk down the aisle in November and why Stan should put his golf clubs in the garage and fight like hell to save his marriage!

At our wedding, my wife and I danced our first dance to the Isley Brothers' "For the Love of You." As Ronnie Isley crooned, "Driftin' on a memory/ain't no place I'd rather be/ than with you," I remember feeling that was the happiest moment of my life. Dancing is fun, but doing it with the woman you love is even more fun. Living the rest of your life with her may be difficult at times, but the rewards make you feel there's no place else you'd rather be.

Women and Power

I was amused when the local news broadcast an interview with a couple who had been married seventy-seven years. The reporter asked the elderly woman what her secret was. The woman replied that it took lots of communication and trust. Yes! That is what it takes for a *woman* to remain married, but success for a man boils down to doing what he is told. I am quite certain the elderly gentleman would have agreed with me, had anyone bothered to ask his opinion. The reporter (a woman), however, barely spoke to him. He sat dutifully listening. No doubt the result of seventy-seven years of training.

Having been married for something less than seventy-seven years, I can honestly say it doesn't take nearly that long for a man to figure out he is not going to get a woman to do anything she doesn't want to do. Conversely, with the right smile, a woman can get a man to do just about anything.

While my tongue is planted firmly in my cheek, there is more than a grain of truth to what I am saying. Women run this world. It's lucky for us guys they don't realize it.

I am not a social scientist and don't have any proof, but my sense is that women used to know their power; they celebrated their femininity. I think things began to go haywire when some guy convinced women to join the sexual revolution. It had to have been a guy. Who else would come up with the idea of multiple sex partners with no strings attached? That he was able to sell this idea to women as "empowerment" makes him the biggest flim-flam artist in history. Men got easy sex while women got sexually transmitted diseases, unwanted pregnancy, and a string of unfulfilling relationships. You tell me who got the short end of that stick. Ever since that time, feminists have been convincing scores of other women that they are powerless and that femininity equals weakness.

Recently, I performed a solo play at a fairly well-known Southern university. In the show, I reminisce about the many women for whom I yearned and who broke my heart while I was a young man growing up at the tail end of the sexual revolution. During the question and answer portion of the evening, a female student, who described herself as a card-carrying feminist, (do they actually give out cards?) declared the abundance of sexual references to women in my play as stereotyping. It should come as no great surprise that I disagreed with her analysis. What was truly fascinating, however, was this woman's very obvious lack of appreciation for the workings of the male mind. This woman was willing to grant me that sexuality was an important element in our social lives, but she disagreed that the sexual dance was *primary* in our social construct, that men's desire of women informs most of our social relationships, and that women are in control of those relationships. Imagine me trying like the devil to explain to a grown woman that guys like girls! At a certain age, the desire for girls is our primary motivation, right after oxygen.

For all of her feminist rhetoric, this student's failure to embrace this fact (I suspect for political reasons) is actually a failure to embrace her own power as a woman. She was accusing me of negative stereotyping while all the time I was giving women props. I shouldn't have been surprised. The mantra of gender empowerment through sexual promiscuity has apparently deadened the minds of an entire generation of young women.

Not long ago, I was speaking to a group of high school students. What was supposed to be a talk about working on television took an odd turn and ended up on the corner of sex and teen pregnancy. As the man caught in the tornado said, "I just had to go with it." The girls in the audience expressed a great deal of distress at the pressure they were receiving from their male classmates to have sex. They explained, "If we don't put out, the boys won't like us." Virginity was weakness. I let the girls in on a secret. "What the boys don't want you to know," I told them, "is that the length of your relationship with a man (or boy) is in direct proportion to how soon you sleep with him. What you have is precious and no matter what they might tell you in whispers and moans, men do not respect women who give it away. Men respect the women they have to work to get."

The boys whooped and hollered derisively, of course (as will some *men* reading this). I was a traitor to reveal such valuable information. The girls, on the other hand, sat silently with blank expressions on their faces. No one had ever told them that they held *all* of the power.

This preponderance of misinformation is not exclusive to high-school students. How many grown women do we all know who are genuinely confused that some guy they met and fell into bed with didn't call them back? Consider that birds with brains the size of peas demand that their mates demonstrate their worthiness. Far too many women today give themselves to men without consideration of that man's worth as life partner or father of their children. The feminist at the university would say that I am blaming the victim. She might also argue that real empowerment for women is in choosing to abort the child that results from such unions. I would argue that true empowerment is in the exercising of greater selectivity in who a woman chooses as a sexual partner. That is real freedom of choice, real control over one's body, real power.

I recently heard of a survey that revealed that ninety percent of men thought a woman who smiled at them was interested in them romantically. I don't know if the study is real, but I don't doubt it. I have known men to ascribe romantic notions to women based on much less than a smile. Whoever said it was a man's world clearly didn't know what he was talking about. Every ounce of power in this society is vested in the smile of a woman and happily, like all men, I am forever at its mercy.

I Am Confused!

We noticed a foul odor coming from the garage. It smelled as if something had curled up and died. Sure enough, a big, fat, granddaddy of a mouse had given up the ghost behind the freezer. My wife never glanced toward the broom nor did she roll up her sleeves to help move the freezer. I am confused. Why is it my job to remove the dead mouse from the garage?

This is called gender role-playing. My wife, who is training for a triathlon, gets up every morning at 4:30 a.m. and runs—she doesn't jog—eight miles and lifts weights. She is strong as an ox. If anyone is in condition to clean rodent nests from underneath the garage freezer, it is my wife. In this instance, however, my wife, who is quick to declare herself a feminist, decided this was a job better suited for the man of the house. Great! The one time I get to wear the pants, it is to get on my knees and clean up dead rodents.

Women are attending graduate schools in unprecedented numbers, breaking through the "glass ceiling" of the corporate world, and sitting in the highest offices of government. Women are working construction, driving cabs, and even playing football. Yet somehow they have still reserved for themselves the right to fall back into those old familiar "gender" roles. I suppose this is what's meant by "a woman's prerogative."

It is no wonder I am confused. The gender roles in my home are turned completely upside down. Perhaps this is an indication of how arbitrary some of these rules can be, or it may be, as a few men have suggested, evidence that I am a girly man. In my home, I do all the cooking. If left to her own devices, my wife would live on a steady diet of steamed broccoli and rice. I do all the gardening and sewing. My wife has no idea what is growing in our garden and if my son's pants need a quick hem before church, I pick up the needle and thread. My wife carried our three sons to term but *I* put on the pregnancy weight. I am also far more emotional than my wife. I love show tunes, cry at movies, and usually am the one who complains of not getting enough attention. Her father, a Viet Nam vet, was more than a bit concerned. But who said real men could not be sensitive?

Further muddying the waters is the fact that my wife works every day while I stay home, waiting for my agent to call. Unfortunately for my wife, the reality of being married to an actor (or this particular actor, at any rate) is that her income is necessary. Unfortunately for me, there have been more than a few years when her income has been essential!

She is part of a generation of new feminists who were raised to believe motherhood was for suckers and that the boardroom was the true avenue to fulfillment. My wife's generation was promised that they could do it all. Actress Jada Pinkett-Smith, wife of actor Will Smith, recently summed up that attitude rather nicely. During a much publicized speech to students at Harvard, Pinkett-Smith remarked: "Women, you can have it all—a loving man, devoted husband, loving children, a fabulous career. They say you gotta choose. Nah, nah, nah, we are a new generation of women. We got to set a new standard of rules around here. You can do whatever it is you want. All you have to do is want it." No doubt the difference between wanting it and achieving it is having a bazillion dollars in the bank as the Smiths do. For everyday women, it is considerably more difficult and the pursuit of such pie in the sky notions results in more than a little confusion.

My wife has run face first into the realization that the new feminists (and Pinkett-Smith) were selling snake oil. She has begun to envy her girlfriends who made the choice to be homemakers. It tears her up inside when she leaves our children to go to work, but you can't be a senior vice president of worldwide marketing *and* a homemaker. She has no designs on becoming Martha Stewart, but she is a terrific mother and loves doing "mommy" things with our sons. She is frustrated by the collision of feminism's promise and reality. Thus, there is a certain comfort in retreating to the "gender" roles of our parent's generation. She is relieved to know that no matter how good I am at making béchamel, I can still be relied upon to kill any creepy crawly thing that crosses our doorstep.

Along these lines, I laughed out loud when I heard the story of the man from Yemen who divorced his wife because she was too loud and bossy. He re-married a deaf mute, no doubt thinking this would bring order to the confusion of gender role-playing. As my grandfather used to say, "Have I got some music for his ears?" Vocal chords or no, my Yemeni brothers' wife will probably still demand that he scrape up the remains of any critter that might be unfortunate enough to die under his refrigerator freezer.

I have no intentions of divorcing my wife but have decided that, as the saying goes, "two can play." The other day while attending a picnic in the park, my son had to go to the bathroom. If there is anything more disgusting than cleaning up dead animals, it has got to be helping your five-year-old use a public toilet. I was actually coping rather well until my son announced he needed to go "number two." At that moment, all bets were off! I marched him back to his mother and told her this was woman's work. At the very least it was not a job for a sensitive man like me. After she left with my son, I sat back down on the blanket and enjoyed another hot dog.

Now, who is the girly man?

The Head and Heart of Little Brothers

As a child, going to the barbershop was unconstrained time spent with my father. The smell of Afro Sheen, witch hazel, and smoke from the rib shack next door filled the small shop. My father would buy me an orange soda pop and I would sit and listen to the men laugh at the lies being told. I'd watch as they ran to the window to ogle the pretty women who passed by. There was nothing feminine about this place! This was time for and about men!

Sadly, there are young boys who will never know the pleasure of this last bastion of maleness and I feel partly to blame. I am part of a generation that has turned the job of raising men over to women. Not too long ago, I was having my hair cut in a shop owned and staffed by women. The owner, a single mother, often brought her son to the shop with her. He was about ten years old and, like so many young boys today, his father was absent from his life. When he wasn't in school or hanging out in the barbershop, he was sneaking into movies or spending money on video games at the arcade.

One afternoon, while hanging out in the shop, his mother caught him flipping milk bottle tops with one of the customers. I have never understood the appeal of milk bottle tops, but he was enjoying himself, as was the customer he was playing with. When his mother scolded him, the other women in the shop joined in and began teasing him. I looked at the little boy's face. He was straining with all the might his ten-year-old body could muster to hold on to some portion of his pride. This was my moment of revelation.

Each man sitting in the shop had probably experienced the unabashed maleness that used to define the barbershop setting. Today—in this barbershop—this boy was being punished for simply doing what little boys do. He should have been safe in this environment, but we men, the guardians of this last sanctuary of testosterone, have surrendered the gates without as much as a whimper.

I joined the Big Brothers program the very next day. It was my way of taking back the citadel.

I participated in Big Brothers for three years. My little brother's name was Jacob. I wish I could say that my relationship with Jacob was the kind of story popular in Hollywood—with happy endings and walking off into the sunset when the music swells as the scene fades to black. But real people with real needs don't often behave like they do in Hollywood movies.

Jacob was typical of the boys involved in the program—bright, talented, sad, and sorely missing his father. It was amazing to see the darkness cloud his face when his father was mentioned and yet he loved his father as only little boys can.

One year, near Christmas, I picked him up and took him to the arcade. We left early so he could get home in time to go to the movies with a friend. During this ride he asked me if God answered prayers. "Yes," I said emphatically. "Absolutely!" "Well," Jacob said, "I am going to pray that we get home in time for me to go to the movies and that my Dad is at my house when I wake up Christmas morning." His father was not there on Christmas morning. His father didn't call on Christmas day. His father didn't send a gift.

I actually had the opportunity to meet his father. He thanked me for being a role model for his son. "These kids need role models," he said. He went on to tell me that he had attempted to join the Big Brothers organization in his community. He was amazed that he had been turned away.

Jacob is sixteen now. I called him the other day just to see how he was doing. The voice on the other end of the phone was deeper, but unmistakable. He was happy to hear from me and, unlike some of the one-sided conversations we had when he was younger, he eagerly filled me in on everything he had been doing these last couple of years. He talked about the computer he built and his goal of becoming a graphic artist. He even talked a bit about his father and the year he spent living with him in New York. Jacob was left behind a grade, has been having fights in school, and will attend a school for students with special needs in the fall. He told me in so many words that he is still looking for a place to drink orange soda while listening to men tell stories, a place where it's safe to be a man.

Rediscovering Innocence

While I was stuck in rush hour traffic, a friend of mine was talking to me about his daughters. Actually, he was bragging . . . you know the conversation. "The girls are in gifted programs at school, they read the dictionary every night before going to bed, blah, blah, blah." I immediately began to wonder, "What's wrong with my kids?" Instead of making insightful observations about life, and pouring through the encyclopedia for nighttime reading, they tell pee-pee jokes. But I don't hate him. I understand him completely.

When I attended Father's Day at my son's school the teacher asked all of the guests to describe what was special about the child they were there to visit. When my turn came, my heart was so full I could barely speak. "I love my son's spirit," I said. "He has the most wonderful spirit of anyone I have ever met. He is my first born and I couldn't love him more if I tried." The lump in my throat was the size of a baseball. When I left the school, I was grinning ear to ear and my heart ready to burst. At that moment, all of my troubles and disappointments melted away. Nothing was as important as my son and the love I felt for him. When that much emotion is bubbling up inside, it is hard to keep it to yourself. A parent is like the newly baptized, wanting to share their experience with all who will listen.

It is not only unconditional love that compels parents to speak. The rediscovery of innocence also demands sharing.

I recall the first time I took my son to the barbershop. The first thing he saw when we entered the store was the bright, shiny bubblegum machine. "Daddy, can I have some?" He pleaded. "I don't have any money," I lied. "I have money," he said holding out his hand to show me his imaginary coins. "Oh you do?" At this point I decided to show him how smart I was. "Well, why don't you go over there and see if the machine accepts that kind of money."

My son walked over to the machine, put in his imaginary coin, turned the handle and pulled out a red ball of gum. That day I was reminded that you never know what you can do until you try.

Age breeds cynicism. We grow older and learn that dreams are fragile and easily broken. We discover that bad things happen to good people all of the time, and that what goes around sometimes takes a long time to come around. All of this baggage weighs us down and blinds us to the blessings of life. Children remind us that there is nothing more precious than innocence, nothing more beautiful than our world viewed through eyes that have not been jaded by life's merciless twists and turns. We forget what it is like to kick a ball just to see how high it will go, or run as fast as we can because the wind feels good in our faces.

We don't recall the quiet delight in hearing dead leaves crunch beneath our feet. We fail to remember that puddles are for splashing and mud is for squishing. I believe God wants us to know purity and to never forget how much fun it is to roll down a hill or lay down on freshly cut grass and look at the sky. Innocence is constantly reintroduced into our lives. We live out our childhood and then have children of our own; we are blessed to relive childhood with them. When our children have children, we once again see the world anew through our grand-children's eyes. And if we are truly fortunate, we get the chance to do it all again as great-grand parents.

At an event over one weekend, I sat next to the young father of a newborn baby girl. He was feeling a bit overwhelmed and amazed to discover that my wife and I were managing to raise three boys. Of course, I didn't tell him that we are con-stantly tired and that our house is in a constant state of disarray. He described the deep love he feels for his new baby and wondered how it was possible to ever love another child as much as he loved his daughter.

I smiled and answered that the human capacity to love constantly surprises. Our hearts have endless reserves and, where our children are concerned, we posses ever-deepening reservoirs of patience, compassion and appreciation. And what we don't have, the Lord will provide.

My children have taught me to love more deeply and more unconditionally than I knew possible. If this is not the meaning of life, perhaps it ought to be.

Of course, no revelation this wonderful comes without challenges. My wife left town not long ago, leaving me alone with our boys. It was the longest four days of my life. Every day was a new opportunity to reaffirm my commitment to not opening the front door and letting the children wander where they might.

I yelled, gave time outs like candy, and threatened spankings until I was exhausted. The end of each day was toasted with a glass of what my sons refer to as "Daddy's special lemonade"—a tall glass of lemonade with a shot of Southern Comfort. Yet for all of the torments, there were also moments that swelled my heart and made me thankful for the time I had with them.

I wrestled with them on the floor and listened to their laughter. I watched as they ran in the yard jumping and leaping, yelling just to see how loud they could be. I read to them and we lay on the floor talking about our days. During these all too brief moments, I felt young again. I felt new in the world.

I hope I never lose that feeling. I want to tap into the child inside of me as often as possible. I am not so certain my wife will understand when I step out of the shower and take off running, butt naked, through the house, hollering at the top of my lungs. Then again . . . you never know. It might take our marriage to a whole new level.

What Really Matters

The very small flue of our chimney prompted my son Connor to ask me how Santa was ever going to fit. I told him that if anyone came down our chimney, he was to call me immediately and I would come running with my baseball bat and pepper spray. My son knows that Santa Claus doesn't exist. I made the decision early on not to indulge my children with that particular part of Christmas tradition.

I figured if I had to stay up until 3 A.M. putting toys together, I wasn't going to let anyone else get the credit. Still, my son likes to play, and for him, the idea of Santa—whether real or not—is all part of the Christmas trimming. Needless to say, he didn't appreciate my sarcasm and looked at me with eyes that pleaded, "Will you please get into the Christmas spirit?"

I wasn't always in need of prompting. As a boy, I used to begin feeling the holiday magic as early as Thanksgiving. It felt like freedom—three more weeks of school until days filled with watching television and stuffing my belly with eggnog, cookies, and peppermint candy. Even as an adult, I used to sing while I walked down the street and greeted strangers with a nod and a smile. However, there have been more than a few years when I felt more like singing the blues than humming holiday carols.

The first drastic jolt came when I moved to southern California. There's something incredibly romantic about waking up on Christmas day with the streets covered with a blanket of crystalline white as I did so often while growing up in Colorado. Compared to that traditional emblem of the holiday, listening to Christmas carols while driving down the street with the top down on the convertible seems almost profane. But it wouldn't be fair to place all the blame on sunshine and short sleeves. My faltering spirit could also be the result of buying (literally) too heavily into the commercialization of Christmas.

During the first years of my marriage, it took me until May to pay the bills incurred during December. My solution was to eschew the superficial rudiments of Christmas and concentrate instead on the purely spiritual side. I didn't listen to Christmas music, I didn't purchase a tree, and didn't exchange gifts. Instead, I went to church and read the Bible. I was miserable!

For some, this may be final proof that I'm as superficial as was suspected all along. But honestly, I didn't feel any closer to the Christmas spirit than I had the year before. If anything, I felt like Ebenezer Scrooge. Bah Humbug!

The following year, we invited friends up from San Diego to visit before Christmas. My wife convinced me to purchase a tree that the families could decorate together. That evening, the children ran around the tree excitedly placing their ornaments. The older kids deliberately spaced their bobbles while the babies rushed to put all of them on the same branch. To set the right mood, I played two Christmas CDs I find essential for the holidays—Nat King Cole's *The Christmas Song* and Luther Vandross' *This Christmas*. After the last bulb was hung, we dimmed the overhead lights and turned the tree lights on. I am not sure which was brighter, the star that sat atop the tree or the faces of the children as they jumped around the room cheering and clapping their hands. A warmth shot through my body. I realized then that I had been searching for the Christmas spirit in all the wrong places. The magic was back. It came through the children's laughter.

My son's playful distress about Santa fitting down our chimney reminded me of that moment. It struck me that in the daily routine of paying bills, parenting and looking for work, I had processed the joy out of the holidays. It was joy, after all, that filled the earth the night the Holy Child was born. It's the same joy that sparkled in those children's eyes when I lit up the tree. Of course, it isn't necessary to buy a tree or spend lots of money to find joy. You don't even need snow. However, I do think it is important to sing. I think it's also important to dance, to hug your friends, smile at folks you don't know, and spend as much time with children as possible.

So, beginning today, I am turning up the volume on the holiday music. I'm planning to go to every Christmas party we are invited to and to talk to as many people as I can. I'm going to indulge my children and kiss my wife longer and more deeply than usual. And if anyone does somehow manage to squeeze down our chimney Christmas morning, I promise I will serve him eggnog and cookies *before* I call the police.

Riding with Dad

No one likes to ride with Dad. If my boys have a choice between jumping in the car with me or their mother, they will almost always choose their mother. Sure, my wife is much more likely to stop at the park where they can play or over at her girlfriend's house so they can swim. But they do neat stuff with me as well. Who was it that introduced them to Jamba Juice, Starbucks, and Krispy Kreme doughnuts? Believe me, their mother did not take them to 7-Eleven and teach them the intricacies of concocting the perfect suicide slurpee!

So why don't I get any company in the car? Beyond children's natural tendency to cling to their mothers, the plain fact is that traveling with her is less stressful. I tend to bark loudly and give orders; my wife doesn't raise her voice when speaking to our boys. My wife strolls with them, whereas I insist that they stop lollygagging. She ignores much of their silliness while I am constantly telling them to sit up straight and cut the horseplay. In other words, I am being a father.

My father didn't yell; he lectured intensely. When I got into trouble as a young boy, my father was famous for saying, "Joseph, I don't want to break your spirit, but. . . ." He would then launch into some hours-long lecture, the point of which I had long forgotten by the time he finished. I, on the other hand, do yell. In fact, I never knew I could yell so loud until I had children. My wife has urged me to speak in more moderate tones and I have tried. I will look at them with a smile on my face and a twinkle in my eye and ask them nicely to pick up their toys from the floor. My sons will just stare at me as if I'm from another planet.

"Did you hear somethin'?"

"Nope."

They assume Daddy doesn't really mean what he says unless the veins are popping out of my neck!

Honestly, I am not so sure I'm cut out for fatherhood. The responsibility is too great, the work too difficult, and besides, my children get on my nerves.

Sure, nobody told me to have three children, but for that I blame my wife. If she didn't look so cotton picking good! Well, as they say, that is why the Good Lord invented birth control. Both of us clearly missed that day in biology class and didn't bother to get the notes. I will tell you what my wife and I tell anyone who asks. We welcomed the first one. We planned the second one and we love the third one anyway. But however they got here, they are here and it is now up to my wife and me to ensure that they become contributing members of society. But here is the difference: My wife has the demanding job of raising three boys; I have the pressure of raising three men. I yell because I take my job seriously.

Recently, I have been yelling quite a bit.

My oldest son Connor is, well, *filthy* for lack of a better word. He returns home from school looking like he has been mining coal.

"Go wash your hands before dinner." Ten minutes later he is back, water dripping all over the floor. "Now go *dry* your hands before dinner."

I am learning that I must be very specific with him as in: "didn't I tell you not to play ball in the house?"

"No. You told Ellis not to play ball in the house."

Ellis is his younger brother and quite possibly the slowest moving little boy I have every met. Good ol' lead bottom! Where is Ellis? Turn around and look to see who is bringing up the rear. When it is time to get dressed in the morning, he moves like molasses in winter. He is liable to take the better part of the day putting his shoes on. The only time I see him move fast is when he is racing through the kitchen at a full gallop in order to do a front flip onto the sofa in the family room. It seems that in order to do a proper full gainer onto the furniture you've got to get up a good head of steam.

The youngest is Sam. No matter how often I scrub Sam down, he seems to have a permanent layer of crust on his face. He is stubborn and ornery! When he isn't whining, he is throwing something: food, Legos at his brothers heads . . . my CDs. When he was a baby we explained his orneriness away because all of his molars had decided to come in at once. His gums turned purple as a result of the teeth cutting through his gum tissue. (To me, that is a reason to ask for Motrin, not to rub oatmeal into your hair.) Now that he is older, we realize he is just cantankerous because it's fun. Sam's favorite food is ketchup. Ketchup and chocolate. He has a sweet tooth the size of Texas. If there is chocolate around, he will sniff it out. He is like an alcoholic. I am certain he has little stashes of the stuff hidden around the house. He would be happy with a mound of chocolate and a bottle of ketchup to pour over it. The remnants, of course, will remain smeared all over his face in a thin layer of ketchupy, chocolate crust.

You have no idea the effort it took to potty train these boys. I have never seen people so determined to mess their pants rather than sit on a toilet. The other day, I realized that I have changed diapers for seven-and-a-half straight years. That comes out to 2,738 straight days of wiping smelly behinds. After the last diaper was tossed into the garbage, I announced, I'm not changing diapers anymore—for anyone—so don't ask!

All of them find every bodily function hysterically funny and they are perpetually silly. Connor will come home from school and repeat some pee-pee joke or make farting noises and all three of them will laugh like little hyenas. My wife is disgusted of course, so I have the task of educating them about why it's not proper to slurp down your juice and then see who can belch the loudest or why it isn't funny to pass gas while the family is eating dinner.

Separately they are a joy. Together they are little maniacs who run around in stores, do karate kicks at each other, and jump off the furniture. They whine and cry. I am constantly refereeing disputes over who's the boss of whom. As far as I'm concerned, Daddy is the boss of everybody! This past summer, my wife and I had the obtuse notion to fly with them to Columbus, Ohio to visit with my wife's father. My sons broke the airplane! I turned away for one moment and when I turned back Connor was holding the window in his hand. I rushed to put it back partly in fear that the glass would pop out and we would all be sucked out of the cabin and fall forty-thousand feet to our deaths. But I replaced it mainly out of fear that I might be charged to repair it. "Honey, here is the bill from our vacation. Ten thousand dollars! We got the super saver air-fare, but the plane repair pushed us way over budget."

I tried, on this trip, to remain calm. I really tried. But after asking them to stop running and sit down a dozen times in calm, soft tones, I invariably reverted to raising my voice and threatening everyone within earshot with some form of bodily harm. My problem is that I just don't brook much nonsense and boys are mostly made of nonsense.

My wife, bless her red-headed heart, has apparently been blessed with an infinite amount of patience. She can also give them a longer leash because she has the benefit of playing the "Daddy" card: "If you don't cooperate, I am going to tell Daddy." They don't want that. "No please! Don't tell the mean man!" If I tell my boys to behave or I will tell their mother, they will laugh in my face.

I am strict because, as I tell my wife all the time, I am laying a foundation. "When they get to be fourteen," I say, "it will be too late." I would love for them to rush to climb into my car, but if the cost is that I loosen the reins, I am not willing to pay. If my sons are to become responsible men of strength and character, they must learn obedience and discipline as boys. They will not learn any of that through coddling or by me whispering sweet nothings in their ears.

I recall a conversation surrounding the efficacy of circumcision I had with Lisa Bonet, my on-screen wife from *The Cosby Show*. Let me preface this story by saying that Lisa is a genuinely nice person. Least ways, she was always nice to me, not particularly warm—we were never going to be buds, but she was friendly and open and we actually spent a great deal of time talking during our down time. Lisa was (still is last time I checked) a bit of a flower child. In addition to the funky clothes she wore, she was a vegetarian who only ate with wooden utensils or her fingers, drank *only* bottled water, and didn't trust childhood immunizations. We couldn't have been more opposite and I took a perverse delight in teasing her. At any rate, during this particular conversation, Lisa was adamant in her opposition to circumcision. I told her that I supported it and when she asked me why, I replied that it taught little boys an important lesson in life: to protect their balls at all times! She just stared at me with a blank look then cocked her head to the side in a way that seemed to ask, "why am I even talking to you." That was the end of our conversation. Come to think of it, many of our conversations ended that way. She just didn't appreciate my sense of humor.

Yet many a truth is said in jest. I don't know that circumcision necessarily teaches any great lesson to baby boys. I do however, believe that part of my job, as father is to teach my boys that the world can be cruel and unsympathetic, and that at anytime, someone is liable to come along with a sharp knife and attempt to take their manhood from them. *That* is why fathers tell boys to "stop crying," to "gut it out!" And most importantly why they tell them "No!"

I actually began saying "no" to my sons when they were still babies. Long after they were supposed to be sleeping through the night, my wife would continue to get up whenever they cried for milk. I suppose it is a mother's job to nurture and cuddle and make the hurt go away. As a father, I didn't feel burdened by any such expectations. My attitude was that reasonable people will not starve before sun-up and by golly, my sons were going to be reasonable people! There would be no bottle to "take the edge off" from me.

I think the mothering instinct leads my wife to try and provide a haven from the realities of the cold world with as many "yeses" as she can afford. "No" is just my way of preparing our sons for the real world. "No" ran off my father's tongue like water! He said no to everything and, as near as I can remember, "'Cause I said so" was all the reason he ever needed. I have a friend whose two teenage sons have nicknamed him "Dr. No." As far as I am concerned, that is a title to be worn with pride.

I have friends who joke all the time about the rigors of raising daughters. I am often told, "You won't have to stand guard with a shotgun when they are teenagers." They are correct. However, raising sons is no picnic, and I think my friends have got the equation backwards. If I raise my sons properly, society won't have any cause to fear for the safety of their persons and property or the chastity of their daughters.

Understand, I don't render discipline and demand obedience because I am on a power trip. I demand it because I know what is at stake. Once these boys enter school, their behavior will be scrutinized like never before. This level of scrutiny will continue for the rest of their lives. There are studies that purport to show that elementary-school-age boys in general (and black boys far more often than white) are labeled with attention deficit disorder and other behavioral maladies at an alarming rate. Boys who engage in horseplay and silliness are medicated. Men (black men) whose behavior goes unchecked by moral and ethical restraints are locked behind bars or shot in the street like rabid dogs.

My friend Gary laughs when he talks about the voice he hears in his head that sounds curiously like his father's voice. As a young man, Gary's father told him, "Do not call home from jail. Your call will not be answered." As a result, Gary has always been careful with whom he associates. As a young man, if he found himself riding in a car and the other boys pulled out drug paraphernalia, he would simply ask that they pull over and drop him at the corner. Taking the bus was preferable to having to explain to his father how he got mixed up in whatever trouble the boys were headed for.

Many of my friends tell similar stories of being in the midst of some adolescent shenanigans only to suddenly see the stern face of their fathers in their mind or hear the deep threat of fatherly reason in their ears. If my sons are to survive, they need to hear that voice in their heads. The common sense Gary displayed is the result of the good foundation his parents laid. It is the same foundation I am attempting to lay in my boys and that my parents laid in me.

By many measures, I should have ended up one more statistic. I was the product of a broken home, my mother committed suicide, and I was something of an under-achiever in school. I had friends who were running away from home, acting out sexually, spending weekends in alcohol or drug induced hazes, yet I somehow managed to avoid these and many of the other pitfalls of teenage life.

So I guess my father got one part of the equation right, the voice in the head part, but quite honestly, he didn't do so well in the motivational department. He was distant and uninvolved, which often seemed to me unsupportive. That said, riding me was not my father's style. When I brought home bad grades or acted silly like my sons do, he most often gave me a look similar to that given me by Lisa Bonet. It was a look that seemed to say, "I don't know if this boy is gonna make it."

It may be that I am hard on my boys not only because I want to protect them, but because I also believe that motivating your children is another important part of a father's job description. The discipline and self-control I demand from them are not only the armor against the blows of an unkind world; they are the tools for success. If only my father had pushed me a little harder, been a little more demanding, insisted that I challenge myself by reaching beyond the stage lights.

I parent the way I do because I want my sons to achieve. I am keenly aware that boys—especially black boys—who are mediocre get lost in the pack.

This may come as a bit of a shock but as much as I love being an actor—performing has been my love for as long as I can remember—I have a sense in my heart that it is a bit of a waste of good brain power. What is this play-acting? Being on television and in the movies is easy. Don't let anyone tell you anything different. You use about one percent of your brainpower being on a television program (the stage requires more of you) and most of that is in thinking how you are going to spend your money. In my quiet moments, I feel I could have done so much more with my life. I could have been an attorney, a judge, or a congressman. My father was a doctor. He never made a lot of money, but he had a standing and respect in the community that an actor—no matter how successful—can never really achieve. My entire life, I was known as Dr. Phillips' son. It was a source of pride for me, but it also carried with it a responsibility I felt the need to live up to. Dr. Phillips' son was supposed to be special, and frankly, I think the path I chose didn't live up to my obligation.

To my wife's horror, I confessed one night that if any of my sons grew up to become television actors I would feel I had failed. Certainly I will support them in whatever they ultimately decide to do with their lives just as my father supported me. When I told him I wanted to become an actor, he just said "okay" and later beamed with pride when he saw me on stage or television. (I was in school with kids whose parents had refused to pay for acting school and had virtually disowned them.) But it will remain a point of fact that I did not put in the years pounding pavement in Hollywood in order for my sons to dance on the end of some Hollywood hotshot's string. "To him whom much has been given much will be required." This bit of Scripture refers to service, but if it is all right with you, I would prefer my sons to serve from the top down as opposed to the bottom up. Senator Phillips! Secretary of State Phillips! CEO Phillips! My wish for my sons is that they be the ones controlling the strings. I don't imagine that makes me much different from most fathers. Because of the blessings bestowed on me and my wife, our children have a duty and a responsibility to lead, not to follow—to stand out from the pack. (Does that make me elitist? Heaven forbid!)

That kind of achievement will demand that as they grow, I be more than just involved, I have to be on top of them every minute. At the same time, I know that men need space so I don't want to hover. Mothers hover. At the park, for instance, mothers hover over the monkey bars, they hover over the slides, they hover around the swings. They hover anywhere there are children in order to ensure that no one scrapes a knee or puts an eye out. I am far more likely to head towards the largest patch of shade and watch from a distance. Mothers also like to run. They run constantly to check on the little ones, inquiring as to their health, brushing sand from their clothes, and kissing boo boos. Unless there is blood, fathers are not likely to pay much attention and even then, they may offer comfort along the lines of: "When I was your age, our heads used to bleed like that all the time. Stop crying and put a little pressure on it."

One of the cruelties of life is that very seldom does someone come along to make things better for you.

It is a fine line I am walking and I am not always certain I am walking it well. I always try to administer discipline with love but imagine I could stand to lighten up a bit, take a few pages from my wife's playbook and temper my teaching with a few more hugs and a little less barking.

As it is, I find myself punctuating my lectures with many of the same dictums my father gave me: "If I didn't love you, I would let you do whatever you wanted" and "the fact that I am punishing you is proof of my love." If their willingness to jump in the car with their old man is any sales measure, my sons are not buying that line anymore than I did when I was their age. I know it may sound corny but it is true. I love my sons enough to do whatever it takes to ensure that they do not stumble on the road to manhood.

But best laid plans right? I have high hopes for my sons just as I know my father had hopes for me. I have all of these theories about parenting and the importance of raising sons into men and yet I find myself not only making some of the same mistakes my father made, I am also breaking new ground in poor parenting.

I sometimes hear my father's voice coming out of my mouth: "Connor, you have a terrific spirit and I don't want to break it, but. . . ." Tell me I didn't really just say that! Oftentimes, I am short-tempered with my sons. I lose patience. In my zeal to instill the proper attitude, I have been guilty of administering punishment that may not have fit the crime. I am sometimes uninvolved. I allow my wife to entertain them with visits to museums and zoos while I sit in my office working on the computer. Much to my embarrassment, I have also found myself giving them the "Lisa Bonet" look when they are telling some rambling story I can't follow with a map. I am girding myself for the day all of my errors come back to haunt me.

In my younger years, I carried quite a bit of anger and resentment toward my father. I had a looong list of all the mistakes he made in raising me! When I was about twenty-five, I shared it with him during a heated long distance exchange. He sat on the other end of the extension, quietly listening to me and when I had finished, simply replied that I didn't know what I was talking about. Well, I did know. How could he have lectured so often and made so many errors? Easy. He didn't know what he was doing then any more than I know what I am doing now.

When my father began his family, he was twenty-nine, six years younger than I was when I began mine. If I was so clueless at thirty-five, why should he have been any wiser at twenty-nine? In spite of all the parenting books on the market, I don't believe there are any real parenting experts. There are only people who love their kids and do the best they can with what they have. They love their kids through all of their own emotional baggage and reach to them through the haze of their relationships with their own parents.

I have heard it said that being a doctor is emotionally expensive. I think that was certainly true for my father. When I was born, he was a pediatric resident at Rose Memorial Hospital in Denver, Colorado. As I grew up, I saw him give so much to his patients. To this day, former patients of my father tell me what a caring and loving man he was. They are right of course. He was. I witnessed it time and again with my own eyes. However, at home, in his relationships with his kids he was somewhat detached. I don't recall seeing him genuinely overcome with emotion but once in my life, and that was in 1989 at my grandfather's funeral. During the service my father stood to sing "Amazing Grace." He was overcome with emotion and it appeared as if he would be unable to finish. The guests in attendance began to sing along in order to carry him through the song. My wife reminded me of the speech he made at my little sister's memorial service. It was almost clinical, as if he were talking to a group of medical professionals. At one point, his voice cracked and he almost broke—almost, but he recovered. That is not to say that my father was without feeling. My father felt deeply. He was devastated by my sister's death and I have come to understand that he carried a sadness over a great many things in his life. One of which was his separation and eventual divorce from my mother. Whatever the problems in their marriage, its disintegration sent him into a depression he carried for many years. He rebounded for a time with his second marriage, but when that marriage too dissolved he fell back into the blues. I am not convinced he ever fully recovered.

About the time Connor was born, I was lucky enough to have another long-distance phone conversation with my father. This one more genial than the one we'd had ten years earlier. I told him he had been right. I hadn't really known what I was talking about because I didn't have all of the information. Well, with a rocky marriage, a pregnant wife, no job, an empty bank account and a prescription for anti-depressants, I suddenly *had* the information. "Daddy," I said, "now I understand. You did the best you could." One of my last memories of him is his large six-foot-four-inch frame sitting on the floor playing with Connor when he was about eight months old. There they sat, the two of them just giggling away. My heart climbed into my throat. But I also wondered if my father ever played with me like that. I struggled to remember.

I do know, though, that in spite of the exasperated tone he used to have with me and my having sometimes been a knuckleheaded little boy, my father thought I turned out okay. Unfortunately, it wasn't until his death that I discovered the depth of his pride in me. Before he fell into a coma he asked the doctor to "call my son." It filled my heart to know that in his most desperate hour, he had thought of me. I knew then that my father thought I had grown into a decent, strong, and responsible man. I wonder if he patted himself on the back or breathed a sigh of relief.

I know that one day I will feel the same way about my sons. Though, with all the whining, crying, and peeing on the toilet seat, that is sometimes difficult for me to see. What is really frightening is that my sons will likely have a lot of complicated feelings about me. They are even now compiling their laundry lists of things I am doing wrong and will no doubt share them with me some day during some passionate conversation. I will promise to try and respond in a similar manner as my father responded to me. I suspect, however, that I will be a bit more animated and use a great many more words and arm gestures. I am liable to explain to them that I was not trying to be popular; I was trying to offer them the keys to the future. The job of a father is not to be liked, but to instill discipline, common sense, and resilience. Dads are full of hugs and advice, but they must also be the guiding hand on the road to manhood. One day they will understand. In the meantime I will count my sons as blessings.

As often as I wish I could stamp them with "return to sender," more frequently I realize I am blessed by having them in my life. When I am traveling, sleep is not the same without a goodnight kiss from them. I envy their ability to dance just because there is music playing and their excitement at the sight of a full moon, a perfect stick, or a puddle of water. Seeing their joy, listening to the sound of their laughter, feeling their skinny little arms around my neck is something akin to being brushed by a cool breeze on a warm summer day. It is there for just a moment and in that moment, it is perfect. They are beautiful, spirited little boys who love to laugh; they are smelly, ashy, and loud just as little black boys should be. I'm confident that in spite of my mistakes, they will grow up to be fine, responsible young men. And if there is any justice, some day *they* will have children who will get on their last nerve.

A Lovers' Photograph
(Love, Marriage, and Divorce)

During a recent family picnic, I commented that I have always found my wife—who I was dating at the time I filmed my role in *Strictly Business*—sexier than Halle Berry. My wife's family greeted this revelation with silence. On the way home, my wife scolded me for embarrassing her in front of her family. I thought I was paying her an honest compliment. Which just goes to prove fellas, that you can't win and you can't get outta the game.

As I write, my wife and I have just passed a milestone—ten years of marriage. I am admittedly in a bit of a daze. I have no idea how I got here. I still remember the first extended conversation I had with my wife on the streets of Brooklyn. I am a foot taller than her so she stood smiling up at me with a big, toothy grin. The last thing on my mind was marriage and if you had offered a wager that I would have married the silly, little redhead I was talking to that afternoon, I would have gladly taken your money. Well, here we are fifteen years and three children later, having just celebrated our aluminum anniversary.

I would be lying if I said I wasn't just a bit surprised we made it this far. No one had a more difficult first few years of marriage than we did. We both spent a lot of time in private session with God during those years asking: "What's the deal?! I didn't know when I agreed to 'For better or for worse' that worse meant *this!*"

It would not be an exaggeration to say that I have had a standing appointment with the Lord for the entirety of my marriage. For the better part of ten years I have wrestled with those forces of destruction that sneak into homes and ruin relationships. I have battled resentment, anger, selfishness, and a host of other ills too numerous to list here. At times, I'm confident I have the enemy whipped and sometimes it seems that after a decade of marriage I am still no closer to figuring out the matrimonial puzzle.

I have been so desperate for answers that I have begun reaching out to my married friends, hopeful they will share their success secrets with me. Out of the insight that has been offered, one response provided me with a surprising bit of wisdom. A couple that has been married for almost twenty years (and has seemed the model of marriage) enlightened me when they announced they were going to divorce after living "twenty years of hell!" (Proof that you never know what is going on behind closed doors.) It seems odd that the tragedy of a friends' divorce would give me valuable insight but let me explain.

I spoke to my buddy on the phone and in one forty-five-minute diatribe, he shared a tale of a marriage riddled with anger and hurt. The woman he described was not recognizable to me. Where was the beautiful, talented, Christian woman I knew as his wife? Similarly, mention of his name during conversations with his wife were enough to send all of that Christian goodwill flying like dust in the wind.

I can remember a time when their eyes sparkled at the mention of each other's name. Indeed, few of us can forget the rush of adrenaline felt with young romances, the way our hearts beat a little faster when we were with the person we loved, the little bounce in our step, the glow on our face when we thought of them, the inside jokes, the smiles from across the room. Where does it all go? How do the whispered phone conversations filled with innuendo and longing turn into yelling matches filled with anger and rage? There is no way to know what demons invaded my friends' home and are now destroying their family. However, I can be fairly certain that somewhere along the way, someone's heart was broken.

The heart is an amazingly resilient organ when you think about it. It bends, breaks, eventually heals, and then eagerly awaits the next boogie board ride on the waves of affection. But resilient as it is, it does have its limits. When a heart is broken enough times, it will eventually be surrounded by scar tissue, walled off from feeling, inaccessible to gestures of kindness and affection. Soft talk and flowers will not work and counseling will just prolong the inevitable. Having surpassed its capacity for healing, the heart will remain an open, festering sore that infects and poisons every healthy fiber of a person's life. Each biting comment, each insult and cruel remark, each failure to do something kind bends your partner's heart to the point of breaking.

I can cite other couples like our friends who have passed this point of no return. The wounds they inflicted on each other over the years are too numerous, too deep and infected to ever heal. Their relationships are dead. The cliché is true: Marriage is hard work. Marriage is even more difficult than raising children! If I neglect my children, they will continue to grow. There is even a possibility that they will be healthy and perhaps even successful. If I neglect my marriage, it will most certainly die.

The heart is also a muscle and like all muscles it can be made stronger. When we want to increase our wind we run sprints. When we want to nurture our marriages we must exercise acts of kindness and giving. It is not enough to simply avoid saying or doing hurtful things. In addition we must build our partner up. Inspired relationships are ones in which couples let each other know how wonderful they are, how significant the other has been in their lives all the time, not just on Valentine's Day. They are partnerships where one partner can be counted on to take up the slack when the other is ailing and where each is willing to sacrifice him or herself for the other.

A long objective look at the sadness and pain my dear friends are now experiencing has strengthened my resolve to make my marriage work. It has also made me realize what I so clearly failed to learn during the ten previous years: Marriage has a much better chance of success if you don't break your partner's heart.

Armed with this new information, I began dispensing relationship advice to anyone who looked in my direction. Since moving to Los Angeles, TJ had been having relationship troubles. I have known him since he was a baby so was only too happy to play the role of wise older brother and offer some much needed advice.

One of TJ's buddies had hooked him up with an invitation to a real Hollywood party. As an aspiring actor, he felt it was the sort of party he needed to attend to network and have his face seen by Hollywood insiders. The problem was the invitation only admitted one and his girlfriend was coming to town to visit him for the weekend. TJ had suggested to her that she stay home the night of the party. Apparently, that didn't go over too well.

My young friend was clearly not ready for prime time. He was making a mess of things. He needed my help fast. "If you want peace, you will give the invite to your buddy. And when you pick your girlfriend up at the airport, have a bouquet of flowers, tell her that you lost your mind, and that you are glad the two of you will have the weekend all to yourselves."

"I may never have an opportunity to go to another party like this," he pleaded.

"Brother," I told him, "you may not get everything you pay for, but you will pay for everything you get! The cost of going to that party is a weekend in Hell." He stared at me blankly. I explained: "Friday night she will step off the plane with attitude. There will be tension all day Saturday in anticipation of you leaving her at home. Sunday, she will be mad that you *actually* went. And you can forget about getting any lovin'! You tell me: is the party worth it?"

To say that I had a bit of swagger in my step would be an understatement. I was quite pleased with myself. Play on Playa! What a fool! I was too busy removing the splinter out of my neighbor's eye to notice the plank in my own.

My marriage has been filled with its share of heartache. If memory serves, the first time my wife mentioned divorce was about two months after we were married and the "D" word, as it came to be known, was tossed around quite a bit for the next two years. We haven't talked about it much since then, but that has not given me any great cause for comfort.

Recently, the cracks in our relationship began to show themselves in a series of arguments over small things that seemed unimportant to me, but somehow took on major significance to my wife. For example, my wife likes to clean the kitchen immediately after we finish eating. Before I have taken my last forkful of food, she is scrubbing dishes and wiping down the table. I am often chewing and lifting my feet as she sweeps underneath the table. I prefer to relax after eating. In my mind, aside from putting leftovers in the refrigerator, there is nothing so pressing that it can't be addressed later on in the evening. We have tried taking turns but she grows impatient. You see, I like to let dishes soak. Sometimes, I let them soak overnight and sometimes they soak for a day or two. But, eventually, they get washed and that is the point, isn't it?

Given all that I do for my wife—all the sexy talk and little gifts—how on earth does my failure to wash dishes become the measure of my love for her?

I approached my father-in-law, desperate for some insight. After all, he raised her. If anyone should understand her twisted reasoning, it should be him. My father-in-law gave me a disappointed look and shook his head. I was obviously "not ready for prime time." "We have known each other for fifteen years," I complained. "This is not some new behavior on my part. If she wants the dishes cleaned on her schedule, then she should clean them. Otherwise, she should get off my back. I will get to them in my own time."

"I am worried about you," he began. "Peace in the home is your responsibility. You sure won't get it by drawing lines in the sand." Sounded like good advice. Where had I heard it before? He continued, "Sometimes the little things that you find insignificant speak more about your feelings for someone than an entire book of love poems."

I was immediately reminded of something my little sister, Carole, told me years ago that I just didn't take to heart. While my sister was in the hospital, my brother-in-law would come visit her. He sat by her bedside and kept her company until visiting hours were over. In his mind, he was the loyal husband. What better way to demonstrate his love than to be by her bedside while she was ill? My sister grumbled that if he really wanted to show her how much he loved her, he should be at home vacuuming the carpet.

Breaking old habits is difficult. I still grit my teeth while cleaning the kitchen. It's a small gesture, I know, but if washing dishes will show my wife that I love every freckle on her face, I will have dishpan hands until I die. Besides, I figure the cost of not cleaning the kitchen is a wife who grumbles, rolls her eyes and who is likely to be tired when I try to snuggle up to her later on in the evening.

I did a little research about divorce on the Internet and I am just a little shaken. According to what I read, the average marriage lasts eleven years. We are approaching eleven. The average age women divorce is thirty-three. My wife is older than that but when we married, my wife was older than the average age at which women marry so that's a push. The divorce rate for women whose parents were married less than ten years is forty-three percent. My wife's mother is twice divorced. My mother was twice divorced and so was my father. I'm waiting for someone to deal me an ace! About the only thing I have working in my favor is the fact that I don't smoke. For some reason, smokers divorce at a higher rate than non-smokers. The problem is that having kids has led me to drink, so I'm sure that has neutralized any advantage I may have had.

I do not mean to be flippant. There are few things as painful or destructive as the break-up of a marriage, particularly when children are involved. I remember well my own childhood and the pain I felt when my parents divorced. The impact of their decision continued to reverberate in my life long past when they signed the final papers. Given the emotional toll, it is still unclear why, once married, people choose to divorce. Eighty percent of marriages end because of irreconcilable differences. What is that, exactly? My wife would say that she and I have an irreconcilable difference of opinion over whether my putting dirty clothes next to the hamper instead of inside the hamper constitutes a material breach of the marital agreement.

My wife always points to her grandmother's marriage as the model of success. Her grandmother has been married for forty years. Of course, the secret to her success is that after the ceremony, she and her husband promptly moved across town from one another. Perhaps she is trying to tell me something.

I watch my divorced friends and it seems to me that many times, divorce requires just as much hard work as does marriage, if not more. My divorced friends are continually on the phone with their exes, dropping by the house to discuss dental appointments or insurance for the kids. There are school functions and disciplinary problems. They're broke, the kids are miserable and their exes are angry. If one must work so hard after divorcing, why not just stay married?

I know some men who are seduced by notions of trading up. The buddy I mentioned earlier has a fantasy that after his divorce he will be in single men's hog heaven. He imagines there will be sports cars and bevies of pretty young women whose sole purpose is to deliver unto him waves of orgasmic pleasure. Chances are much greater that he will be sitting in a one-bedroom apartment, watching television on a thirteen-inch screen (his wife will get the big screen in the settlement), and getting drunk on cheap merlot. The game is a bit different at forty than it was at thirty. I got a dose of this reality the other night while out to dinner with my wife. I informed her that our young, pretty waitress was smiling at me. "I still got it," I boasted. Later, the waitress informed me that she had seen me on a rerun of *The Cosby Show* the night before and couldn't believe how young and slim I looked *way back then.*

There is now something called a "divorce ceremony." The ceremony attempts to use ritual to bring closure and healing to the divorced couple. Family and friends attend and the divorcing couple makes a new covenant to be kind to each other, be good co-parents, and other positive things. I suspect if a couple had been capable of being kind to each other, they wouldn't be getting divorced. I realize there are some people who just can't live with each other and for whom divorce is a blessing. But I remain convinced that marriage is supposed to be forever, that marriage can work, and that married couples can be happy. Happily my wife shares that belief.

Marriage demands persistence. Our diligence may be driven by our love for each other and our resolve to be a family or maybe it's just that we are both obstinate. I'm sometimes tickled by the notion that the real reason we have remained together is that each of us is determined to outlast the other. Or perhaps it is to out-love the other. More often than not, we feel that we have found the groove that evaded us early on. Still, I wouldn't term our marriage a success. I don't know that anyone can really say their marriage has worked until they are preparing to leave this earth. Marriage is one of those highly-combustible mixtures of ego, temperament, sex, and emotional baggage that is liable to go poof! at any moment. It's my guess that in the end, if we make it, our last words will be, "Whew!"

Approaching this milestone got me reminiscing about the evening I proposed. I asked my wife what she remembered about my marriage proposal. I expected her to blush and then smile. Maybe she'd sidle up next to me and give me a kiss. She hesitated then told me it was distinguished only by how forgettable it was. After taking an honest look at my effort, I am forced to agree with her.

It was April 1993. We were boyfriend and girlfriend. I picked her up from her Brooklyn apartment and we walked around the corner to have dinner at a new Italian restaurant. During appetizers, I asked her what she was doing the following May. She responded, "I have no idea. Why?"

"I thought we could get married," I said in response.

Thinking I was joking, she kicked me under the table. "Don't do that."

"I'm serious," I protested, and added, "I'm asking you to marry me." She smiled, said "yes" and the rest is history. No drama! No romance! No professions of love and longing! And no ring! There was not one bit of thought put into the entire event. It was an absolute disaster from beginning to end and my wife is right to be disappointed.

It wasn't that I took the moment lightly. On the contrary—I had been anxious about the prospect of asking for her hand for weeks. I blurted out the proposal lest my nerves would get the best of me. On the other hand, I have friends who did things the right way. My best buddy proposed to his girlfriend on New Year's Eve. He took her on a trip to Lake Tahoe. As the clock struck midnight, he gave her a huge diamond and asked her to be his wife.

I have another friend who took his future wife to their favorite Thai food restaurant and arranged for the waiter to present the ring on top of her dinner plate. The entire restaurant applauded as he got down on one knee and she accepted his proposal. Still another proposed to his wife while on a carriage ride through Central Park. I should have called one of those guys and asked for advice. Instead, when it was my turn at the line, I threw up a brick.

It's not that the proper proposal will guarantee a successful marriage. I know too many men who made great proposals and had rotten marriages (my soon-to-be-divorced buddy is one of them). There are however, certain elements in a proposal that are important and their significance is not lost on today's women. R & B singer Beyonce Knowles is quoted in a recent *US* magazine as saying that she is an old-fashioned girl who wants her man on bended knee with a ring in hand. (Are you listening Jay-Z?) I discovered this in hindsight of course.

Historically, marriage was a way for women to guarantee support for herself and her children. Even with women working outside of the home and men sharing more of the child-rearing responsibilities, this is still true today. Generally speaking, married women with children enjoy a higher standard of living, better health, and suffer far less domestic abuse than do their single sisters. Their children are also provided with better and healthier opportunities. It may be fair to say that the institution is for, by, and about women. The act of the proposal, then, is really a request by the male for permission to enter into this completely feminine world. Getting down on one knee is not essential, but again, the symbolism is important. It is a man saying that from this moment forward, his life and his happiness will be secondary to hers. Like at the moment in the New Testament when Jesus stoops to wash the feet of his disciples, a man humbles himself before his bride as an act of adoration and submission. To love is to serve.

Similarly, the ring—no matter the size—is a warranty that the promise of submission is backed up by the full faith and credit of United States currency. Talk is cheap! Diamonds are not!

It's also terribly romantic. I have not met a woman yet who did not dream of a man on bended knee, placing a band of gold on her finger. I have also never heard tell of a woman who didn't feel just a bit cheated when her intended neglected to offer his knee and this token. My wife is no exception. As we reminisced, she made sure to let me know that any other woman would have rejected my weak proposal based purely on GP (general principle)! I count myself lucky.

I am serious when I say that this failure on my part—more than any other moment in the past—is my greatest regret. As Cher sang, "if I could turn back time," I would give the moment the respect it deserves and give my wife a proposal to remember. Maybe I would take her to the top of a mountain and let my proclamation of love echo across the valleys below. Maybe, I would fly her to Paris and ask her at the foot of the Eiffel tower or hire a plane to write her name across the sky during the seventh inning stretch at Dodger stadium. Or one night, when we were strolling down a quiet street, I would take her hand, get down on my knee, tell her how deeply I love her, what a terrific mother she would be, and ask her if she would please allow me the honor of spending the rest of my life with her.

Last year, the father of a very good friend of mine passed away. The local paper published an article about his life—his experiences as part of the civil rights movement in Mississippi, moving to Denver and being one of the first black families in Southeast Denver, and so forth. At one point in the article, my friend's mother describes her late husband as a hero. It brought tears to my eyes. It wasn't the depth of her mourning that moved me. I was touched because, in that moment, I felt the deep respect, tenderness, and heartfelt love a woman can have for her man after fifty years of marriage. From that moment, I became convinced that every wife should feel that way about her husband. By the way, I also feel that a man should feel similarly about his woman. In our eyes, our wife's beauty should transcend years. Their softness should only grow more comforting and our respect and admiration for them should only deepen.

I looked at my wife the other day. I mean, really looked at her. I surprised myself at how often I have looked at her over the years without really seeing her. I wondered, as well, how often I had listened to her without really hearing. I studied her face, counted her freckles. I traced the shape of her lips. I looked at her hair. I looked into her eyes and strained to see if the years that passed had enhanced my ability to read the complex thoughts and emotions hiding behind them. They haven't.

Seeing her with new eyes, as it were, was a bit like seeing her for the first time. Three children have changed the shape of her body somewhat. Time has changed the color and texture of her hair. There are lines on her face that weren't there fifteen years ago, but she is just as beautiful as the day I first saw her. I saw her in her totality and concluded that I have been blessed with a terrific partner and friend.

Our children have also been blessed with a terrific mother. She makes sure our boys go off to school with teeth brushed, ears clean, and bellies full. She works a full-time job and then comes home only to have the kids jump all over her fighting for her attention. Although she is tired, she manages to make each feel special by listening and responding to them even though they're all talking at once. After dinner, she bathes them, reads stories, tucks them in, and then staggers into the bedroom only to have her attentions demanded by me, when I ask her, "Honey, read this essay," or "Come here and give me some lovin'." On the weekends, she finds time to run errands, take the boys to the beach or the museum or maybe to a farm where they can pick strawberries. Every once in a while, she gets a break—a dinner with girlfriends or a business trip, but generally speaking, that is her routine and she does it every day with little complaint.

I try to let her know how much she is appreciated. I realize that quite often I take her for granted. It's a shame I have looked at my wife for years and yet somehow never seen her.

You know, on second thought, maybe I don't want to get out of the game. Maybe I am a bigger winner than I realize.

When my father passed away, I sat through a funeral service in Mississippi and a memorial and internment in Denver. By the time the services in Denver were complete, I was emotionally drained. I felt dry, there was not one tear left inside of me, or so I thought. As we stood outside the church and the priest began to pour my father's ashes into the columbarium, tears began to flow from some deep reserve inside and my knees buckled. My wife, all five feet of her, wrapped her arms around my waist and held me up. That was the lowest moment in my life. It was also the same moment that I grasped my wife's devotion to me and understood why I am choosing to spend my life with her. We each need someone to keep us company and give us shelter from the storms. Life can be a scary place to be all by yourself.

FAITH

Power of Faith and Religion

"Practice virtue yourself then encourage it in others. This is the armor, my friends, that makes us invincible."
—Patrick Henry

While channel surfing one night, I came across George Carlin on HBO's *Real Time* with Bill Maher. During discussions that ranged in topic from the FCC's crackdown on indecency in broadcasting to the war on terrorism, both the comedians stressed the undue influence of religion on American Culture. Carlin asserted: "At the base of most of the evil in the world is religion of any kind." Maher added that, like politics, religion plays on fear. The audience cheered their appreciation. Later in the program another panelist, former Canadian Prime Minister Kim Campbell mocked the religious faith of President George W. Bush and then added, "It [religion] gets in the way of morality." Again, the audience applauded loudly and shouted their agreement.

Carlin's attack on religion didn't surprise me—this is his "shtick." For forty years, he has railed against convention, setting himself up as a bemused observer of the quirks of American culture. I know very little about the former Canadian prime minister except that she was only prime minister for four months before leading her party to a massive defeat at the polls, and that as a politician she is a staunch pro-abortionist who supported more restrictive gun laws. I could have predicted her retort. It was the audience's enthusiastic embrace of both these sentiments that shocked me and convinced me that there is an ever-growing hostility to religious faith in general and Christian faith in particular.

The story of Stephan Williams, a teacher in the Cupertino Union School district here in California's Silicon Valley illustrates this antagonism rather nicely. Williams, a self-described orthodox Christian, has been prohibited by Patricia Vidmar, the principal of the Stevens Creek School, from providing his American

History students with a portion of the Declaration of Independence because that portion of the document contains references to God. Read it again just so you are clear—a public school principal is objecting to students reading certain portions of the keystone document of our republic because it mentions God.

This nonsense is not unique to the West Coast. Similar absurdity has spread like the flu into every community in the nation. Maryland public school teachers are forbidden to mention that the first Thanksgiving was a religious celebration. Charles Ridgell, public schools curriculum and instruction director of St. Mary's county public schools says, "We teach about Thanksgiving from a purely historical perspective, not from a religious perspective." Other statewide administrators agree, proudly offering that religion never coincides with how they teach Thanksgiving to students. What remains unclear is how one teaches this holiday from a historical perspective without mentioning religion. The pilgrims, a deeply—some would say orthodox—religious people, (and, not coincidentally, the authors of the Mayflower Compact another document central to the ideals of popular government, which begins: "In the name of God, Amen.") set aside the day to give God praise and thanks for his benevolence and mercy.

It is clear that a war is being waged on faith. It is also clear that those of us who believe in the foundations of faith upon which this nation was built have been far too complacent for far too long. In the name of political correctness, we have, as they say, allowed the inmates to take over the asylum without so much as a whimper.

Writing about America's strength in 1835, French Nobleman Alexis de Tocqueville, said: "I sought for the greatness and genius of America in her commodious harbors and her ample rivers, and it was not there; in her fertile fields and boundless prairies, and it was not there; in her rich mines and her vast world commerce, and it was not there. Not until I went to the churches of America and heard her pulpits aflame with righteousness did I understand the secret of her genius and power. America is great because America is good. And if America ever ceases to be good, America will cease to be great." Tocqueville, understood the importance of religious faith in America. It is too bad more Americans (and one Canadian I can think of) do not.

Faith, of course, is not really what the panelists on Maher's program and those in the audience that night find objectionable. Nor is it the source of the left's discomfort. If one were to ask, most of them would describe themselves as having faith in something. They might describe a belief in some vague greater energy, or, as one of my neighbors suggested, in their families, or in their fellow man; faith in any number of things except that which is greater than themselves. Their argument is with organized religion, the translation of Judeo/Christian faith into doctrine and ritual.

Syndicated columnist Dennis Prager offers this definition of Judeo/Christian faith: ". . . a belief in the biblical God of Israel, in His Ten Commandments and His biblical moral laws. It is a belief in universal, not relative, morality. It is a belief that America must answer morally to this God, not to the mortal, usually venal, governments of the world."

Some may argue the veracity of a belief in one Supreme Being that gave life to all things and in whose judgment the fate of the world hangs. It seems a stretch, however, to argue that this conviction—whose tenants celebrate love of God and service to one's fellow man—or that the institutions organized around that belief are evil. You don't have to look far to see the good work on behalf of the poor, sick, and elderly performed by church—or religious-based groups. Organizations like Catholic Charities, Christian Children's Fund, The Salvation Army, the Episcopal Migration Ministries, Lutheran Immigration and Refugee Services, the Hebrew Immigrant Aid Society and literally thousands of other religious, faith-based organizations minister on a daily basis by providing healthcare, education, and comfort to people all over the world.

The panelists on Maher's program, of course, were quick to point to all the death and misery that has been caused by those who invoked the word of God. Those familiar with the New Testament will remember that when Jesus ventured into the desert and fasted for forty days and nights, he was tempted by Satan, who quoted Scripture. "Satan himself masquerades as an angel of light." Put more plainly, the exploitation of faith is not religion but a violation of religion. The Bible calls it taking the Lord's name in vain.

The worst evil of the twentieth century was not the result of faith, but the cynical grab for political power and wealth by those who, in fact, lacked religious faith. Hitler, an atheist, is responsible for the extermination camps of The Third Reich; Stalin, another atheist, the Soviet Gulags. Marxists were responsible for the re-education camps of Cambodia; Maoists China's cultural revolution; fascism the poverty of North Korea and the mass graves in Iraq. Faithful people committed none of these atrocities. As a matter of fact, Christians and Jews died at their hands. Further, the great evil of the twenty-first century—terrorism—is committed in the name of religious zealotry, but Al Qaeda, Hamas, and other terrorist groups are not spiritual orders. Yes, they demand that the world bow before Islam, but their concern is not with bringing anyone closer to God, but with bringing power and resources under theocratic, tyrannical control. They are fascists hiding behind keffayahs. And just as it was the American Judeo/Christian sense of justice and liberty that was responsible for the defeat of Hitler, the Soviet Union, and Saddam, it will be those same values that will defeat this new twenty-first century enemy of freedom.

The apostle James said, "I will show you my faith by my works." What then has religious faith produced? Simply some of the greatest victories in human history. (Though if you are a student in the Cupertino Union or Maryland Public School districts, this information may have escaped your attention.) Men and women who invoked the moral authority of faith to free their fellow man led the Emancipation movement in America, which led to the effective end of the slave trade in the western world.

Harriet Beecher Stowe's novel, *Uncle Tom's Cabin* is credited with illustrating for the entire nation the moral repugnance of the cruel system of slavery. Legend has it that in 1862, when she visited President Lincoln, he greeted her as "the little lady who made this big war." Harriet Beecher Stowe came from a family of ministers. The entire family shared her abolitionist sentiment and was active in hiding runaway slaves. They lived by the creed that "the best way of serving God was to take action in society to make a better world."

America has become great in part because we have unleashed the intelligence and creative power of women who number roughly half the members of our society. The leaders of the women's rights movement, who continue to influence women in other cultures around the world, found the righteousness of their cause in the Judeo/Christian values of Biblical faith. The very first women's conference was held in a church in Seneca Falls in 1848. Elizabeth Cady Stanton quoted Scripture in her address to those present: "In every generation God calls some men and women for the utterance of truth, a heroic action, and our work today is the fulfilling of what has long since been foretold by the Prophet—Joel 2:28: 'And it shall come to pass afterward, that I will pour out my spirit upon all flesh; and your sons and your daughters shall prophesy.'" Susan B. Anthony's sense of justice and morality were certainly also the result of her religious upbringing.

Similarly, the struggle for civil rights and human dignity in this country was led by men and women who believed in their soul that freedom for all men was to be found in God's eternal law.

On December 5, 1955, just days after Rosa Parks refused to give up her seat on the bus to a white man, a twenty-six-year-old minister delivered a speech at Holt Street Baptist church that set the tone not only for the year-long bus boycott that was to follow, but also for the entire civil rights movement. The minister was Reverend Martin Luther King, Jr., and that evening he called for a nonviolent movement based in Christian love. Not "free" love or love simply, but *Christian* love! "He called for unity and said he felt that future generations would have to pause and say that there lived a people, a black people, a great people, who injected a new meaning into our civilization." Joe Azbell editor of the *Montgomery*

Advertiser writing about that momentous evening said, "A flame had been lit that would go across America." That flame of faith as demonstrated in non-violent protest and prayer is present throughout the Civil Rights Movement.

Ten years after the Montgomery bus boycott, six hundred men, women, and children began a march from Selma, Alabama to Montgomery for the right to vote. The march began at Browns Chapel. As the marchers crested the Edmund Pettus Bridge, a wall of white state troopers armed with tear gas, horses, and clubs greeted them. Bracing themselves for the police onslaught the protesters kneeled to pray. Seventeen demonstrators were hospitalized for injuries suffered at the hands of police. Another forty were given emergency treatment at Good Samaritan Hospital. Many others licked their wounds back at Browns Chapel. More importantly—while they were down—they were not discouraged. They prayed and began planning the next march across the bridge. The courage and the *faith* demonstrated by these brave souls on that Bloody Sunday and many thousands more like them who faced death and injury were the inspiration for freedom movements throughout the world. It is not by accident that the Chinese students in Tiananmen Square faced Communist tanks while singing the Christian hymn, "We Shall Overcome."

Most significantly, however, faith was central to the founding of this great republic, this "shining lantern on a hill." This nation's founders had a vision of a free and just society based on a belief in the God of Israel and laws based in biblical morality. The words on the Liberty Bell, "Proclaim Liberty throughout all the land . . ." are from the Torah. The men recognized as our founding fathers not only publicly practiced their faith, but also wrote openly of it, thus codifying it into our national consciousness. It was James Madison who said "We have staked the whole of all our political institutions upon the capacity of mankind for self-government, upon the capacity of each and all of us to govern ourselves, to control ourselves, to sustain ourselves according to the Ten Commandments of God."

The framers of the Constitution believed that governments are necessary because men are flawed. The more virtuous men are, the more liberty they have from government. In an eighteenth-century world governed by kings and czars, these men believed that men could govern themselves. But liberty, they argued, could be had only if built upon a strong moral and religious foundation.

Is it possible for men to be moral without a belief in something greater than themselves? Where does goodness come from? It may be an interesting philosophical exercise to debate, as Maher did on his television program, if morality exists outside of an objective truth. However, that will be quite separate from the fact that the founders didn't believe it possible. This nation was thus founded on the principle of faith that the rights of all men flow from God and are not handed out at the discretion of the state or potentate. If there is no God, then from where do we obtain inalienable rights? And without these natural rights, the purpose of government cannot be to secure them for individual men.

Tocqueville also wrote: "Liberty cannot be attained without morality and morality without faith." Far from being an impediment to morality, as the prime minister suggested, faith provides the fertile ground from which morality springs. Without the belief in an objective truth, which applies to all men, regardless of their station, morality and law become subject to whim. Whether Principal Vidmar or the Maryland public schools like it or not, these founding principles are the essential notions on which our importance as individuals, the importance of our free will, and the importance of liberty is based. (And quite honestly, if you object to this notion you have no business in the public schools teaching our children!)

The plain truth is that what Carlin, Maher, and the rest fear is not man's inhumanity to man, but that citizens and leaders will consider well-established moral principles embodied in the teaching of the great religions of the world when voting and legislating. Whether standing in solidarity with disenfranchised blacks in Selma, or hiding slaves on the Underground Railroad, Americans have been moved by biblically based values to fight for what is morally right. What remains unclear is why they should not now be led by that same sense of compassion and justice when they enter the polling booth or the state capital to debate issues like abortion or national defense. It is here the rubber meets the road. The notion of a citizenry motivated by the moral values embodied in their religious faith is incompatible with the current political agenda of the left. One cannot support abortion on demand, homosexual marriage, and the confiscation and redistribution of wealth while standing under an umbrella of faith. That is the reason Maher mocks religion on his program and why the left is hell bent on removing it from the vicinity of our public schools. Their solution is to simply close the umbrella, erase notions of right and wrong, and proclaim morality relative.

A belief in God is not necessary to conclude that life begins at conception. Many an atheist has come to this very conclusion. To the religiously faithful, however, there also exists the notion that the sexual act is sacred and thus so is the life that results from it. Life is valued because it is created in the image of God. The notion that the power over that life is left to the whims of a woman because it grows in her body runs counter to faith-based principles of the sacred nature of birth. Abortion then is the unjustified killing of children, which is the desecration of God's holy work, and is difficult for a religious community to countenance.

Similarly, the argument over radical redefinition of marriage is not as some would have us believe about the hatred of homosexuals or the rights or ability of homosexuals to love and cherish one another. A biblical worldview holds marriage as the holy bond between a man and a woman for the purposes of raising children. The marriage vows are not delivered in a void but are spoken before God. Marriage therefore becomes the answer to a higher calling that brings its participants into God's blessing. For millennia, states have encouraged the traditional institution of marriage, recognizing that it is an anchor offering a crucial standard of behavior, a stabilizing influence on society primarily because this traditional family unit is the chief source of moral education.

The very principle of liberty that this nation was founded upon is faith-based and includes the idea that the fruits of a man's labor and creativity belong to him and are not the property of the state or of other men. The left would have us believe that, in the name of fairness and charity, the government must take from those who the government determines have more and give it to those who the government determines have less. Having no money of its own, every dollar the government gives away to the deserving in order to fulfill this noble objective must first be coerced away from someone else. When this happens in a back alley we call it robbery. Charity is moral and worthy of praise because it is the voluntary choice to respond to those in need. When government makes that choice for us it is not charity but despotism.

Upon being freed from bondage in Egypt, the Israelites begged Moses to be their king. Moses declined. The people of Israel had God's law and therefore did not need kings. Obeying the law would bring God's blessing. This great and good nation was founded on a similar notion that good and virtuous people needed less government. John Adams stated, "We have no government armed with power capable of contending with human passions unbridled by morality and religion. Avarice, ambition, revenge, or gallantry would break the strongest cords of our Constitution as a whale goes through a net. Our Constitution was made only for a moral and religious people. It is wholly inadequate to the government of any other."

Those on Maher's panel and the nodding heads in the audience that evening would have us believe theirs is a call for a higher morality when what they are really offering is the rejection of morality and the embrace of tyranny. There can be no morality in a world where right and wrong is subjective. Without a clear choice and a measure that is the same for every man, everywhere, people cannot make true moral decisions. When there is no freedom and the state and those in charge make the decisions, the preferences of a few supplant the interests and the objectives of the rest of society. The subjugation of the many by the few is Socialism. And to those with a biblical world view that is a sin.

As Tocqueville noted, the goodness of America begins with faith. A friend of mine describes faith as stepping out into the void to meet God. I like that image, but the notion I prefer is one of faith being a bridge from us to all that is greater than us. It is across that bridge that we discover concepts like justice, compassion, and liberty. America was founded on such a bridge and our lasting greatness depends on our continued determination to traverse that void.

I am not a regular viewer of *Real Time*, however, my sense is that the program is very similar to *Politically Incorrect*, Maher's previous program. The audience tunes in for a bit of irreverent entertainment with just a touch of substantive debate thrown in for good measure. Hey, sounds good to me! The difference with this particular episode was there was very little offered in the way of humor and no debate. All on the panel were in agreement that religion was bad and that people of faith are simpletons. The audience cheered their derision, never challenging the delusions arrogantly spouted by the panelists. My guess is that those who seek to convince us that our society would be better off without religion just don't like the competition. They would like to have the power of God for themselves.

Being Blessed

I was feeling sorry for myself. It had been more than a month since my last acting job and I was feeling down because this was my first audition in weeks. To make matters worse, the job I was reading for was so small, it didn't even merit an identity. The role was one of those characters so inconsequential to the story that screenwriters simply label them "Attorney" or "Man Number 1."

I had been talking to myself all morning, trying to correct my attitude. Actors are not unlike athletes in that we need to get psyched up before a reading, and I was desperately trying to put on my "game face." I was too busy with my pity party to have much success. How could this have happened? Why am I—good-looking, talented me—reading for "Man Number 1"?

When I get in moods like this, the unpleasantness I feel inside usually comes through on my face. A friend once told me I had a habit of walking around looking as if I hadn't quite decided whether or not to kick some a—! If that was true, it was no wonder people (casting directors included) occasionally tend to cut a wide path around me. Who wants to be in the vicinity if and when I decide to kick a little tail?

So I sat in my car outside the audition taking deep breaths and quietly muttering a short prayer, "Please, God, adjust my attitude before I get upstairs." I even tried smiling. I read somewhere that using the muscles that turn your mouth into a smile releases a hormone into your bloodstream that actually improves your mood. It didn't work and what was worse, I looked like a mental patient sitting there wearing a stupid grin. I finally grabbed my script and headed toward the entrance to the building.

As I reached the elevator, a young woman dashed into the lobby and dropped her picture and resume into a cardboard box on the floor next to the elevator. The box was filled to overflowing with the photos and resumes of actors who were hopeful their smiling faces or something in their cover letter would earn them an invitation to meet the casting director upstairs. As the young woman turned to leave, she saw the script in my hands, smiled at me and said, "Oh, you're one of the lucky ones. You get to read."

I have always been told that the Lord speaks in a quiet voice. That's not true. Sometimes the Lord roars because sometimes He needs to do so. We cloud our lives with so much "spiritual" white noise, it's a wonder we ever hear Him at all.

There had been nothing but noise since the moment I woke up that day. I turned on talk radio and the kids wanted to watch TV. I checked my e-mail, listened to old-school jams, and talked on my cell phone. My day was filled with chaos and confusion and not once did I take a moment to listen for a quiet voice that might have calmed me or given me comfort or direction. But why must I strain to hear Him? I so wish the Lord would speak to me as He did to Moses— loudly and boldly. Where is my burning bush? Where is my pillar of fire, guiding me as I wander? Standing in that lobby, I discovered the answer. If I would just keep quiet long enough to let Him speak, He would reveal blessings in the tiniest of moments. The role *was* small but I *was* going upstairs. I wasn't dropping my photo in a box that would more than likely be emptied into the trash bin.

As it happens, I had another audition later in the day. Unfortunately for me, the producers chose to read actors at the height of rush hour. I sat in bumper-to-bumper traffic for more than an hour. Perhaps it was out of boredom, but I'd like to think I turned off the radio and rode to the audition in silence so I could listen again for that quiet voice. My earlier revelation in no way made the ordeal one big laugh fest. Blessed or no, sitting in Los Angeles traffic is a miserable experience! But whenever I felt like complaining about the poor timing of this audition, I reminded myself that I could have been home watching reruns of *Judge Judy*. Instead, I was given an opportunity many other actors don't get because I was truly 'one of the lucky ones.'

Uncovering What's Truly Important: The Dunking

My wife and I have been looking for a church to join for quite a few years. I grew up in the Episcopal Church—I sang in the church choir, was an altar boy, went to church camp, the whole nine yards. My wife was baptized Catholic, but did not grow up in the faith. Both of us had neglected our spiritual lives as young adults. I always told myself that it was because I couldn't find a church as special as the one I grew up in. The truth is that I never really looked. I preferred to sleep in on Sunday.

As Brad Pitt quipped to Edward Norton in the film *Fight Club*, "How's that workin' out for you?" The unfortunate truth was lazy Sundays weren't working out for me at all. I was wrestling with depression, anxiety, and feelings of inadequacy. Women didn't cure it, celebrity didn't cure it, and I couldn't medicate it away with fast food. Marriage brought an entire new set of concerns. My wife and I struggled to find our footing and the shadows simply grew darker.

I reasoned that faith was what was missing and my wife agreed. We talked a lot about going back to church; however, we didn't begin looking for a church in earnest until we were pregnant with out first child. We wanted desperately to raise our children in faith. I remembered the comfort and joy I found in church as a boy and wanted to give my children that same gift.

I was also mindful of the futile battle I had attempted to wage without God and wanted my sons to be better armed. I am convinced that faith leads to a fuller and richer life. My wife and I felt it important to imbue our children with a sense that there exists in the universe something greater than them and that the choices they make during this life—no mater how small—mean something.

Turn on the television, listen to the music, or just drive down the street and you see what children are up against. They are inundated with images of sex, violence, and all manner of anti-social behavior. What is more, these images are not only shoved down their throats, they are celebrated! Celebrities who are on the cutting edge of dysfunction are touted as "beautiful." Young women take off their clothes in public and Barbara Walters introduces them to the world as "the most fascinating people." Men father multiple children out of wedlock and are spread all over the magazines as "the most intriguing people" or given image awards. It goes on and on and on. If not with faith, what will we arm our children with? (What will we arm ourselves with?) We should allow Britney Spears, Jay-Z, and Snoop Dog into our homes and keep the knowledge of a loving and merciful God out? Should we sit our children down before reality television programs or introduce them to biblical concepts that form the foundations of civilized society; equality before the law, the sanctity of life, and the dignity of the human person, the individual conscience and personal redemption, collective conscience and social responsibility, peace as an abstract ideal, love as the foundation of justice? As my neighbor says, "Without a foundation of faith, acts of evil become all too easy, and acts of good become moot because they lack roots in a cosmic theme and purpose." Joshua was keeping it real when he said to the Tribes of Israel, I don't know about y'all, but "as for me and my house, we will serve the Lord."

So we began looking.

This being Hollywood, we were in for quite an experience. For instance there was the church where the pastor cursed from the pulpit and then proclaimed that it was just his "cross to bear." At another church we sat through a sermon wherein the pastor asked the congregation to purchase his wife a new Cadillac Escalade. We heard later that she got it. We chose not to visit one rather popular church in town when we discovered that they preached that Jesus was or was not the Son of God. Along with the virgin birth and the resurrection, this seemed an important element for any church, Christian or otherwise, to be absolutely clear on. There is also a church that has VIP parking for celebrities. This didn't sit well with us. Church should be one of the places those distinctions do not exist. Besides, I wasn't on television at the time. . . .

Let me just say that my style when visiting a church is to sneak in and sit in the very last pew as close to the door as I can get. I don't want anyone watching me worship and if the service is bad, I want to be able to leave without anyone watching me leave. Oddly enough, I don't want to be *seen* in church!

My buddy Courtney invited me to attend a men's service at his church. We arrived late and rather than sneak in the back as I would have done (and wanted desperately to do), Courtney walked in the front door waving at folk and calling attention as we sat down right up front in the second pew.

When we arrived, the choir was singing and though I was a bit self-conscious, I was enjoying myself. You know tapping my feet and clapping my hands. I even dropped a little money in the basket. Next the guest preacher got up to deliver the sermon. And man did he start to preach. Folks were yelling out. I was even getting my praise on a bit. (Episcopalians can get down when we want to!) After a period, the emotion in the room really began to rise. I looked up and much to my amazement and utter confusion I saw folks starting to sprint around the church. I mean run like at a track meet. I turned to say something to Courtney and who was out front leading the pack? He left me by myself! I was sitting in the pew alone, people were running around, a woman was at my feet trembling and crying, there were women whose jobs (I guess) were to move the people who lay in the isle trembling out of the way of the people who are running. . . . I just sat there thinking to myself, "well I guess we won't be joining this church."

The church we finally did decide to join is a little place down the street from our house. One of my fraternity brothers sends his children there for school so we decided to check it out. Thankfully, the pastor didn't curse or ask us to purchase a luxury car for his wife and parking is first come, first served. Most importantly, the boys love it! They look forward to Sunday school and my eldest even asked for his own Bible. It is a place small enough for us to feel comfortable and active enough for us to be involved.

When Glen Kirby, the pastor of the church, first spoke to us about joining, he encouraged us to consider being baptized. I was baptized as a child but this was something different. Being baptized as an adult—being born again (with all the political baggage that entails) was something different and I felt fearful. I wondered why I didn't feel motivated. I read the Bible, I prayed (I prayed all the time. You know: "Please God let me get this job." "Please God let me get my mortgage paid this month." The usual.), I went to Bible study. Yet something was missing. I was waiting for some voice to speak to me. I saw other people moved to tears or raise their hands in joyous praise (sprinting around the church), filled with the Holy Spirit, but in spite of all my desire I felt, well, I felt nothing.

During one Sunday service while watching a baptism, all of that changed. My eyes welled up with tears. Something inside me moved and I wanted that cleansing, I wanted the change. I had professed my life for Christ before, but it had always rung hollow. In that moment, I knew I truly meant it. I knew that I was ready to change my life.

I informed my wife of my decision. It was something I had wanted us to do together, but I told her I couldn't wait for her. (It did cross my mind that perhaps she may have been waiting for me to take the first step.) I called Glen and informed him of our decision to officially join the church. He asked if I was going to be baptized and if so, would I be prepared for the service on Sunday. I told my wife who replied, "I knew once you told him we were going to join, he would try to dunk you in that water as soon as possible!"

During the recitation of my wedding vows, I was overcome with emotion. After taking the vows I knew my life would be forever and irrevocably changed. I was entering into a new phase of my growth as a man. Pledging one's life to another being is a tremendous responsibility, one I did not take lightly. The same was true as I stepped into the baptismal at our church. I was pledging my life to Christ and after going under the water I would emerge—reborn—as a different man.

The intensity of the moment choked me with emotion and my eyes filled with tears.

My wife had an altogether different experience. She was much slower to come to a decision, but once she decided to allow Pastor Kirby to "dunk her in that water" she was joyful. While my baptism took me inside myself and I was slow to let people know of my decision, my wife called all her girlfriends giggling with the happy news. She was the same way when we were married. She was much slower to embrace the concept of spending the rest of her life with me but once she made up her mind she was joyous. Prior to our wedding ceremony, my wife was filled with the excitement of a child. During the ceremony I was in tears while my wife smiled up at me—even whispering at one time, "What's wrong?" When she was baptized, I cried and she looked at me in puzzlement and asked, "What's wrong?" Where our experiences were similar is that we emerged on the other side of both rituals forever changed. The way we interact with each other has changed, as has the way we interact with the world.

Our story is not unique. Others have come to know the Lord in similar fashion. What surprises me is how many people still look for healing and inner peace in all the wrong places. My wife and I recently became fascinated with the reality series *Extreme Makeover*. So transfixed are we by the stories on this program, that we have abandoned a far more popular Thursday night program in order to watch everyday people submit themselves to expensive, time consuming, and extremely painful cosmetic procedures.

On the show each week, two people are chosen to travel to New York or Los Angeles in order to spend six to eight weeks with top cosmetic surgeons. Participants receive everything from liposuction and breast implants to complete dental makeovers and skin peels. After the swelling wears off, they are teamed with personal athletic trainers and hair and make-up stylists. At the end of the show, they arrive back home via a limousine and reveal their new self to family and friends, who, of course ooh and ahh over their transformations.

Sometimes the stories are truly touching, as when a woman born with a cleft palate received corrective surgery that gave her a beautiful smile. Mostly, the shows are merely fascinating—like watching a train wreck, or pathetic as when an eighteen-year-old undergoes liposuction and breast enhancement to look better in her swim suit. Everyday folks—many of whom have often neglected to get enough exercise or visit the dentist on a regular basis—tweak themselves to perfection or a close approximation of it.

The program is just one of a slew of makeover programs currently on the air. Another program, *The Swan*, offers cosmetic surgery to a series of women and then, in what seems the definition of superficiality, pits them against one another in a beauty pageant at the end of the season.

The contestants on all of these programs seem to agree that the changes they see are nothing short of miraculous. Now that they look better, they feel better, and are able to interact in the world with more confidence. All of these programs are based on the connection between self-perception and self-esteem. As one plastic surgery text puts it, "beauty is not only in the eye of the beholder, but in the mind of the beheld." This may be true when it comes to corrective surgery for a cleft palate or extreme scaring on the body. I imagine a fix like that can do wonders for a person's self image. There is in my mind, however, something a bit unseemly about breast implants or liposuction being necessary in order to lift ones self-esteem. I can't help but be amazed at the often quite painful lengths to which people will go in fixing their outer selves so as to make their inner selves feel better.

Medical texts from the 1940's used to teach that patients who presented themselves for plastic surgery were suffering from a variety of psychiatric problems. I don't contend that cosmetic surgery patients are in need of long-term psychiatric care. I do, however, find it intriguing that people see themselves as physically flawed or "ugly" (as the patients on the programs do) while being surrounded by family and friends who think they're beautiful and witty. Undoubtedly, they have husbands, wives, and significant others who find them attractive and I would presume sexy. No. The finger that scratches that itch cannot be removed with a surgeon's scalpel.

But it's difficult for me to fault the patients on *Extreme Makeover*. Like so many of us, they are merely consumers of our "glamour culture." We are bombarded daily with images of young, chiseled bodies that are almost impossible for most of us to achieve (and are often the results of plastic surgery) and told that this is the beauty standard to which we must aspire. Magazines tout Hollywood types as the "most beautiful" and "most intriguing" no matter how vapid or unpleasant their personalities, and we buy, buy, buy! What these programs miss is that in addition to being physical creatures, we are spiritual animals. We are coaxed into believing beauty exists in the sphere of the physical, but it is altogether spiritual. A smile always makes one more attractive while the prettiest face worn with a scowl almost never is. Lust is based on a physical attraction, but love is built through intimacy, through spiritual communion.

Perhaps the networks should consider a series where patients receive makeovers from the inside out. I am not talking about some Dr. Phil knock off, but a reality program where the participants really begin the deep difficult work of transforming their spirits, of becoming comfortable being children of God, made in his image and, as Bruce Wilkinson, author of *The Prayer of Jabez* says, "to become wholly immersed in what God is trying to do in us, through us, and around us for his Glory." Of course, a substantive makeover such as this is time-consuming and requires real commitment on the part of the patient. Here in Hollywood, we don't have time. In television city, peoples' lives are fixed in an hour's time—less if you allow for commercials. And in our quest for instant gratification, beauty is now being packaged and sold like skin lotion. No matter how painful, it is much easier to simply lie down and have beauty done to you. If you're fat, for a few dollars, you can lie down and a doctor will suck the fat out of your body. Have bad teeth? No need to improve your dental hygiene. Lie back and for a small sum, a dentist will replace all of your teeth with porcelain veneers. Lacking confidence? No need to develop personality or read a book to have something to talk about, just write a check and the doctor will noticeably enlarge your breasts. Want to be beautiful? Just open a bottle and rub it on.

Of course, I understand the desire to conform to socially acceptable standards of physical beauty. Believe me, I go to church on Sunday and want to look my best when I get there. I live in Hollywood and I too want to be one of the beautiful people. I didn't join a reality makeover program but I did join a diet center to lose weight.

It was confided to me that I was not going to be hired for an acting role because the director thought I looked chubby. "There is a good reason for that," I responded. "I am chubby!" I then mustered as much indignation as I could and said, "Is he trying to say that forty-year-old men with pot bellies can't be sexy? It might be to his surprise, but I have been told by plenty of women that I'm very sexy." I couldn't think of any names right at that moment, but that was beside the point. However, my indignation rang hollow and my source just shrugged. As difficult as it was for me to admit, I wouldn't have hired me either.

Yep, looks matter! And like some of the contestants on the makeover shows, I had let myself go. If I were a character actor, one hired to play old men and wacky sidekicks, the additional inches on my waist might not matter. In fact, they might actually help. However, I am still seen as a leading man and when directors are casting for leading men to play the romantic interest of their sexy leading ladies, they don't want a guy with a spare tire around his waist.

The writing had actually been on the wall for some time. Not too long ago, I appeared on a television program with Boris Kodjoe, who was one of the stars of the Showtime series *Soul Food* at the time. As we were sitting in the green room chatting, several of the young ladies in the office "dropped by" to see if we (Boris) needed anything. Frankly, I didn't blame them. Boris is a good-looking man. If I were a woman, I too would have asked if he needed anything. Like the gunfighter who has lost his nerve in the film *The Magnificent Seven*, I confided to Boris that "time was, not too many years ago, the young ladies used to 'drop by' to see if I needed anything." I chalked the change up to age, but the truth remained, I was getting fat. And I didn't feel good about it.

I began to gain weight when my wife was pregnant with our first child. Some call it "sympathy weight," and it's not uncommon. Should women get to have all the fun? When my wife was pigging out on pickles and turkey sandwiches over the kitchen sink, I was right there by her side packing the calories away along with her. In fact, I was so sympathetic that I was also sneaking out at night to eat ribs and hamburgers. I matched her weight gain pound for pound! What could be greater proof of my devotion? Unfortunately, it is much easier to put the weight on (and a lot more fun) than it is to take it off.

I managed to shed the weight but eventually gained it back. I had grown to hate my job on *General Hospital* and my unhappiness manifested itself again in an increase in junk food and sweets. Once I left (was fired from) *G.H.*, there was a brief window of opportunity to correct some of this destructive behavior. The problem was that while I was happy not to be hoeing rows on the Wendy Rich Plantation, I was now unemployed! Financial pressure replaced job stress and put a strain on my marriage, and after the death of my father I was back in the drive through at McDonalds. There were a few halfhearted attempts at getting back in shape, but when you are forty, you have to work out twice as hard just to stay even. I grew tired of fighting what seemed like a losing battle. "No," I thought. "It is much easier to simply buy bigger pants." I just resigned myself to the idea that I was going to be a big man.

You would think the effect of my weight and eating habits on my health would be enough to motivate me, but it was of little concern. I was unmindful when I noticed that conversations with my male friends tended to veer away from the topic of women and sports and instead covered such juicy subject matter as prostate exams, high blood pressure, and heart disease. I remained unfazed even when four of my good friends—all my age and all a bit overweight—were diagnosed with diabetes. This should have been enough to open my eyes but leave it to my vanity to draw attention to the matter and provide me with the wake up call I needed. Whatever works, right? If my size is preventing me from getting acting work, if I am not seen as beautiful anymore, it would behoove me to find a way to lose weight and keep it off. And hey, if it means that as a leading man, I might get another shot at kissing Halle Berry . . . well that should be motivation enough for any man.

My diet worked. I dropped the weight (and so far I have kept it off). I look younger, feel healthier, and sure enough, the young ladies are noticing me again. One young lady in particular was very happy with the change—my wife. She has been much friskier since I lost the tire around my waist. I love wearing tight shirts again. I had a black tie event to go to not too long ago and I wore the tux I was married in. The outer change felt great! I was a new man—born again—attacking the world with a newfound confidence.

Alas, it was short-lived as is the euphoria the patients on *Extreme Makeover* will no doubt feel soon after the novelty of their reveal wears off. The demons that created our weight problems cannot be exorcized through plastic surgery or dieting. I was soon struggling with the same issues I had when I was heavy. The melancholy was there, the career frustration, the feelings of inferiority. All of the things I have gone round and round with most of my adult life could not be sweated out by running hills or eating steamed broccoli. The real problem, the thing that made me eat my way to a forty-two-inch waist in the first place, and the factor that makes people surrounded by love, lust, and support feel that they need bigger boobs or a smaller nose to feel pretty is a crisis of the spirit. The culprit in the never-ending battle with life's demons is not deficiency of physical perfection but lack of spiritual health. And there is only one way to bring light where there is darkness. You can't do it by sucking the fat out of your butt. You must give your life over to something greater than yourself.

These television makeover programs are a reflection of our ongoing struggle to find the connection between self-perception and self-esteem. However, the perception—and more importantly the acceptance of ourselves as children of God—should be all we need to lift our self-esteem. The smiles that greeted me after my baptism were more meaningful than the oohs and ahhs and "oh, you look so goods" that greeted me after I lost weight. I was beautiful in the eyes of the congregation no matter what I looked like. More importantly, much as my wife has enjoyed my new body, the love she had in her eyes for me that day was as great as it has been in our eleven years of marriage. That day affirmed my beauty in her eyes and conversely she was never more beautiful to me than after her baptism.

The relatively simple task of Pastor Kirby (as my wife says) "dunking me in that water" produced changes in me that are deeper and more substantive than those executed by the surgeons on the makeover programs. I made a commitment not just to change but also to grow closer to my family, closer to my neighbors, and closer to God from the inside out.

There was a small poster that my father hung in our home when I was growing up. The poster read, "I know I'm beautiful 'cause God don't make no junk!" He doesn't. Sure, we may take what the good Lord has given us and ruin it through abuse and neglect, but what we start out with—no matter how removed from "socially accepted standards"—is art and our beauty radiates from within.

All of us are taught as children that what we put on to our bodies is not nearly as important as what comes from our hearts. In the end, when we leave this earth, no one will remember our wonderful abdominals or our fabulous jaw line. No tombstone ever recounted the deceased's great nose. Our legacy will be etched with kind words, compassionate touches, and warm smiles. What a wonderful world this would be if we all spent as much time and energy cultivating our inner selves as we do working on our outer appearance. Inner beauty is, after all, something that will not fade with age or when ratings disappear.

The Muscle of Faith

Not long ago, I was asked to contribute to a collection of essays detailing how faith can carry one through hardships. After many starts and stops, I finally begged out of the project. I am a bit embarrassed to admit that I could not readily think of any time in my life during which I could point to faith as the lifeline that pulled me to safety or sanity during a difficult time. That is not to say that I have never experienced painful episodes or struggled with disappointment, grief, or temptation. Nor is it to suggest that I somehow feel I was able to find my way through the darkness by myself. There is no doubt in my mind the Lord carried me through those times. It is simply that I do not recall any time that my ultimate triumph was due to any overt (or covert) act of faith on my part.

I have heard others talk about moments of epiphany in their lives when they were gifted with clarity or filled with the needed strength to overcome. Where was my ah-hah! Moment—the big, grand, magical event that could illustrate the power of faith? Alas, faith does not always come in plaids. Sometimes it works in pastels. Neither is faith magic. Most often it is hard work.

I recall a particularly bad stretch my wife and I were having in our marriage. Both of us were frustrated in our careers. Both of us were tired from taking care of babies and both of us were angry with the other for any number of reasons. We invited discord into our home and he had taken up residence, disrupting our relationship. I do not know what other couples do when destruction and conflict camps out in their homes. My wife and I fought, offering up our best imitations of Ali-Frazier! Had it not been for our children, it is quite possible we would have gone our separate ways.

The Psalms say that the Lord is our refuge, our light, and salvation. But God also demands that we do more than simply believe in things that are unseen. He asks that we be active. God asks us to worship; He asks us to trust, to love, to honor each other, to sow and to reap. We are asked to sing, to sacrifice, to forgive, and to knock with the expectation that the door will be opened. Those who are strong in their faith have recognized that faith is a muscle that must be worked.

To find our way back to each other, my wife and I decided to renew our commitment to each other, to our family, and to God. We joined a local church. I began visiting a men's group. We reached out to friends who vowed they would not be passive in support of our marriage. I had one friend in particular who called me daily from the set of his television program just to pray with me. Most importantly, my wife and I began to pray with each other.

Some years later, we are still together. We are not quite Rob and Laura Petrie, but neither is our marriage the Thrilla in Manila. Like all couples, we still have disagreements and frustrations. However, our marriage is stronger, our love is deeper and we are more determined than ever to keep discord at bay and instead invite peace into our home.

That is my aha moment—the realization that faith did not pull my wife and me through that painful period. It was the *exercise* of faith that made the difference. And through exercising our faith, my wife and I discovered we had more than we ever knew.

Living Good or Living Well?

I can't lie. I like nice things.

I love fine wine, gourmet foods, and well-tailored clothes. I wouldn't mind a few more thousand square feet of living space and before I die, I am going to own a Mercedes CL 600 coupe. This is known in the vernacular as living fat. I prefer to call it living well. "Living fat" conjures up too many images of big bellies, cellulite oozing out of spandex pants, and long lines at Mickey D's. The irony is that living well often leads to being fat. The high lifestyle encourages us to indulge our sensual selves until we have grown flabby, both physically and spiritually. There is, however, another way to live—to live "good."

I have been tremendously blessed of late. I have been working steadily and making money, several more newspapers and websites have picked up my column, and I am anticipating the release of my first book (which you are now reading!). I am on my way to living well. It is just a matter of time before I am dancing to the tune of a twin turbo charged V-12, intoxicated by the smell of glove-soft nappa leather and polished chestnut wood trim.

Typically for me, rather than simply saying "thank you" and going about my business, I began to worry. Things seemed too good to be true. I scheduled some one-on-one time with God and asked: "Okay, what's the catch?" God, of course, tends to operate on a need to know basis and judging by the silence that followed, I apparently had all the information I needed.

Soon afterward, I found myself screen testing for a new television series. My competition was an old friend with whom I'd had a bitter falling out. We had not spoken to each other in two years. (Yes, in good Christian fashion, I chose anger instead of forgiveness and reconciliation.)

That was the moment God decided to fill me in. It was suddenly clear that all my recent blessings had nothing to do with God wanting me on television or thinking I would look sooo good driving a Mercedes. God is remarkably unimpressed by the trappings of high living. Fame is fleeting, cars are stolen, and big houses are swept away by mud. God is about relationships—our relationship with Him and with those made in His image.

Moreover, as my friend and I embraced like a couple of schoolboys, it occurred to me that the Lord is not blessing me in order for me to rush out and buy more stuff. A fancier car—while adding substance to my lifestyle—would not add greater substance to my life. God would prefer that I direct my energies into building stronger relationships with my family and with my community. These are things of lasting significance. I am receiving His blessing in order that I may bless others and in so doing give glory to the Father—that I begin living good.

That is not to say God doesn't want us to have nice things. Hunger, thirst, and ambition are also God's gifts. God wants us to have abundance. In fact, when I stop whining about what I want long enough to begin thinking in terms of what I already have, I realize my life has been tremendously blessed. Even in the leanest of times, I have never wanted for food, clothing, or good friends. I have a beautiful wife, three spirited, healthy little boys and a sturdy roof over my head. It seems I have been living well all this time and didn't even know it.

With God's help, I can now begin living good.

Finding Strength and Renewal

Often, my faith walk seems more like a faith crawl. I remind myself of my sons when they were infants—I am always taking a few small, uncertain steps before falling on my well-padded bottom. Therefore, I am making only one resolution for the New Year: I'm going to renew my faith.

It's mostly in moments of great despair and heartache—when, without a doubt, my faith is needed most—that I reach for the surety of faith and find myself wanting. But the small things derail me as well: A job I didn't get, a toy I can't afford, or even a party invitation that doesn't arrive. After every tragic loss or when a dream fails to materialize, I begin to wonder if, while I am on my knees, my prayers are simply echoing anonymously and unheard into the void.

I have great admiration for those who, rather than feel abandoned during times of hardship, see each trial as a sign that God is working in their lives. That's rock solid faith. Like them, I aspire to have a level of belief that doesn't disappear at the first sign of bad weather.

For a time, I believed that a great many of my Christian friends and acquaintances had faith like that. Many of them witnessed my ongoing battle and offered to council me. They invited me to Bible studies, and emailed me daily Bible verses and sermons by famous preachers. If you don't know these people by name, certainly you recognize them by their behavior. They pepper every conversation with references to Scripture and some of them have even been known to speak in tongues while praying before dinner. One piece of wisdom I garnered from looking up to these good Christians is that it's unwise to put your faith in men, they will let you down every time. It's not that I expected them to be perfect in their faith, it is just that with all their praying and Scripture quoting, I didn't expect them to lie, cheat, fornicate, and divorce with such abandon. Their falls from grace were disheartening to me. If these folks—who outwardly seem so secure in their faith—can so easily engage in un-Christian-like behavior, why am I even bothering?

One Christmas season, as I rode in my car listening to the endless stream of Christmas carols over the radio, I had my answer.

"The First Noel" is one of my favorites. How can we relate it to today? As shepherds lay asleep in the fields, an angel appears proclaiming the good news that prophecy has been fulfilled. A star appears in the Eastern sky guiding travelers to the site of the miracle birth. Three wise men travel with gifts they will lay before the newborn king. But the three wise men were not the only ones who traveled to see the child. Those same shepherds in the fields set their burdens down and set out to witness the miracle as well. I was listening to the chorus of this beautiful song when it struck me that this hymn is not only about the birth of The Messiah, it is also about a faith walk.

It was more than belief that roused those shepherds from their sleep and bade them follow a star wherever it led. It was commitment. Without the journey, their belief meant very little. More importantly, each man walked alone on his path and had to overcome different obstacles to reach the now holy town of Bethlehem.

True faith is more than just belief; it is the willingness to turn our lives over to something greater than ourselves and to honor that offering with the struggle to become something better than we were. It is a long road to travel and part of the Christian teaching says that all men will fall short during their journey. My Bible-quoting friends only proved themselves human. I must continue to toil in spite of their shortcomings because falling short is not as important as making the journey, as making the daily commitment to live a righteous and humble life. I may not be as adept at quoting Scripture as many of my Christian friends, but they are laboring just as I am. The difference is that while I have chosen to see my labor as a lack of faith, they rightly see theirs' as an affirmation of their faith.

So, perhaps I misspoke earlier. This holiday season, I'm not going to renew my faith but continue on my journey. It's my goal to walk it with the same enthusiasm and commitment displayed by certain poor shepherds more than two-thousand years ago.

Idealism

Black Conservatism, Black Pride

While attending a conference on race and culture sponsored by the Manhattan Institute, I ran into Professor Glen Loury, a prominent social critic, award-winning author, and public intellectual. Although Loury has recently begun to move left on certain social issues, he was one of the pioneers of the contemporary black conservative movement. As we chatted at the coffee station, he no doubt wondered what in the world I was doing on the same dais as him. I assure you that while we chatted, I was wondering the same thing. As we spoke, he apologized for not knowing who I was, but understood that I was a conservative. He then asked me my definition of conservatism. I felt as though my father was grilling me after arriving home after curfew. I nervously began rambling on about economic freedom and traditional values before, thankfully, we were called into the conference.

I had been reading the work of men like Loury, Thomas Sowell, Walter Williams, and Shelby Steele for years. Their opinions seemed to make a lot of sense to me. Once confronted with the question, however, I realized I had not actually given much thought to what exactly a conservative was. Moreover, I was suddenly at a loss to explain exactly what it means to be black and conservative. I know what a lot of people think black conservatives are, and most of it is rather unpleasant.

Most people would define a conservative as someone who seeks to preserve the status quo. Liberals would define a conservative as one who is opposed to social progress, opposed to gender and racial equality, opposed to economic fairness . . . opposed to little old ladies and cute, little puppies with wet noses. . . . They then usually add descriptions like uptight, stuffy, and sexually repressed. This is precisely why, for most of my life, I have eschewed these types of labels. They seem designed only to give the user a point of reference—"Oh, I know who he is. I know what he is about." Once able to identify the labeled person as abnormal, the identifier can then effectively dismiss any argument that ensues. "Well, you know, he is one of *them*." I don't deny that there is something to be said for having a point of reference. Unfortunately, these labels seem so sweeping and rarely say much about who we are and what we believe, effectively stifling the real exchange of ideas as opposed to beginning it. For instance, I do not think of myself as uptight or stuffy and it is only on the rare occasion that I make love to my wife with my wingtips on. I am not opposed to change; I am opposed to change for the sake of change or in order to achieve some bureaucrat's notion of utopia. It may be that I need a more elastic definition of conservative, one that allows for P-Funk as well as for Johnny Mathis. What is interesting to me is that for the majority of my life, the *label* I put on myself was that of liberal. If I'm now a conservative, it's certainly a conservatism grounded in the same common sense and independent thought that was encouraged by my parents—both of whom were life-long Democrats.

My sisters and I were raised to believe that we, as black people, had a right to the mainstream economic and educational institutions of this nation. Our right of ownership was purchased by the toil of millions who came before us. That claim, however, also came with an obligation to achieve. We were taught that life is not fair and that hard work will accomplish more than complaining. A constant refrain in my home was that there *is* no monopoly on brainpower. My sisters and I were taught that we (along with other black children) could compete academically with white children. If black students are challenged to compete on an objective scale of merit, in time, through hard work, they will rise to that challenge and excel. We attended church regularly and were taught that Christ loves us and that Christianity is more than a belief; it is a responsibility. We should love our fellow man and evil is to be confronted and not endured.

Those ideals learned in childhood have matured into a belief in personal autonomy—a smaller, less intrusive federal government; a belief in empowering parents when it comes to educating their children. I believe in the traditional institution of marriage and in raising children in households in which God is at the head. I believe in American exceptionalism because this nation is good, truly "the last best hope of man on earth." I know that this makes me a Republican. Quite frankly, if that now also defines conservatism, then I am proud of it! And I might turn the question around and ask liberals, to what are you progressing?

The liberalism I knew growing up supported our constitutional notion that our government ought to act in defense of individual rights. In the name of social progress, liberals have now replaced the sacredness of the individual with group rights and victimology. Our government is no longer securing rights for individuals, but ensuring that rights will only flow to individuals by virtue of their membership in a group.

While in college at NYU, liberal-minded administrators created something called the "Third World Project" or more accurately, liberalism gone terribly astray. As a means to provide minority students with acting opportunities, they earmarked one play every year for the black second- and third-year students. I couldn't help but be a bit offended at the rather colonial notion that in spite of being raised in Colorado, my blackness meant I couldn't rate "first world," wasn't even "second world" (with my pitiful self), but just "third world." And let me remind you, these were New York liberals, not "Reagan Republicans," behind this so-called initiative. Rather than enforce open casting or choose plays with black characters that would require the casting of black students (who had paid the same amount as the white students for an equal education) they adopted a "separatist" policy. The real madness was that now the white directing students had a *legitimate* reason not to cast us in their projects; they didn't need to cast us because we had our own "project." But as the Supreme Court stated in *Brown v. Board of Education*, separate is not equal! The initiative had a crippling effect. By separating us, they not only ensured that most of the black students' *only* opportunity to perform would be with the Third World Project, versus the two or three opportunities afforded the white students, but they also denied us an important opportunity to build relationships with directors, several of whom have gone on to great professional acclaim.

Twenty years later, programs like this exist all over the country. In addition, liberalism now celebrates separate dormitories for black students, separate courses of study, and—dare I say it after we have celebrated the fiftieth anniversary of *Brown v. Board of Education*?—separate schools! And not only for black students. The same is now true for Latino students, Asian students, as well as gay students or any students who can claim group victim status.

Here in California, the State University at Long Beach holds a graduation ceremony for its African American students. The University will tell you that this is really a cultural celebration and is not meant to replace the school's official commencement ceremony. However, the black student graduation mirrors the traditional commencement in every way save the official conferring of degrees. But why quibble? Students wear caps and gowns, they are called to cross the stage and receive *certificates of participation*. The black faculty participates in cap and gown. There are keynote speakers and family and friends attend the event.

But wait. There is also a separate ceremony for American Indians, Chicano/Latinos, Cambodians, and Pineoy or Filipino students. More bizarre is that a portion of this ceremony is paid for with student funds. Every major school in California has a similar ceremony and the trend is spreading to most major universities in the country. All of this is happening under the vigilant and encouraging gaze of liberalism. Can you imagine what would happen if a bunch of white kids got together and decided that they were going to have a white graduation ceremony and pay for it with student affairs dollars? The liberal editorial writers are even now sharpening their pencils to decry the systemic racism permeating our nations' colleges and universities. It would be funny if it weren't so tragic.

After my parents' generation fought to extend the reach of the American ideal of freedom and opportunity, how in the world could I not shake my head in disgust at these events? Why would I not grow impatient with the promotion of a society that defines individual excellence down to the lowest common denominator? That rejects individual responsibility and accountability in favor of claims of victimhood at the hands of some specific "ism"? Why wouldn't I reject out-of-hand government interference in my personal life or public policy that punishes hard work and creativity? How could I not resist and fight tooth-and-nail against the increasing hostility toward religious belief that seeks to break down the moral foundation laid in me as a child in order to forcefully transfer a relativist or amoral culture onto my children?

I think Professor Loury would be tickled to discover that I'm not really a conservative, more like an abandoned liberal who came home to find that my family left with no forwarding address.

I was not an ideological orphan for long, though. The '80s were the time of the Reagan revolution. While I was not part of it, I certainly felt its effects.

I did not vote for Ronald Reagan. In 1980, as a college sophomore, I cast my vote for independent candidate John Anderson. Undaunted, four years later I tossed my vote into the abyss that was the Walter Mondale campaign. I was never above telling a good "Ronny the Ray Gun" joke and as a good friend was quick to remind me, I spent more than one evening railing against that doddering old man in the White House. But Reagan's vision struck a nerve in me. The conservatism of Ronald Reagan was a dynamic conservatism that advocated American virtue and strength, believing that lower taxes and smaller government would unleash the productivity and creativity of the American people. What is more, Reagan communicated a unifying vision of what it means to be an American. (His two resounding victories at the polls and the tremendous outpouring of grief at his passing suggest his vision resonated with a great many Americans.) A short four years after Reagan left office, I was arguing for the re-election of George Bush amongst friends with whom I used to share Reagan-bashing sessions.

Reagan was able to simply and clearly communicate the difference between conservatism and liberalism. More than anything, however, it was the vitriol from the left (of which I had been party for the eight years of his administration) that distinguished the difference most clearly for me. Today's liberals believe that in the interest of fairness, it is government's duty to take from those who have more and give it to those who have less. Wealth, wisdom, and righteousness have been doled out unequally and even though God did not make life fair, liberals believe that with a little tinkering on their part, they can create equality where none exists. Conservatives on the other hand are far more willing to accept the inherent inequality of life. Recognizing that "the real destroyer of the liberties of the people is he who spreads among them bounties, donations, and benefits," conservatives believe the people of this country are capable of solving their own problems. Of course, that faith is what earns Republicans the reputation of being cold-hearted and selfish pessimists.

However, the week-long national mourning of former President Reagan requires us to consider: Who was the most optimistic president of our time? Conservatives are optimists by nature and liberals seem unable to comprehend that it is that optimism that makes conservatives popular. I believe the vast majority of people like the notion that they are capable of solving their own problems and that if given the opportunity, they will be able to create for themselves lives of significance. It is a cruel irony that our faith in individuals is characterized as pessimism, while the belief that the American people need the government to provide for them makes liberals progressive.

In a *New York Times* interview, Donna Brazile—former Al Gore campaign manager (and current thorn in the Democratic party's side)—was asked to comment on "speculation that she would jump across party lines." Brazile responded that she could be a friend with Republicans but had a fundamental disagreement with Republicans on the role of government. "Government has a duty to take care of the least of these [the poor and downtrodden]," she asserted. (The declaration of independence—the foundational document of our republic—states that the role of government is to secure individual rights. It mentions nothing about taking care of folks from cradle to grave.)

At the 1964 Republican convention, Reagan pointed out so brilliantly in his speech, "A Time for Choosing:" "anytime you and I question the schemes of the do-gooders, we're denounced as being opposed to their humanitarian goals." He added, "They tell us we are always 'against,' never 'for' anything." I see this as one of the major problems in today's political debate. We do not seem able to begin the discussion from the premise that all of us are interested in helping the less fortunate. Does Brazile truly believe Republicans do not care about the poor and afflicted? It certainly appears so and to my ears it sounds as if most liberals concur. Which also proves the axiom that when conservatives disagree with liberals, liberals are wrong. When liberals disagree with conservatives, conservatives are evil. How else to describe people who, as Brazile suggests, do not care for their fellow man?

Republicans are not without compassion. We just believe government is an inefficient tool for addressing the problems of suffering. The best way to help the "least of these" is not through an expanding federal bureaucracy, but by limiting government, decreasing obstacles, and securing the natural rights of life, liberty, and the pursuit of happiness, thus freeing citizens to reach whatever heights their talent and drive can carry them to.

I shared this opinion with my dear friend Karen. She responded by saying, "I think if we rely on the goodness in men's hearts to share wealth, wisdom, and bread, we will starve. I think people have to be made to share more equitably." (Didn't this experiment fail miserably in the Soviet Union?) She was clear that she didn't mean to *support* people "who can and should be working for their income, but to amend and encourage those who have been kept down." What liberals never seem able to explain is how they know what is fair. On what mountaintop were they anointed with superior vision to know how much is too much and who deserves more? Understand that I am not in complete disagreement with Karen. The populace does sometimes need a little prompting; I just disagree on where that prompting should come from. I prefer the minister's tongue to the government's bayonet.

Nor does my conservative realism share her liberal cynicism. Churches, fraternal and professional organizations, women's auxiliary groups, and school children donate time, goods, services, and millions of dollars to aid the homeless, drug addicted, abused, elderly, sick, and lonely. Following the murders of September 11, 2001, there was an unprecedented outpouring of generosity on the part of the American people. Charities raised more than $1 billion. Following the death and destruction brought about by the tsunami in southeast Asia, American corporations and individuals gave another $1.2 billion in cash and assistance. Americans gave so much that relief organizations had to ask that the giving stop. After the devastation created by Hurricane Katrina, Americans gave more than 1 billion dollars in cash donations. This is proof that there is something inherent in our American character that encourages us to help our fellow man. We are not a secular people (not yet anyway) and the Christian faith of our founders still courses through the veins of our culture. My fear is that our spirit of nobility, compassion, and charity is being bred out of us. That, as a culture, we will continue to numb ourselves on drugs and alcohol, lattes and reality TV until we no longer recognize the suffering around us, that the ACLU and others will succeed in purging God from our public square, supplanting objective morality with nihilism. I worry that the more we depend on government, the less we will look to that better part of our American selves.

Reagan suggested to those listening in 1964 that "we're told that we must choose between left or right, but I suggest there is no such thing as a left or right; there is only up or down. Up to man's age-old dream—the maximum of individual freedom consistent with order—or down to the ant heap of totalitarianism." The belief that government redistribution of wealth and opportunity will create the mythical "level playing field" naturally leads to paternalism. When some seek to use the government to force their notion of fairness onto others, oppression and bloodshed will naturally follow. I shared these thoughts with my friend Nancy, a liberal commentator. She was appalled. She asked, "Is it fair that some people, because of their wealth, will always be able to afford access to better services than those of lesser means?" I had some fun by sending her this quote from Winston Churchill: "The inherent vice of capitalism is the unequal sharing of blessings; the inherent virtue of socialism is the equal sharing of miseries." She is probably still sucking her teeth.

These are generalities of course. There are conservatives and liberals (my friend Karen included) who are working daily at the grass roots—with very little money—to change and inspire people's lives. It is the noble work for which Americans are known, and their concerns are not of fairness, but of a government whose priorities often seem out of place. Ultimately, we must all answer the question: What is the best way to unleash the talents and imagination of the populace? It is, after all, that dynamism that will cure sickness, extend life spans, and raise the living standard of the "least of us."

The query, then, of ethnic conservatives in America is whether the nanny state or policies that make individuals responsible for their own destinies is the best way to unleash the dynamism of black and brown communities that have for so long numbered among the least of us? This goes to the heart of what Professor Loury was really asking me.

There can be no question that the removal of state and local government-imposed barriers to education and the political process along with the enforcing of equal protection laws have paved the way for black success and made possible the leisure that allows me to ruminate on such things. It is also a sad fact that there was a period in this nation's history when Republican conservatism seemed content to institutionalize blacks as second-class citizens. The Party of Lincoln lost its vision. I dare say I would not have been a conservative fifty years ago. My stake in the American experiment being a success would have demanded that I lock arms with fellow artists and writers and march for civil and human rights. But times have changed. Oh how they have changed! And it is this change that led me to become a conservative. Liberals are no longer the champions of civil and human rights, they now fight to ensure that rights are allocated on a group basis. It is now conservatives who have taken up the mantle of individual rights.

Removing government barriers and enforcing existing law is in line with a true conservative ideology, as is the celebration of traditional moral values, which provide the foundation for strong families, strong communities, and a strong nation.

My friend Michael Bowen describes himself as an "old-school" Republican. He has a list of what he calls the core of the old-school values. They are not particularly ideological, but I can't see how you could be considered Right if you don't conserve these principles:

Liberty—We believe in the rule of law and rights of people to be free and to determine their own fate. We fight tyranny and oppression of all kinds, keeping in mind the battles of those who struggled and died that we might be free.

Patriotism—The United States of America is our home, not simply by default, but by choice. We take our duty to our home seriously and we defend it. We seek to improve it by our work and values and leave it better than we found it.

Family—We are extended families and we put family first. It is the primary organization to which our lives are dedicated. We fight for the proper upbringing of our children. We demand respect and consideration of our elders. We love and support our brothers and sisters.

Pride—We are Americans of all backgrounds and ethnicities. We are proud of our heritage, and respect the lives, triumphs, and tribulations of our forefathers in this country and beyond. We aim to represent their greatest hopes for us and honor their memory.

Industry—We work twice as hard and sometimes get half as far, but we work with dignity and we expect and enjoy our rewards. We are not materialistic but we know the value of a dollar. We seek self-improvement through creativity, dedication, and effort in our jobs, businesses, and partnerships.

Piety—We have abiding faith in God and the principles of righteousness. We strive to be true to transcendent values and take the long view of our purpose on earth. We conduct ourselves as vessels of spirit and we guard our own souls and the souls of others from corruption, tolerating all forms of religious expression and faith.

Pluralism—We believe in a tolerant and open society, and we welcome all people to enjoy its benefits and responsibilities.

Liberals will often ask, rather mockingly, "exactly what is it that you black conservatives are seeking to conserve?" We ought to answer that we seek to preserve those principles and values taught us by generations of black folk who demanded that America live up to the meaning of her creed. That's right. Far from longing for the good old days of Jim Crow and tap dancing, black conservatism means embracing the concepts of self-reliance and individual rights and responsibilities. That is black pride, baby! Black conservatism affirms the ability of black fathers to lead and provide for their families. Black conservatism insists that black children are as creative, industrious, and academically capable as any other children. Black conservatism proclaims to the world that our American culture benefits when the creative energy of individuals is unleashed.

The anger with which the black left greets this conservatism is a reflection of how corrupt black liberalism has become. Liberal black leadership would apparently rather see black children condemned to substandard public schools and substandard educations rather than break their allegiance with the teachers' union and empower black parents with school choice. Welfare nurtures dependency and kills initiative. Black liberalism sneered at welfare reform and cried that work for benefits programs were unfair. "According to the Department of Health and Human Services, welfare reform helped to move 4.7 million Americans from welfare dependency to self-sufficiency within three years of enactment, and the number of welfare caseloads has declined by 54% since 1996." As the "Personal Responsibility and Work Opportunity Reconciliation Act of 1996" nears expiration, black liberalism is fighting its renewal. Black liberalism rejects any attempt to empower individual citizens with control over their own retirement dollars through personal retirement accounts, thus keeping the black community wedded to a system that transfers millions of dollars out of black hands and into white. Remind me again who it is that is against change?

The anger from the left is also demonstration that progressives—who have an unhealthy tendency to confuse the health of the progressive movement with the health of black America, and to define civil rights as whatever they say it is—have co-opted political debate in the black community. How, for instance, did they manage to convince so many in our community that black people suffered under Ronald Reagan, in spite of fifteen years of uninterrupted economic growth, that saw an eighty-four percent increase in black household income? By trotting out the bogeyman of racist white conservatives and Tomming black republicans rather than engaging in serious debate on the merits.

My attempts at discussing this topic have largely been fruitless. I used to spend time on the computer going to chat rooms and participating in discussions on African-American message boards. I had to stop. I grew tired of the abuse. Discussions quickly deteriorated into street-corner yelling matches replete with "playing the dozens." My conservative ideas were not rejected on their merits; they were summarily shouted down. Noticeably absent from the challenges were any real facts. Moral indignation and claims to historical victimization were deemed sufficient argumentation. And if that wasn't enough, sooner or later someone would tell me I was a lousy actor.

Certainly, this is to be expected when conversing over the Internet with ordinary folks whose domain is not the world of ideas. However, it is maddening when this same street-corner strategy is used by those we entrust with the job of moving cultural dialogue forward through thoughtful analysis and debate.

While surfing the net, I came across several essays critical of black conservative thought. The essays differed in the amount of vitriol leveled at black conservatives, but all seemed to agree on one thing: We are up to no good. Our beliefs are manufactured, not organic, and we all have some ulterior motive. What exactly is that motive? If you are James Dixon, writing for *Black World Today*, it is nothing short of the "exclusion of blacks [and other ethnic minorities] from full participation in American society." Exactly how this will benefit those of us who are "ethnic in spite of our politics," he doesn't say. My guess? His answer is the same as the general explanation he and others offer for the existence of black conservative thought—appeasing the white man.

Even respected intellectuals like Dr. Cornel West, professor of black studies at Princeton University, are not immune. A few years ago, West published an article in the *Christian Century* entitled "Unmasking the Black Conservatives." In all fairness to West, he believes the emergence of the black conservative to be a healthy development. After ceding that there has indeed been a cultural and moral decay in the black community, however, he proceeds to argue that black conservatism is really a quest for white peer acceptance. Let me get this straight. We strive to deny opportunity to our fellow black citizens, at the cost of opportunity for our children and ourselves, because at the end of the day we want the white man to pat our nappy heads, give us our thirty pieces of silver, and send us on our way. Alas, this is the progressive notion of thoughtful, intellectual engagement.

Both West and Dixon claim that our small numbers are proof of our ignobility and that there is a disconnect between black conservative ideology and what is happening in the black community. A study recently released by the Joint Center for Political and Economic Studies revealed that support for the Democratic Party has dropped eleven percent among black voters. Meanwhile, the number of blacks who identify themselves as Republican has more than doubled. It would appear that we conservatives are not as out of touch as some would hope.

But, as the fellas on the street say, "who's zoomin' who? If we gon' talk, let's talk!" West, Dixon, and other critics of black conservatism are not interested in the conservative position on gun control or tax reform. When they talk about "repugnant" ideas, they are referring to the black conservatives' failure to embrace a liberal doctrine based on deference to past victimization. No, a belief in free markets and a lean federal government will not earn the wrath of the liberal elite (black or white). Moving against the tide of that wisdom—to hold that white racism is not the primary impediment to black success—will get you called a "Tom" every time.

Alas, this was a lesson television star (and staunch liberal Democrat) Bill Cosby learned the hard way. Cosby created a firestorm with remarks he made at an NAACP-sponsored celebration of the landmark Supreme Court decision, *Brown v. Board of Education*. The comedian criticized segments of the black community about issues ranging from out-of-wedlock births to literacy. A partial transcript of Cosby's remarks:

> People marched and were hit in the face with rocks to get an education, and now we've got these knuckleheads walking around. . . . The lower economic people are not holding up their end in this deal. These people are not parenting.
>
> I am talking about these people who cry when their son is standing there in an orange suit. Where were you when he was two? Where were you when he was twelve? Where were you when he was eighteen, and how come you didn't know that he had a pistol? And where is the father?
>
> People putting their clothes on backward: Isn't that a sign of something gone wrong? . . . People with their hats on backward, pants down around the crack, isn't that a sign of something, or are you waiting for Jesus to pull his pants up? Isn't it a sign of something when she has her dress all the way up . . . and got all types of needles (piercing) going through her body? What part of Africa did this come from? We are not Africans. Those people are not Africans; they don't know a . . . thing about Africa.
>
> We have millionaire football players who can't read. We have million-dollar basketball players who can't write two paragraphs.

With names like Shaniqua, Taliqua, and Mohammed and all of that crap, and all of them are in jail. *Brown v. Board of Education* is no longer the white person's problem. We have got to take the neighborhood back. . . . They are standing on the corner and they can't speak English.

People used to be ashamed. . . . [Today] a woman has eight children with eight different "husbands," or men, or whatever you call them now.

The idea is to one day, get out of the projects. You don't just stay there. We, as black folks, have to do a better job. . . . Someone working at Wal-Mart with seven kids, you are hurting us. We have to start holding each other to a higher standard.

The incarcerated? These are not political criminals. These are people going around stealing Coca-Cola. People getting shot in the back of the head over a piece of pound cake and then we run out and we are outraged, saying, "The cops shouldn't have shot him." What the hell was he doing with the pound cake in his hand?

We cannot blame white people.

Detractors charged that Cosby's comments were elitist. Many responded that the remarks were insensitive and judgmental. Others expressed concern that this airing of the black community's dirty laundry will only arm conservatives with more ammunition in their effort to roll back civil rights. (Who is it again that is concerned with what white folks think?) Those who missed the point—that black people need to begin taking responsibility for their personal lives and stop blaming the white man—have insisted that "The Coz" should have admitted that discrimination still exists.

Black conservatives, of course, have levied criticisms similar to those of Cosby for years and for their troubles, the left has lambasted them. Once again, the reaction of Dr. Cornel West is fascinating. During a radio interview, West explained that the painful truth of Cosby's remarks must be put into the context of who Cosby is (or more accurately, who he is not). He noted that Cosby has been a friend of the people's struggle for years. His words, therefore, were spoken out of great compassion. "We know he is not from the right wing. He is not Clarence Thomas," West intoned.

I see. So the issue then is not correct or incorrect or, as some would have it, left versus right. It is not a question of class, but about how to speak truth with compassion and being for the common man. According to West then, the arguments of black conservatives would have been met with less derision had they only reasoned using more tenderness.

Fifteen years ago, Shelby Steele published the award-winning book, *The Content of Our Character*. He quickly became the whipping boy of black "progressives" who took umbrage with his challenge to black people to abandon the pride of victimization. But Steele's book is filled with faith in our human capacity to seize opportunity as individuals in order to uplift the black race. He writes: "Uplift can only come when many millions of blacks seize the possibilities inside the sphere of their personal lives and use them to take themselves forward." If I didn't know any better, I would swear I was listening to Cosby at the NAACP gala.

In the same vein, the left has mercilessly hammered Ward Connerly because of his opposition to affirmative-action preferences. Connerly, however, does not oppose preferences simply because he wants to deny opportunity to minorities. Connerly "believes that hard-working, high-achieving women and minorities should not have to live under the cloud of affirmative action and its insulting premise that we are incapable of winning in an open competition." The same is true of favorite villain Clarence Thomas, who says, "These kids are bright, they are capable. For the life of me, why don't we tell them the same thing we tell all the other kids in our society." It's not Shakespeare, but it sounds like love to me.

The fact is that the painful truth Cosby spoke was no truer and no more compassionate than that spoken by conservatives like Steele, Connerly, and, yes, Clarence Thomas. Cosby's critics may be gentler in their rebuke of him because he's their political bedfellow—involved in the people's struggle and all that. Their quarrel with him, though, is very much ideological. They may be loathe to admit it but, like black conservatives, Cosby has apparently grown tired of the worn-out notion that until the last vestige of racism is eradicated, black success is impossible and any success black people do attain is either the result of luck or the benevolence of others.

One thing that critics of black conservatism have correct, however, is that they recognize the black community's growing disenchantment with the liberal establishment. There are issues of great concern in black communities that need addressing (as Cosby attempted to point out). Solutions will require new ideas and fresh perspectives. The traditional leadership, grown fat on the politics of victimization, has failed. West refers to liberal black leadership as "inadequate" but black conservatism as "unacceptable." After a generation of progressives teaching socialism instead of capitalism and scorning independence in favor of dependency, I would argue that it is time to once again embrace the old school conservative values of pride, patriotism, family, industry, piety, liberty, and pluralism.

In the final paragraph of his *Christian Century* essay, West expresses hope that a principled and passionate political discourse will emerge, highlighting the issues of poor and working-class blacks. But so long as black liberals prefer insults to honest engagement, there will be no discourse, which will sadly leave our community recycling the same tired, inadequate ideas.

I, for one, would welcome open, rational debate. It sure would be nice to engage in discussions without being perceived as a non-thinking boob or worse, a cancer in need of excising from the black cultural body.

Professor Loury and I didn't have the opportunity to finish our conversation. If I'm lucky, I'll get another chance. I won't be so nervous and certainly I will be better prepared. To be a conservative is to accept that human nature is flawed and that the role of government is not to facilitate equanimity among an imperfect people but through the rule of law to protect its citizens. However, it is also to embrace the notion that our American republic thrives because it is nurtured by the American spirit. To be black and conservative is to go one step further. We know firsthand the corruptibility of the human species. We look backwards to the failure of so many to live up to the promise of this great nation, but also look forward, not with hope but with the certainty that the American ideal is the best guarantee of liberty on earth.

Why Don't We Want What We Fought For?

A few days after September 11th, I raised my flag alongside the dozens that flew in my neighborhood. As my four-year old son looked on, I explained that we were flying our flag because we were proud to be Americans.

A week later at the Chicago Black Expo, I presented an award to a former marine for his contributions to the black community. I was shocked when, after accepting it, he turned to the audience and delivered a diatribe about America that covered everything from slavery to hanging chads, then declared that he would never wear the flag or fly it at his home.

I was further troubled when a few days later, I read a newspaper account of black firefighters in Florida who refused to ride on their fire engine while it flew the American flag. And I was perplexed by statements made by people like Julianne Malveaux: "Black people need to examine carefully if we have any stake in this war"; Alicia Keyes: "I see lies in that flag"; and Al Sharpton: "Black people don't owe this country anything."

Why do so many blacks feel comfortable voicing sentiments that are anti-American at their core? And why aren't there equally fervent black voices denouncing them?

Anti-nationalism is not new in the black community. For Black Americans active in the civil rights movement of the 1960's, it was only natural to reject a flag that represented a legacy of slavery and Jim Crow. Though times have changed, it is not surprising that blacks who came of age in the sixties would be prone to spouting anti-American rhetoric. What baffles me is hearing it from the mouths of the younger generation.

Alicia Keyes, for instance, is hardly a poster child for the repressed black masses. On the contrary—she represents a generation that has never suffered the indignities of Jim Crow, and which presently enjoys more opportunity and wealth than most people of *any* color *any* where in the world.

In January, my father-in-law attended a Martin Luther King Day program at his city's convention center. While a man in full military dress sat on the dais, a black high school student delivered a fiery speech vilifying America and condemning our war on terrorism. The 3,000 mostly black audience members applauded the speaker and nodded in agreement. No doubt there were those in attendance who disagreed, but they sat in silence.

Perhaps those audience members with dissenting opinions kept quiet because they, like many in the black community, believe that we make progress only when we have a unified voice, when we let an anointed few speak for us all. The trouble is, now anyone who openly disagrees with the rest of the group risks being ostracized and labeled a "Tom." It has happened to me.

A few months ago, I went online to discuss the events of September 11, 2001 with some of the members of my fraternity. When I took exception to the characterization of the destruction of the Twin Towers as "chickens coming home to roost," I was shouted down and my racial pride was called into question.

It's true that the flag represents a nation that once enslaved and denied rights to a segment of its population, but it also stands for the revolutionary idea that every individual has God-given and inalienable rights. Focusing on the fact that America hasn't always lived up to its ideals misses the point: it is the very existence of those ideals that has allowed this country to eradicate slavery and segregation. Previous generations of Black Americans understood this, perhaps better than their oppressors. The poet Langston Hughes describes America's commitment to press forward toward the ideals expressed by the founding fathers as "keeping our hands on the plow."

Black America's stake in this land has been earned through generations of sweat equity. Not only did our forefathers shed blood fighting in America's wars, they also contributed food, fashion, language, music, and art to its culture. Our ancestors understood that they had a vested interest in this country's future; they were struggling so that their children could be Americans in the fullest sense of the word. For the younger generation to suggest blacks ought not embrace America is to take the position that those "old time Negroes" just were not as sophisticated as we are today and simply didn't know the deal.

The other day, my son came home from kindergarten and proudly recited the Pledge of Allegiance. Did I tell him that America is a hoax? That he should not claim ownership of a land bought with the struggle of those who came before him? No. I told him the truth—that America is by no means a paragon, but warts and all, it is still the best thing going.

The Arrogance of Reparations

We were looking forward to meeting our friends for dinner. We chose a nice, intimate Italian place, just right for doing a lot of catching up. During the evening's conversation, our friend's wife broached the topic of equal opportunity. According to our friends who are black and quite wealthy, there is no such thing. For black folks, the deck is stacked. If you have never experienced it, there is nothing quite as bizarre as millionaires sitting around, sipping Merlot, and talking about the lack of equal opportunity and how the system doesn't work. Needless to say, that is when the fun stopped and the throbbing in my temples began.

My wife and I headed home where I began popping Excedrin like candy. The elitism on display had given me a monumental headache. Was their accomplishment an accident? A gift from some benevolent patron? No. They had not inherited their wealth or won the lottery; they had worked and sweated their way into successful careers. I wondered why the standard of discipline and hard work that they had demanded of themselves and that they currently demand of their children was too much to demand of "those other people." They were too smart, too beautiful, and too successful to claim victimhood, and yet they slipped into its well-worn visage with ease. Of course, they were merely victims by proxy. The cloak they wore as they sipped their wine was donned on behalf of all the regular folk—people not as smart as they. It was from this vantage of superiority that they saw clearly enough to fix what is wrong with the world.

It was arrogance that made me angry that night and this same arrogance and egotism is at work in the current movement for slavery reparations.

Reparations advocates argue that this current generation of black people has not shared in the bounty that is America *and* that any pathology in the black community is rooted in the legacy of slavery. How a monetary payment will address either wrong remains unclear, as does the morality of taking money from people who never owned slaves in order to pay people who were never enslaved. But reparations are not about righting historical wrongs; it is about massaging the egos of those leading the movement.

Consider the words of Randall Robinson, one of the leaders of the current push for reparations: "Do not be fooled by individual examples of conspicuous black success. They have closed neither the economic nor the psychic gaps between blacks and whites, and are statistically insignificant." Or those of John Hope Franklin: "Most Americans do have a connection with slavery. They have inherited the preferential advantage if they are white, or the loathsome disadvantage if they are black, and those positions are virtually as alive today as they were in the nineteenth century." Like the man whose wife caught him cheating, Robinson and Franklin say, "Are you gonna believe me or your own eyes?" In Robinson's view, it is insignificant that seventy-five percent of American blacks live above the poverty line, with fifty percent of us solidly in the middle class. It is of no consequence that the median-income gap between white and black married couples continues to close. We should ignore that blacks are wielding political power at the highest levels of government and in every major city in the nation. What else but ego would lead a man to tell black people that, in spite of mountains of evidence to the contrary, we are sick and hobbled by our ancestors' enslavement?

Proof of America's systemic racism is to be found in statistical disparities in housing, healthcare, and the justice system. Reparations activists toss these statistics out as though they were truly objective measures. Of course, statistics don't tell the entire story and establishing a factual connection between said disparity and bigotry, not to mention slavery, is often difficult to do. You will not, for instance, hear the reparations crowd talk about the statistical disparity in the number of blacks playing basketball or why there are so few American blacks running long distance races as opposed to sprints. It is not my intent to trivialize disparities in housing or income. Many of the gaps the reparationists point to are very real, however, in addition to racial bigotry, there are all sorts of things that influence disparities: age, regionalism, diet, individual choice, *height,* and culture.

Disparities in income, for instance, are far more complex than one is led to believe. Incomes vary depending on occupation and do not remain static over a worker's lifetime. As a worker gains more experience and maturity, his income will grow. Older workers quite naturally earn more than workers just entering the job market. In the eleven years my wife and I have been married, my income has fluctuated quite a bit. I have had years when I was in the top two percent of wage earners and years when I was in the bottom. Such are the financial realities of a career in the arts. During this same time period, my wife's income as a marketing manager has doubled. Had she majored in finance in business school rather than marketing, she would be earning twice as much as she is now. Conversely, had she majored in the humanities she would be earning half as much.

Marriage is also a prime factor when looking at income, poverty, education, healthcare, and a host of other issues. Generally speaking, couples that marry before having children and stay married have higher incomes and do not live in poverty. If both parents work, the chances are greater that the family has health coverage. Children with fathers living in the home do better in school, are less likely to suffer from anxiety or depression, and are less likely to act out with drugs or sexual promiscuity, all behaviors that can lead to situations that hinder a person's ability to earn.

Of course, when pointing out these statistical disparities, we are never told who is being polled, whether the workers are young or old, whether all those in the sample work in the same discipline, or if they are married or single. I suspect one reason is that once controls are put in place for things like age, education, and marital status, those statistical gaps begin to close or disappear all together.

These pesky little details are precisely why Robinson and the rest discuss statistical disparities only briefly. They are in a rush to get to the meat of their argument: psychic damage. It is much easier to talk about feelings because emotions require no objective proof; they are subjective and proven true by virtue of the accusers' righteous indignation—the more the better.

But wait a moment. Robinson, Representative John Conyers, Charles Ogletree, Johnny Cochran, and the others in the forefront of this movement have clearly not been hobbled by slavery's legacy. Robinson was born in Richmond, Virginia. He attended Norfolk State College before serving in the U.S. Army. He went on to receive a B.A. from Virginia Union College in 1967 and later, a law degree from Harvard University in 1970. Today he is a well-paid professor, writer, and public speaker. Charles Ogletree graduated Phi Beta Kappa from Stanford University. He went on to Harvard Law School, rose to the rank of Deputy Director of the Washington D.C. Public Defender's Office, began a private practice, and worked as an Associate Professor of Law at Harvard Law School. Today, Ogletree works as Faculty Director of Clinical Programs, Associate Dean for Clinical Programs and is the Jesse Climenko Professor of Law at Harvard. John Conyers served in the United States Army Corps of Engineers, the Michigan National Guard, the United States Army, and the Army Reserves. He received a law degree from Wayne State University and became a congressman in 1964. The late Johnnie Cochran was born into modest means and rose to become a multimillionaire attorney, one of the most famous in the nation.

Phi Beta Kappa? Multi-million dollar life styles? How is this possible for a people who are suffering "social wreckage"?

These men don their victimhood by proxy for the rest of us. Slavery would not be blamed for the promiscuity or poor school performance of their children. It is only *our* children that are so simple-minded as to suffer the effects of an institution more than one hundred years removed from them.

Like my rich friends who slipped on the raiment of victimhood over veal piccata and red wine, these men and women view the world through the lens of superiority. Witness Robinson's call for an urban Marshall plan for reparations.

For all those expecting cash in hand, Robinson says no: "Public initiatives, not public checks!"

Similar pomposity was displayed in the class action suit filed by Attorney Deadria Farmer-Paellmann in a New York Federal Court on behalf of 35 million descendants of slaves. The lawsuit, which was filed in 2002 (and was eventually thrown out of court), charged three companies—Fleet Boston, Aetna Insurance and CSX (and hundreds of corporations to be named later)—with profiting from slavery. The lawsuit overlooked that fact that, during the time of slavery, CSX wasn't even in business. Moreover, the business these companies conducted was perfectly legal, and holding current shareholders responsible for the practices of people long dead and forgotten is on rather shaky moral ground.

Taking a slightly different route, the Chicago City Council recently passed a law that requires all companies doing business with the city to disclose any involvement they may have had in the slave trade. The Chicago City Council requires these corporations to turn over all paperwork going back 150 years. The information will of course be forwarded to a team of lawyers preparing a class-action reparations lawsuit similar to the suit filed by Farmer-Paellmann. Other metropolitan cities are following suit. I can only feel outrage and a deep sense of sadness.

Is there no more pressing business that our elected officials need attend to than this?!

But the idiocy of this bit of extortion masquerading as law is not what troubles me. It is that it is being committed in my name, but not for my benefit.

The lawsuits don't seek money for individual descendants of slaves. Farmer-Paellmann's attorney, Ed Fagan, pointed out that the 1.4 trillion dollars sought in settlement would be placed in a welfare fund for black Americans. Remember: public initiatives. Not public checks! No matter that welfare kills initiative and breeds dependency. No matter that one could reasonably argue that the welfare state has done more to hobble the black family than Jim Crow ever did. No matter that this government has already spent trillions of dollars on poverty programs and the current black poverty rate is essentially unchanged from what it was in 1970. These folks confidently reason that a few more trillion administered by *them* will solve the problem. But here's the thing: Didn't Robinson say that my success was insignificant? Why should all that dough go to only twenty-four percent of the black population? Farmer-Paellmann filed a suit on behalf of *all* thirty-five-million African-Americans, which, in spite of my political beliefs, no doubt includes me. If I am one of the walking wounded, shouldn't the reparations money belong to me to do with as I choose? My wife and I have had our eye on a hot tub for the backyard, and I certainly wouldn't mind cruising the neighborhood in a brand new Escalade. Not to mention we have three boys that will need college tuition in the not-too-distant future. Who are these people to decide who among us is deserving and who is not? Who are they to determine how money due me because of my *suffering* is best spent? Is my brother now my master? Or is this nothing more than a huge money grab by a few elites who identify a cause and then don the noble garb of champion for profit and ego gratification.

Pass the Excedrin!! Extra strength, if you please.

Rex, my white neighbor, who is about twenty years older than me, attempted to console me by explaining: "There is a deep sense of hurt and we have to get past it. We have to talk about these things and sometimes that discussion is going to get insane, but I much prefer this to those days of segregation."

I am not certain Rex was aware of it, but he had just articulated the subtle shift that is emerging in the debate. Facing an uphill battle in the courts, advocates are now claiming that actual money damages are beside the point. What they are really looking for is some sort of symbolic gesture by the United States government—an apology perhaps—that would help black people to bring some closure to the legacy of pain. They also feel the need for a national dialogue on race. Some have even suggested the establishment of a national commission similar to South Africa's Truth and Reconciliation Commission, which was set up after the fall of apartheid to examine all the effects of apartheid and its human-rights abuses on the South African people.

I suggested to Rex that this notion of having a national discussion reeks of EST (Erhard Seminar Training) and other group-awareness programs begun in the 1970s. Do we really need one big national encounter group? In junior high school we called them rap sessions. A teacher would moderate the discussions, which largely consisted of black students accusing the white students of harboring racist attitudes. The white kids would nod their heads with understanding and promise to do better if the black kids would stop intimidating them in the hallways. Everyone would shake hands and eat a donut before heading back to class.

Or perhaps they mean the kind of conversations we had in college classrooms. We (the black students) would stand up and make loud, angry speeches detailing every instance of racism we had ever encountered. The white students would sit quietly sipping their Tab and nodding their heads in sympathy. Before heading back to class, they would promise to do better.

Maybe they mean the kind of conversations they have at Democratic Party fundraisers. Black "leaders" stand and make quiet, passionately intellectual (if not completely accurate) arguments decrying this racist, sexist, homophobic nation. Their white counterparts nod in agreement and then stand giving detailed accounts of their lifelong commitment to rid the world of racism and inequality. Before driving off in their Town Cars, they all agree that the real problem is Republicans.

Or it could be that they mean conversations like the one I had during a recent meeting of my investment club. One of the other members argued that America was racist. I made some comments along the lines that racism, while still very much in existence, did not have the social power that it once held. He then became very animated, reaching back ten years for an example to prove how wrong I was. I sat quietly nodding my head in astonishment and then promised never to have this discussion again.

Good Lord! Haven't we talked about race enough? We have been discussing race since the earliest days of our republic. It seems sometimes as if we have talked about nothing else.

The conversation began during the first Continental Congress in 1787. It continued until it erupted into civil war in 1861. After the destruction of the South, the conversation hardly abated. If anything, it became more passionate. We flapped our jaws through Jim Crow, *Brown v. Board of Education*, the civil rights movement, the great society of Lyndon Johnson, and affirmative-action quotas in the 1970s under Richard Nixon. The race card has been played so often, it is torn and dog-eared from use. We have talked until we are all blue in the face. Quite frankly, I am tired of talking about race! More accurately, I am tired of a conversation about race that, according to reparationists at least, has borne so little fruit.

My neighbor Rex then told me a story about his growing up in a segregated Los Angeles. He described watching his high-school football team play the black school from across town. "I used to look across the field when we played San Fernando and see all the black cheerleaders with white gloves. It was a spectacular sight," he told me. "I always wondered, 'Who are those people?'"

I understood his point; this is just part of the ongoing struggle to cleanse the stain of our nation's original sin—slavery. But don't we get any credit for the monumental progress we have made? Or is John Hope Franklin correct, and "those positions are virtually as alive today as they were in the nineteenth century"? As sincere as these folks may be, how exactly is digging around in corporate closets for evidence of a 150-year-old injustice going to make things better? How is looking in the faces of our children and telling them that they are damaged goods going to move us forward?

I know something of the world Rex described. In 1969, my family moved across town. If we weren't the first black family in our neighborhood, we were certainly the second. I didn't trust white kids. The first day of school, when they gathered around to say hello, the first words out of my mouth were, "Black is beautiful, brown is hip, yellow is mellow, but white ain't sh**!" They were amazed. Those white kids had never heard anything like that before.

I attended high-school football games with my father and I too remember the segregated stands when the all-white schools played the all-black schools. Those were the games from which the police escorted my father and me a few minutes early to avoid getting caught up in the riot that was expected to follow. Funny thing is, by the time I got into high school a short six years later, all of those schools were completely mixed. The police no longer escorted my father from the field to avoid the race fights that followed games because there were no fights. It wasn't that the world suddenly became something out of a Disney movie, but things had changed. The quarterback on our varsity football team was black, the student council was mixed, as was the social scene. If my neighbor had attended high school with me, not only would he have known those dark-skinned girls with white gloves, he may have even dated one or two of them.

My children will know of those days only through history books. Unlike the days of my neighbor's youth, or even those of my own, there is no place that my children cannot go, nothing they cannot do. In a world with such incredible opportunity for our children, a world so far removed from the world of even twenty years ago, how sad is it that we have some who not only choose to spend their time discussing slavery, but who seek to force the rest of us to discuss it with them? Every day I see with my own eyes people of different races and ethnicities working, laughing, worshipping, and loving together. On September 11, 2001, I saw them mourn together. I will not believe that all I see is a fabrication. I refuse to tell my children, or any child, that they are "psychically damaged" and that the only way to relieve their suffering is through welfare paid with reparations money.

Some time ago, I sat on a television panel discussing the pervasiveness of racism in America and shared some of these thoughts. One of the panelists expressed a belief that I was not living in the same world as everyone else. Perhaps he was correct. The world I live in is filled with struggle, but there is hope; heartbreak, but also joy; injustice, but also a great deal of compassion! At any rate, my world is more vital than that of the Chicago City Council and Deadria Farmer-Paellmann.

That said, if talk is what advocates for reparations want, then let's talk. But rather than discuss race in the context of who is owed what and by whom, I would prefer we concentrated on our common ground and focus our energies on how to address some of the issues and concerns that we all share. A trillion-dollar black welfare trust fund administered by Ogletree, Robinson, and a few of the other anointed is clearly not the solution, nor is a national rap session conducted by and among some politically chosen elites. However, a smaller federal government and a renewed focus on personal responsibility will do more for the black and the poor than treating us as psychically crippled children. Let's talk about that.

Reparation activists have long contended that the crippling economic effects of slavery have prevented the black community from passing wealth from one generation to the next. They are partially correct; there has been an economic drain from the black community. The solution, however, is not reparations. If there really is an interest in building generational wealth, a more appropriate front on which to fight is the reform of Social Security. At its core, slavery represents the usurping by force of an individual's labor or property for the benefit of another individual. By this definition, Social Security is economic slavery and its impact on the black community continues to be negative.

Social Security began in 1935 as a progressive redistribution system whereby each generation pays for the previous one and those who have more, pay for those who have less. Like most liberal programs, their hearts were in the right place while their hands were in our wallets. The monkey wrench in this whole business is life expectancy and birth rates. Americans are living almost fifteen years longer than they were in the '30s and therefore draw on payments longer. Indeed, when Social Security became law, almost half of the eligible recipients died before they were able to collect. Today, people are also having fewer children. In 2020, Social Security will begin to pay out more than it collects in taxes. In order to fund its obligation, the government will have to turn to the Social Security trust fund. Unfortunately, the only things sitting in the trust fund are IOU's. As the Clinton Administration's fiscal year 2000 budget explained: "They (IOU's) do not consist of real economic assets that can be drawn down in the future to fund benefits." Keeping Social Security solvent will require either an increase in taxes, a decrease in benefits, or a combination of the two.

Mortality rates have also had the effect of transferring huge amounts of wealth away from the people it was intended to help. The wealthy live longer than the poor, married couples live longer than singles, and whites live longer than blacks. This last fact means that on a per capita basis, social security transfers between $2,000 and $21,000 out of the black community and into the white. This is precisely why private ownership is so important to the black community.

My grandmother was seventy years old when she opened her first checking account. Until that time, she paid everything in cash. When the electric bill was due, she would walk to Con Edison in Brooklyn and pay cash. When I tried to talk to her about mutual funds, she would nod her head, "Yes, baby." That was her way of telling me that I could go on talking but she was through listening.

For a time, she did all right. Her needs were few. She liked to sit at home and watch her "stories." She liked the chicken from the Chinese place around the corner and she sent me down the block for an occasional Champale. She was not a big spender and it was a good thing, too. The average Social Security benefit is $8,300 per year and her meager Social Security checks would not have afforded her much more of a lifestyle. She was poor as are most of the elderly who rely on Social Security.

The black community is overwhelmingly—some might argue detrimentally—dependant on Social Security. Rather than wean our community off the drug of dependency, a tactic that might really empower our community in the manner they desire, our black leadership prefers scaring the elderly and the poor by saying that Republicans are playing fast and loose with privatization schemes. The "scheme" the Commission on Social Security Reform is working on is seeking a way to allow workers to voluntarily invest their retirement money in private accounts. Republicans are discussing the gradual dismantling and transfer of a bloated and ineffective bureaucracy into the hands of individual citizens. This is an important distinction the Democrats are reluctant to make. My grandmother is no doubt the very woman Democrats claim to be saving from us bloodthirsty Republicans who want to give people who rely on social security an opportunity for ownership and greater autonomy. When the truth is relative, I guess it is acceptable to scare the bejeezus out of the electorate by saying Republicans want to turn Social Security into Enron.

The argument against ownership is delivered from the same vantage of superiority as reparation advocates. They share a common a belief that their good intentions (or outrage) grant them a moral right to transfer the wealth of one man to the pocket of another. And like reparationists, when the facts do not support them, righteous indignation and calls for fairness (their version of it anyway) will suffice. Democrats, for example, argue that personal accounts are "more like Social Security roulette. Democrats are all for giving Americans more of a say and more choices when it comes to their retirement savings. But that doesn't mean taking Social Security's guarantee and gambling with it."

In 1960, the Supreme Court held that individuals have no right to the funds they pay into the system. Contrary to common belief social security is not an insurance program, it is a tax, and as such the money paid into social security belongs to the federal government to do with as it wishes. This effectively means that politicians can, at any time, cut or eliminate benefits. Oddly enough, their prescription for social security solvency is "a little increase in taxes, a little decrease in benefits and a little increase in the retirement age and social security is good for another 100 years." That guarantee they keep referring to is subject to the whim of politicians and bureaucrats.

As to ownership, they respond, "Any introduction of individually owned retirement accounts would be detrimental to the nest egg that many Americans, particularly minorities, depend on in their retirement." They are no doubt referring to that whopping $8,300 per year nest egg. Those of us who favor private accounts argue that without ownership of our social security dollars, there is no choice, no say, and no guarantee!

My father passed away when he was sixty-six years old. He paid into the system for forty years and drew out of the system for one year. When he died, rather than that money being divided amongst his heirs like the rest of his estate, it remained in the coffers of the federal government. Forty years of Social Security payments, at an interest rate of four percent (twice as much as current Social Security returns) compounded over forty years. What kind of difference can that much money make for a family? What difference can that kind of money make to a community? Advocates preach about an economic legacy and economic empowerment. Well, here is a real opportunity to put their money where their mouth is.

Critics are quick to point out that personal accounts will lead people to make bad investments. Not to mention that a down turn in the market could wipe out gains earned in previous years, leaving people with nothing. Mind you, this concern has not led them to take their own retirement money out of the market.

I was recently discussing private accounts with a colleague who expressed concern that there are people who can't handle their 401(K)'s. Not him of course, but all of those *other* people. His sentiments were reflected in the words of former Democratic congresswoman and vice presidential candidate, Geraldine Ferraro: " . . . If you don't have the knowledge and the wherewithal to manage your own private funds," said Ferraro, "well, you know, you're gonna be out of luck."

There it is in a nutshell. Private accounts are not "a tragic mistake" as some have charged, because making Americans owners of their retirement dollars is risky. The major objection to offering Americans choice is that the American populace is simply not smart enough to manage its own money. I guess one could say: Public initiatives! Not personal accounts!

There is no way I expect women and men of my grandmother's education (which is to say no education) to sit down to morning coffee and a copy of the *Wall Street Journal*. I do, however, believe that Americans who are clearly capable of creating businesses and paying taxes, who are sufficiently skilled to run households and raise children, are capable of making decisions about where to put their retirement dollars when given a few narrowly defined choices. I also give average Americans enough credit to believe they should own the money they work so hard for, whether they chose to invest it or not.

But no matter. This is the new liberalism! Under the guise of creating more opportunity for Americans to lead ever greater and more enriched lives, new liberalism favors an ever-expanding involvement of government. It is not enough that government secure individual rights, it must also oversee individual lifestyles from birth to grave. Self-reliance, individual responsibility, and autonomy are distractions that cloud this vision of a citizenry with no worry or need that government cannot address. In the end, it can only be because if left to our own devices, we average folks do not have it in us to create lives of value and worth without the aid of a few elites in Washington.

The truth is that through higher returns, personal accounts will give workers more, not fewer, retirement benefits, which means a more secure retirement for today's workers. The average return on Social Security taxes is about two percent, and that stellar return is expected to decline for younger workers. The Social Security administration estimates that a balanced portfolio of stocks and bonds could expect to earn returns of approximately 4.7 percent, net of administrative costs. According to the Cato Institute, "a worker earning $30,000 per year will pay roughly $120,000 in Social Security taxes over a forty-year working lifetime. A two percent return on that money yields Social Security benefits equivalent to $185,000. But a 4.6 percent return would yield $344,000, nearly twice as much."

Americans are counting on the promise of Social Security being kept; prudent leadership demands that this very serious problem be addressed. Republicans are in favor of turning Social Security into a legal asset (in the form of personal accounts) while Democrats—the party of the little guy—in their arrogance, favor propping up a system of political entitlement leaving the destiny of our nation's elderly to the whim of politicians and bureaucrats.

This difference in philosophy is seldom so clearly drawn. And it is instructive as it relates to race and the relationship of race to power in this nation. On the one hand, you have a party consistently portrayed as anti-black, which is saying to black people we want to give you a better "new deal." You should own the money you spend a lifetime earning. The funds "guaranteed" under the current system are a fraction of what you would receive if your money were conservatively invested. Investment and ownership will create wealth in your communities and wealth will change the equation in discussions of healthcare, education, and a host of other social ills. Ownership will give you greater autonomy and a greater stake in the American dream.

The other side, the side that, year after year, paints itself as the party of uplift for minority communities, preaches government dependency. (We just don't know how good we got it!) They say ownership is a risky scheme. You die earlier; you work for lower wages so let us take care of you. Sure, the returns may be lousy, the benefits may not be there when you are ready to take them, and you may not ever build generational wealth, but hey, we're feeding you.

I have been waiting for someone to tell me why, with so much for the black community to gain, Randall Robinson, Charles Ogletree, the NAACP, Congressional Black Caucus, and others have turned their backs on Social Security reform, a winnable battle, but embraced the idea of reparations, a quixotic dream if ever there was one. Perhaps divine inspiration has anointed Robinson, et al. with a superior vision. I doubt it. I can't shake the image of the group of them sitting around a table, sipping expensive wine, practicing the speeches they will give when they are inducted into the Black Folks Hall of Fame. "This is for all the nameless, faceless people of color who have a chance now that *we* have opened this door."

Reparations advocates and Social Security reform opponents are always talking about fairness. They must put their egos aside and recognize that there is nothing fair about converting the fruit of one man's labor into the property of another man. Slavery does not cease to be repugnant because it is washed with indignation or good intentions. It is immoral whether committed with whips and chains or by forcing reparations *from* people who were never slave owners *to* people who were never slaves. It is immoral, too, under cover of altruism to redistribute wealth from one community to another at the same time preventing that community from achieving economic autonomy.

Diversity and Institutional Variety

Several years ago, while contemplating a career change, I took the Law School Admission Test. While sitting in the lecture hall, I looked around the room and took note of the great variety of people taking the test. Some of my fellow test-takers looked to be on the ball, others looked out to lunch, and there were many of us in between. I realized that there was a law school out there for each of us. No matter how each of us fared on the test, if we were willing, there was a law school willing to accept us.

But that's the thing. Law schools nowadays aren't just willing to accept some, of us they *have* to. Former Supreme Court Justice Lewis Powell reasoned in the 1978 decision, *Regents of the University of California v. Bakke*, which upheld the use of race in college admissions, that in order to get past race we must first take race into account. I am no legal scholar, but I would argue that this was not one of Justice Powell's most lucid moments. Reducing individuals to the sum of their ethnicity is the very definition of racism. Powell, of course realized this. The back door he left open was based on the rationale that a diverse student body provided a greater educational opportunity for all students and that the chance to encounter a mixture of cultures was a benefit that outweighed the harm to students who were denied acceptance under Affirmative Action policies.

Invoking the spirit of Powell, the University of Michigan Law School argued to the Sixth Circuit Court of Appeals that diversity is so necessary for an enriching academic experience, the state has a compelling interest in allowing them to continue discriminating by race in their admissions policy. Silly me. I had no idea the racial makeup of a law school classroom was essential to understanding torts or evidentiary procedure.

The Supreme Court followed suit a year later in *Grutter v. Bollinger*, holding that a "critical mass" of black, Hispanic, and Native American students is important to the "substantial, important, and laudable educational benefits that diversity is designed to produce, including cross-racial understanding and the breaking down of racial stereotypes." The Court further held that diversity better prepares students for an "increasingly diverse workforce" and that "the skills needed in today's increasingly global marketplace can only be developed through exposure to a widely diverse people, cultures, ideas, and viewpoints."

For what its worth, I much prefer the good ol' days when affirmative action policies were, in the words of Julian Bond, "necessary to fight a history of slavery and segregation." All of this talk of diversity is giving me Jim Crow flashbacks.

What exactly does "critical mass" mean?

Diversity proponents define "critical mass" as "enough minority students to ensure that minority students don't feel isolated or like spokespersons for their race; to provide adequate opportunities for the kind of interaction upon which the educational benefits of diversity depend; and to challenge all students to think critically and to reexamine stereotypes."

I have a few questions. If need be, I am willing to sit and be spoon-fed because I truly want to understand.

Who quantifies the point at which "critical mass" has been reached? And what scientific method is used to determine the exact racial mix necessary to achieve "critical mass"?

Jeffrey Lehman, Dean of University of Michigan's Law School, explains in his *New York Times* editorial, "Our philosophy is a matter of predictive judgment, not science." Aah yes. Empirical evidence be damned! With little more than their superior wisdom and judgment, these social engineers have determined that twelve percent of each first-year class should be African-American. The incoming class would only be four percent African-American without preferences.

How is diversity different from integration? For example, there are approximately two-hundred families living in my neighborhood, six of which are black. This means that roughly five percent of my neighborhood is black. Do I live in a diverse neighborhood or merely an integrated one? If it's merely integrated, at what point does it become diverse? (At twelve percent?) And how many black families can move into this neighborhood before it tips and becomes a black neighborhood? (Thirteen percent?) Is there a tipping point at the universities at which there are too many minority students on campus?

Maintaining the correct ratio of black students to white necessarily means we must count the number of minority students on campus. Once we begin to quantify, we walk the fine quota line. It may be a fluid quota system, but it is a quota system nonetheless. And black folks are all too aware that quotas are ceilings, not floors!

A friend of mine recalled her days at Rice University during the mid-'80s. "The university admitted eight black students per year," she tapped her finger on the table for emphasis. "We used to line up in the dining hall and count them as they came in." She was outraged. Amazingly, she was not equally outraged at the word games played by the U of M. Officials of the U of M have already told us that the correct racial mix is twelve percent. Period! Those waiting for a banner year that will produce a first year class at U of M with black enrollment at fifteen percent are waiting in vain.

It is also worth remembering that segmenting by race also means segmenting by class and that begins to beg the question of how to admit the "right" kind of black student.

Harvard, a school that prides itself on its outreach and dedication to diversity, has recently fallen subject to this very criticism. It seems that of the five-hundred or so black undergraduates, two-thirds are either African or West Indian immigrants or have mixed parentage. The American-born students actually refer to themselves as "descendants." According to the Reverend Jesse Jackson, "Universities have to give weight to the African-American experience because that is for whom [sic] affirmative action was aimed in the first place. That intent must be honored." I'm sorry. I understood us to be working for diversity in order to enrich the educational experience. I gather that even in those institutions where diversity is king, there are still some black folk that are more diverse than others.

Racists of another generation used the same twisted logic to reach only slightly different conclusions. To them, race mixing was a *distraction* to quality education and so the numbers of blacks and Jews who entered their institutions had to be strictly controlled. Today's race consciousness concludes that the number of blacks and Jews who enter institutions of higher education must be manipulated in order to achieve some ideal race ratio. And like the racists of old, who were always on the lookout for ways to circumvent anti-race laws, the racist of the twenty-first century claims their racial *sensitivity* is necessary for the common good. Bull Connor must be smiling in Hell!

Advocates claim that diverse classrooms force students to think more critically. Historical evidence would tend to disprove this argument. There are students being educated all over the world in homogeneous classrooms, without benefit of sitting next to black and Hispanic students.

For years, I've listened to friends who attended historically black colleges brag to me that they received a superior education to that of black students who attended white-majority schools. They are quick to produce studies proving that black students perform better academically in a homogeneous environment. If diversity is bad for black students, why is our leadership demanding it? Conversely, if the educational benefits of a diverse student body are great enough to warrant putting the Constitution on hold for another twenty-five years, shouldn't the black community demand that Spelman immediately begin recruiting and enrolling a "critical mass" of white and Asian women? If diversity is truly essential to providing skills for work in "today's increasingly global marketplace," can the black community afford to let our children be left behind?

The notion of forced "diversity" despicably suggests that what black students contribute to the university environment is merely cultural and not intellectually significant. Frankly, I find that rather insulting. Equally offensive is that liberals continue to frame the current debate over racial preferences in the language of civil rights. Congressional Democrats in the house and senate accused the Bush administration of being "opposed to civil rights and opposed to diversity." The *New York Times* editorialized that the charges of a quota system at the U of M were groundless and that the Bush administration and "their conservative supporters" were "attempting to turn back the clock [on civil rights]."

I find this liberal line rather patronizing. What's more, none of the demagoguery answers any of the questions many of us have—some of which I posed earlier. Furthermore, there are rational, objective arguments to be made against race-based affirmative action policies. There are also race-neutral policies that attempt to address the concerns of affirmative action advocates. The bottom line is: Either we are a nation that is struggling to move beyond race or we are not. In a nation that loudly proclaims its desire to move into a new paradigm free from racial bias, questioning race-based preferences does not make you a racist. On the contrary, it would seem to make one downright "progressive."

However, rather than discuss the merits of any alternative solutions or offer any rational defense of the ever-expanding *raison d'être* for affirmative action, liberals choose to simply identify any and all opposition as anti-black and racist.

The current debate over affirmative action is not about opportunity; there is no ongoing racial bias against blacks and Hispanics at the U of M. The University has admitted that its policy is not designed to counteract a pattern of systemic racism, nor does it concern itself with issues of equal access or segregation. It's about getting the correct racial mix. Lehman writes in his editorial, "[Our policy] was not designed to compensate for segregation and discrimination in American society past or present." Perhaps, Dean Lehman, that is the problem. The original goal of ensuring equal opportunity for all students was an admirable one. However, that noble goal has given way to this pernicious notion of diversity, which is only bigoted soup warmed over.

Diversity advocates worry themselves silly over aesthetics while graduation rates go ignored. Black students admitted under racial preferences (which invariably means lowered academic requirements) drop out at a rate twice that of white students. For those who stay, their GPAs rest in the bottom eight percent of the class and their failure rate on the bar exam is six times greater than that of whites. Ahh, but now they have opportunity! Yet opportunity was never denied them. Failing acceptance to Michigan, most of these students could, if they chose to, distribute themselves among law schools at which they would be better suited academically and no doubt find greater success.

I'm not the first to raise these arguments, but they continue to go unanswered. I suspect the reason is that affirmative action/diversity advocates don't really believe their own propaganda. All this talk of diversity on our college and university campuses is a cover for what liberals don't want to say and for what conservatives are demonized for pointing out: On average, middle-class black students continue to score two-hundred points below their white and Asian counterparts on the scholastic aptitude tests. The time has come to give a polite "thanks, but no thanks" to the diversity salesmen and begin to deal with what can only be described as "underperformance" by our children.

Don't misunderstand me. I'm not saying that black students are incapable of competing; in fact, I am saying just the opposite. There is no monopoly on brain-power! I am begging that our children be allowed to compete—to fail or succeed—on their own merits.

There's a long history of black academic achievement in this country. The annals of black history are filled with scholars, artists, and statesmen who were products of schools like Dunbar High School in Washington, D.C., P.S. Five in Harlem, Frederick Douglass in Baltimore, Booker T. Washington in Atlanta, and many others. Generations of black men and women somehow managed all of this achievement with far less money while facing more pernicious racism than today's black students and without the benefit of affirmative action policies. History provides proof positive that when excellence is demanded, excellence is what is delivered.

So what has happened? Why is it now acceptable to this community that our children scoot into universities as part of a "critical mass" of ambient culture rather than step boldly onto university campuses as representatives of a long and honorable academic tradition?

Interestingly enough, Powell also wrote in that same *Bakke* decision, "the guarantee of equal protection cannot mean one thing when applied to one individual and something else when applied to a person of another color. If both are not accorded the same protection, then it is not equal." On this, Powell was correct! Denying opportunity to students based on their race is wrong; it doesn't suddenly become right because the students losing out are white or Asian. Additionally, lowering academic requirements for black students is crippling. So long as black students are not required to compete on an objective scale of merit, they will never develop the skills necessary for real academic success. Lowered standards would also seem to imply that blacks are simply not up to the intellectual task and need the proverbial thumb on the scale. If we keep the bar high and steady, given time and commitment, our children will rise to the challenge. Diversity will happen naturally and in a manner that will allow all students to celebrate admission to elite universities without suffering the stigma of preference.

The Golden Rule

I wanted to know the definition of diversity so I wrote to a friend of mine who is knowledgeable about these things. My friend e-mailed me back about the 1978 Supreme Court decision in *Regents of the University of California v. Bakke,* wherein Justice Lewis Powell held that diversity offered a compelling motive for a university to use racial preferences. "No, no," I wrote back. "I am familiar with that. What I am trying to decipher is what is meant when, during a conversation, someone tells me that they are excited because a program offers diversity or when a company says that they encourage diversity in the work place." My friend confessed that he wasn't sure.

In this context, diversity should mean a variety of people, experiences, and ideas. The sad fact is that rather than fulfilling the aims of the civil rights movement and unshackling the individual to reach whatever heights his or her ambition, talent, and diligence could take them, it has turned individuality on its head. Diversity is now synonymous with "group identity."

A recent advertising insert in the Sunday *New York Times Magazine* solidified, for me, the vacuity of the diversity movement. For eight pages, various corporations discuss their concerted efforts to recruit diverse candidates on the basis of "race, gender, ethnicity, age, disability, religion, and sexual orientation." I imagine work and life experience falls in line somewhere lower on the list. Antoinette Malveaux, president of the National Black MBA Association, says diversity is necessary because as companies target different segments of the population, it "helps to have individuals inside the company who understand those [cultural and ethnic] nuances." This makes perfect sense. Joe Ramirez down the hall may be able to add value to a discussion of marketing to the Hispanic community. What I question is the assumption that, simply by virtue of his ethnicity, Joe has some expertise. Our middle class neighborhoods and public schools are filled with an ever-broadening mixture of races, ethnicities, and interracial combinations. This generation of kids dresses the same, listens to the same music, and speaks the same language. Do we want to suggest that Latinos automatically know how to market more effectively to Latinos because of their race? Do all blacks like soul music? Do all Chinese know Kung Fu? Experience teaches that if race is the determining factor in who adds value and who does not, soon blacks will work only on black projects, Asians on Asian projects, and good ol' Joe Ramirez down the hall will only work on Hispanic projects whether he speaks Spanish or not. This racial pigeon-holing would set us back forty years.

The source of this erroneous analysis is revealed on the first page of the ad where, in big bold print, a diversity expert boasts: "The problem with the Golden Rule is that it makes the assumption that everyone likes the same thing. In a multi-cultural society, you teach people how to make the Platinum Rule—that is, treat people the way *they* want to be treated." Apparently, these experts are not satisfied with undermining the spirit of the civil rights movement; they must now rewrite Scripture as well.

Doing unto others as you would have them do unto you (the apparently passé Golden Rule) demands the very sensitivity to others the diversity experts claim to be seeking. Just how do black employees want to be treated that is different from how white workers wish to be treated? I am fairly certain that, if polled, employees of every ethnic stripe would say that they want to be treated with respect and dignity. Concentrating on my cubicle-mates' color or sexual preference is unnecessary in order to meet this small request.

Consultants consistently cite diversity training as an ideal way to overcome stereotypes, but a review of their work suggests that they actually encourage stereotyping. Andrew Erlich, a cross-cultural psychologist (whatever that is) is quoted as saying, "I try to get people to understand the process of stereotyping, as well as some key points about culture and how it affects the way each of us act." Call me silly, Mr. Erlich, but there are diversity workshops teaching white supervisors that African American culture may be responsible for the tardiness of their black subordinates. This sounds more like a stereotype being reinforced. It also doesn't seem to jibe with Kodak's Diversity Manager Gary Voelkl, who believes that "we need an environment where people feel free to express themselves as individuals." Interesting. I am curious to know what he thinks of the diversity program at Coors?

This diversity management program has set up a total of eight affinity councils: the African American association, Hispanic network, Native American Indian council, Lesbian and Gay resource, women at Coors, the veterans group, the Asian network, and the silent group. Are they mad? How exactly does one "feel free to express themselves as individuals" when they are forced to declare membership in a group as soon as they walk through the door? What's more, the groups are not assembled based on interests or values; there is no Christian group, Republicans of Coors, or Trekkies council—groups that ostensibly would be racially mixed (or dare I say, diverse). These programs seem to fly in the face of individuality and demand an embrace of the ugliest of stereotypes, namely that people of certain races, genders, or ethnicities all think and act the same.

What is meant by diversity? I don't know and I am not so sure any two diversity experts would agree. It's all such a convoluted mess. Authorities on diversity should be applauded for developing a vernacular of inclusion and awareness, but in my mind they have yet to demonstrate how so much emphasis on our differences has brought us any closer together.

Attack of the Hollywood Liberals

Love/hate properly describes my feelings for Hollywood. I love to perform and I love performers. What I hate is when performers step off the stage and use their celebrity as a bully pulpit to unleash the narcissism that is so much a part of the current liberal Hollywood activism. Lest anyone think that I exempt myself, I do not. The difference is that I am an unemployed actor—a semi-celebrity. I am not using the power of celebrity to preach my conservatism. I have been writing a weekly column for more than three years. To paraphrase the old Smith Barney commercials, I got my soapbox (small as it may be) the old fashioned way: I earned it. Truth is, I would much rather be on stage. If Hollywood wants to shut me up, all they have to do is give me a weekly television series. If I was pampered, paid, and praised like the liberal Hollywood elite, I would, to paraphrase Laura Ingraham, Shut my mouth and sing!

There exists, however, a cadre of Hollywood celebrities, who have no such reservations. They have work aplenty and their celebrity status gives them a ready platform from which to offer their opinions. Not that anyone asked.

It is a huge irritation that America's post 9/11 foreign policy has proven the catalyst for so much Hollywood caterwauling. Hollywood liberals are currently scurrying about like red ants on sugar candy attacking conservatives as they go.

Dustin Hoffman weighed in on the Bush administration's Iraqi policy, accusing the president of dishonesty and of exploiting the nation's grief over 9/11. "I may be wrong," Hoffman said. "I am no expert. This war is about what most wars are about: hegemony, money, power, and oil." Well, Mr. Hoffman is partially correct. He is no expert, and yes, he is wrong. What America is fighting for is liberty.

Another Hollywood anti-war protester explained the purpose of our war in Iraq as follows: "This is a hegemonistic [sic] mission to spread the American way of life far and wide in order to protect and guarantee U.S. interests and leverage worldwide. Iraq is only the beginning of a plan for global domination." Global Domination? (Cue the scary music.) Spoken like someone who has been reading too many B-movie scripts.

The problem with this characterization is that it makes little distinction between nationalism and this country's very real national security concerns. (Not to mention, it simply ignores twelve years of diplomatic pressure and about fourteen United Nations resolutions.) It seems to me there is a difference between the quest for global domination and the desire—as the world's sole superpower—to meet our global responsibility for leadership.

We Americans could always withdraw from the world but it's very difficult, if not impossible, to lead from the rear. America has a duty to promote the ideals of liberty and a right to protect her security and economic interests from a fundamentalist Islamic movement that seeks isolation from—and the destruction of—western culture and from regimes that fund, promote, or supply safe haven to those movements. Terrorism is not the figment of some right-wing conservative imagination. It is a real and present threat to the liberty we value so dearly.

Make no mistake; the battle we are engaged in *is* for liberty. Some may be reluctant to couch it in these terms, but at the center of it, that is what's at issue. This nation believes in liberty and justice. Those who are waging war against us believe liberty leads to immorality and that America is immoral and therefore must be destroyed by any means necessary. It became crystal clear after 9/11 that enemies of America are not only actively seeking weapons of mass destruction but will gladly use them on American citizens. It should also be clear that these zealots are aided in their efforts by outlaw regimes that not only terrorize their own people but which also seek weapons of mass destruction in order to export that terror throughout the world.

Hoffman and others suggest that by actively working to replace these dictatorships with democratic rule we are arrogantly forcing our worldview on the world. This argument misses the point. It also presupposes that there is no moral or practical difference between our capitalist democracy and the totalitarian regimes of North Korea, Iraq, or Syria. In comparison to the poverty and hopelessness present in these parts of the world, our American way of life is pretty damn good!

It is a fact that in those areas of the world that embrace the ideals of free trade, free speech, and freedom of the press, there is stability, peace, and rising standards of living. Those regions that reject these ideals in favor of isolation and repression are hotbeds of despair and incubators of terrorism. It's not immoral to suggest that democracy will lead to peace. Nor, in this context, is it unreasonable to believe that from time to time, America must demonstrate her military might and her political resolve to use it.

And what is the real world alternative? Subjugate our national interests and security to the will of the U.N.? The U.N.'s record of protecting people from tyranny is hardly stellar. This is the same body that stood by idly while one million Hutsi's were slaughtered in Rwanda; that is still dickering over minutia while tens of thousands die in the Sudan.

Should we continue to negotiate with regimes that fail to honor agreements and have no respect for the rule of law? This strategy was a terrific success in North Korea. Perhaps we should follow Washington Senator Patty Murray's advice and build some day care centers.

Attempting to secure a toehold for democracy in the Middle East is a courageous step. It requires a faith that says democracy, not appeasement, is the way to battle terror. It's a faith that recognizes that the winds of change have already begun to blow in Syria, Libya, Lebanon, and Iran and will begin to blow in Saudi Arabia and elsewhere in the region. It's a faith that democracy will provide the foundation for a lasting peace between the Israelis and the Palestinians. It's a bold vision and frankly, I feel proud we have a president like George W. Bush who was willing to take this step and stand up to terror, as opposed to buying it off or merely sitting on his hands and leaving the heavy lifting to others. As he has so eloquently stated, "The liberty we prize is not America's gift to the world; it is God's gift to humanity."

Hoffman is by no means the only culprit guilty of failing to "get it." In addition to the usual suspects—Alec Baldwin, Mike Farell, Martin Sheen, and Susan Sarandon—The Dixie Chicks have demonstrated their lack of nuance. Our not falling in line behind the French made them ashamed of their President. George Clooney and Julia Roberts have also decided to add their opinions to the mix. Actor/economist Ben Affleck and Cher, Rosie O'Donnell, and Janeane Garofalo, Bruce Springsteen, and Puff Daddy have all decided to share their wisdom with America. Harrison Ford even chimed in about the evil of George W. Bush as he made his way overseas to deliver an Oscar—Hollywood's highest honor—to Roman Polanski, a convicted child molester. Still others have offered more pointed condemnation. Harry Belafonte launched an obscene attack on Colin Powell. Prior to the war with Iraq, actor and director Sean Penn visited the country to . . . what exactly did he go there to do? He then placed an ad in the *Washington Post* exhorting the president to "save America from a legacy of horror and shame." Danny Glover has toured the world proclaiming President Bush a racist, Woody Harrelson wrote a rambling op-ed piece in a London tabloid blaming America for all the evil in the world, and of course Barbara Streisand has continued attacking Republicans in general and the current administration specifically. These Hollywood liberals fascinate me, if only because the louder they yammer, the more they reveal their warped view of the world.

These celebrities share a worldview awash with arrogance and enamored of symbolism. It is also a view that will not countenance a difference of opinion. Those who disagree with them are not simply of a different mind; they are evil!

After making derogatory remarks about then Secretary of State Powell on a San Diego radio station, Belafonte appeared on *Larry King Live* to "put his words into context." "I did not refer to him as an 'Uncle Tom,'" he said. He's right; he didn't. He simply referred to Powell as a "sellout" and a "house slave" doing the bidding of his master. (I don't know about you but I sure am glad that hair has been split!) In Belafonte's world, a black man serving a Republican administration is not an intelligent individual exercising objectivity, he is a pawn subjugating his desires to the will of the white man. Not satisfied with questioning Powell's veracity (those who disagree have no conscience!), he then dismissed any significance of National Security Advisor (now Secretary of State) Condoleezza Rice, a black woman, ascending to the highest corridors of education (Stanford provost) and of government. "Yes, we've come a long way," Belafonte said, "but that does not diminish how far we still have to go." What? Wasn't this the destination of the civil rights movement? Doesn't the fact that Rice holds one of the highest offices in this administration (not to mention that this administration is the most diverse in the nation's history) indicate that something is *right* in America? But to Belafonte and others, she is an aberration. I guess once you admit the system is working, it's hard to make the case—as Belafonte does—that there is continual and systematic oppression of the masses.

Liberals have criticized Powell because he walked out of the 2001 Racist—I mean, Racism—Conference in Durban, South Africa. "The United States should have been in attendance," Belafonte said, "and given us the benefit of thought on a very grievous set of conditions that affect the human family." To Belafonte, the fact that the conference itself was engaged in bigotry and hatred was less important than the symbolism of America's participation and Powell's presence. Call me crazy, but I think the United States made a very strong, symbolic statement by walking out. The "grievous set of circumstances" the United States commented on was that we are not going to be part of any conference that blames America for the world's suffering while embracing Fidel Castro (one of the keynote speakers.) And further, America will not take part in the disparagement of Israel and the support of the murder and devastation wreaked by the neighboring Muslim countries in the region.

Hollywood liberals love Fidel! After dining with Castro, Steven Spielberg described the dinner as "the eight most important hours of my life." (This Castro must really be something. Eight hours with him beats eight hours romping in the hay with Amy Irving?) Actor Jack Nicholson told *Daily Variety*, "He [Castro] is a genius." Model Naomi Campbell declared that Castro was "a source of inspiration to the world." This is an opinion clearly not shared by the hundreds of Cuban citizens who have sought asylum in the United States. Other Hollywood celebrities who have visited Cuba and Castro include Robert Redford, Spike Lee, Sidney Pollack, Oliver Stone, Woody Harrelson, and Danny Glover. These free-thinking Hollywood types betray their moral confusion when they embrace a dictator who eschews the very democracy they claim to hold dear. They praise what they believe is the vast equality present in Cuba, forgetting that said equality was bought at the price of liberty and that the vast wealth they enjoy here in America would not be available to them under a dictator like Castro. Danny Glover has been spotted all over the world screaming into a bullhorn that George Bush is a racist. I wonder what kind of conversation Glover has when he sits down to dinner and cigars with Fidel Castro. Castro has routinely had political opponents jailed and murdered. Castro's dictatorship rejects the ideals of freedom of the press, freedom of speech, free markets, and private property rights. I suppose it's not a big deal until one realizes that these are the very tenants upon which *our* liberty is based.

Harrelson titled his op-ed "An American Tired of American Lies!" He then proceeded to tell a couple of whoppers himself. Harrelson accused the United States of causing the deaths of millions of Iraqi children and claimed the war on terrorism is racially motivated. "The warmongers (that's us) have hijacked a nation's grief and turned it into a perpetual war on any non-white country they choose to describe as terrorist," he wrote. It is quite possible that Harrelson has not been keeping up with current events, so let me fill him in: beginning with the take over of the American Embassy in 1979, the destruction of the marine barracks in Lebanon, the embassies in Kenya and Tanzania, the USS Cole, two attacks on the World Trade Center (1993 and 2001), the most recent episode of C-4 packed into a pair of Chuck Taylor's, the beheadings of journalist Daniel Pearl, and contractors Nick Berg and Paul Johnson (to name a few), it has been open season on Americans and the culprits have all been Muslim Extremists. The Swedes have not declared jihad on America!

I find the constant blaming of the United States for the poor policy decisions of despots tiring. If half a million Iraqi children died as a result of sanctions put in place by the world community, their blood is certainly on the hands of Iraqis who purchased arms instead of medicine or diverted foodstuffs to army personnel instead of children and who used precious resources to line their own pockets. Or perhaps the United Nations officials who were complicit in the Oil for Food scandal should bear some of the blame. What about the French and German officials who participated in the scandal with bribes and kickbacks? None of this seems to matter to Harrelson. Like Belafonte, he views America's cup as half empty and seeks to indulge the mythology of an oppressive, evil, and racist United States, any evidence to the contrary be damned!

The ranting of these celebrities also exposes their utter contempt for the American people. True to their liberal natures, they think they are smarter than everyone else. Belafonte blamed the public's criticism of his remarks on the fact that the "public doesn't come from the same sophisticated sense of history" that he does. Well, excuse us. Meanwhile, Streisand dashes off memos on political strategy to our nation's leaders as if she were the Queen. Many of these celebrities-cum-political-pundits have claimed to speak on behalf of a public that has been manipulated. (Everybody except them, of course.) While the rest of us brain-dead zombies are doing George Bush's evil bidding, they are the only ones with enough sense not to be fooled. Of course, they can't stay out of rehab, but they can see right through the conservative attempt to manipulate the masses.

And what is it with liberals and Shakespeare? In his ad in the *Post*, Penn pleaded with the president to "read Shakespeare." Belafonte evoked the Bard on *Larry King Live*, and during a Democratic fundraiser, Streisand thought she was quoting Shakespeare. (It turns out she was quoting from a Shakespeare hoax circulating the Internet.)

Well, we conservatives know a little of the Bard ourselves. In fact, Shakespeare could have been referring to Hollywood liberals when he wrote in part two of *King Henry VI*, "Away with them! Let them be clapped up close and kept asunder."

Don't misunderstand. I do not begrudge the opinions of celebrities. After all, everyone from the grocery clerk to the gardener has an opinion. The difference is that the grocery clerk is not getting airtime to share their uninformed views. Because they are stars, celebrities are given a platform and a microphone. The press dutifully records their every word, not because they know what they are talking about, but because they are famous.

Today's Hollywood stars feel an "obligation" to speak out on issues and cannot fathom that their view of the world—a view born in '60s radicalism, fed on Marxism, and now wed to moral relativism—is not shared by a majority of Americans.

I understand the sense of self-importance. I also understand that all of this activism is hardly organic.

There is no question that there is a history of political activism in Hollywood. Paul Robeson was a Hollywood star who put his career on the line to fight for human and civil rights. The dirty truth, however, is that most of this current activism has little to do with the spirit of Robeson and much to do with the narcissism of Hollywood and the need to garner publicity.

I can testify firsthand that the first thing the publicity machine in Hollywood recommends to stars is that they attach themselves to a cause. I hired a publicist during my first year on *The Cosby Show* and that was one of the very first things suggested to me. But don't take my word for it. Actress Alley Mills, from the hit series *The Wonder Years*, recounts the exact same experience in the book, *Hollywood Interrupted*. She was counseled by her high-powered public relations firm to associate herself with a cause. Like me, she was told to pick anything, whether she knew anything about it or not. She could then go to the events, get her photo in the magazines, and show up on talk shows to push her "cause." That is what the writers of *Hollywood Interrupted* call fashionable activism and it is only the beginning. Once a star appears before a congressional sub-committee to talk about some issue that was highlighted in their latest film, their egos convince them that they must have something of equal value to add on more pressing issues of the day. "How do you keep the boys on the farm once they have seen Paree?"

The Hollywood star system is the narcotic that lulls these celebrities into their arrogance. The city of Los Angeles revolves around celebrities. Successful performers are showered with special treatment: first-class air travel, complimentary meals, gifts, and days filled with the pampering of sycophants and fans who are constantly telling them how brilliant and funny they are. Hey, it's a great life, which is why I've been in the game for twenty years!

The day after the November 2002 congressional elections, a local radio host was railing (in typical Hollywood liberal fashion) that the Republican sweep signaled an end to the civilized world. Suddenly, he had to break away because the Winona Ryder jury was back from deliberations. Yes, the world can be going to hell but in Hollywood we have to break for Winona Ryder. And she hasn't had a hit film in years!

Anyone who has been in L.A. during Oscar night can testify that the world stops. It doesn't matter what is happening anywhere else. The only thing you will see on local news is who's wearing what, who won which award, and who's showing up at the "hottest" parties. Is it any wonder that a celebrity's sense of self-importance is completely at odds with reality? During the American Music Awards, recording artist Sheryl Crow wore a T-shirt with the slogan "War is not the Answer" written on the front. I dare say war and its accompanying ugliness *was* what freed 4.5 million Black American slaves, rescued European Jews from the Holocaust, and throughout history has delivered many millions more from tyranny. What else but ego would prompt her to emblazon her ignorance on a T-shirt and parade it in front of an international audience?

But there's something else at work here, namely hypocrisy. In spite of their obligation to speak out, these Hollywood activists remained quiet when President Bill Clinton was launching cruise missiles into Iraq, raining bombs down on Kosovo, and sending troops to Somalia. Did they not think people were dying in those conflicts? These same compassionate promoters of peace also have not seen fit to protest the parade of homicide bombers killing innocent Israelis.

And what of the Iraqi people?

Saddam and his regime routinely engaged in the torture, murder, and terror-ism of the Iraqi people. Are these defenders of human rights uninterested in the liberation of an oppressed people? Do not be fooled. The recent arousal of the Hollywood Left is not in response to American aggression or motivated by com-passion. It is about politics. They are protesting George W. Bush, conservative principles, and the celebration of this nation as the economic, military, and moral leader of the world.

I'm having a protest march this Saturday. I am protesting a man who *chose* to spend millions on weapons while his nation starved, who *chose* to invite invasion by thumbing his nose at the U.N., who *chose* to nurture a relationship with Al Qaeda and other terrorist groups whose stated goal is the destruction of the United States and Israel. I am protesting that warmonger Saddam Hussein.

Do you think Mike Farrell, Martin Sheen, Alec Baldwin, or Sheryl Crow will show up? Can I get Barbra Streisand to sing? Don't hold your breath.

Picking At Scabs

Years ago, I performed in a production of *A Raisin in the Sun* with the wonderful, late Esther Rolle. One evening, the cast was gathered in Esther's room and, as often happens when black folks get together, the conversation turned to the subject of racism. Esther described the topic as being like a scab she picked so it would never heal. It always struck me as odd that anyone would want to preserve an open sore. This seemed a kind of noble suffering.

I was reminded of this story after reading the text of Vernon Jordan's (former Head of the Urban League) speech to students at Howard University. Jordan didn't stray far from the standard Democratic Party line: the Supreme Court elected President Bush, Enron, John Ashcroft, etc.

Obviously, that was enough to get my jaw tight, but what I really took exception to was Jordan's assertion that since 9/11, "America is now grappling with the kind of terrorism that blacks have been forced to endure throughout American history." One of the examples he cited was the bombing of an Alabama church, some forty years ago, in which four little girls were killed.

Historically, Jordan is correct. In the twenty years from 1947 to 1965, the city of Birmingham suffered some fifty instances of destruction of property by dynamite. These criminal acts began as a means to scare and "terrorize" black citizens away from moving their families onto the fringes of white neighborhoods. In 1963, the campaign of violence and intimidation led to white supremacists bombing the Sixteenth Street Baptist Church, killing four little girls and wounding dozens of others. It was a wicked act and certainly not one of the finer moments in American history.

I would also agree with Jordan that there are similarities between American terrorists and those Islamic fascists who are now at war with the west. America's homegrown fanatics were hoodlums who used inhumane torture and murder to intimidate blacks, Jews, Catholics, immigrants and any other infidel who differed from them racially, religiously, or ideologically. Today's Islamic radicals seek to use terror to intimidate their Arab brethren and break the spirit of the American people. The beheadings carried out in Iraq—like lynching—are committed in order to shock and frighten. Like the Ku Klux Klan and White Citizens councils of another generation, they assume their inhumanity and brutality will dampen the thirst for liberty and like the Klansmen, they miscalculate. Klansmen wore hoods and burned crosses. Islamists peek out from behind a keffeyah covering their faces and invoke the name of God. True righteousness, however, has no need of a mask and is not cloaked in darkness. The Lord's work is done in the light of day, shining for all to see and those who love the day have nothing to fear from the night.

Hatred fuels their actions, but it is more than hatred that informs their irrational convictions. Like the white supremacist, they share backwardness and a fear of the forward progress of civilization. They look at their lives and reason that their inadequacy could only be due to the presence of "the other." American's demonized the Negro. In the Arab world, it is America, Israel, and the whole of Western civilization.

During a speech at Vanderbilt University, National Security advisor (now Secretary of State) Condoleezza Rice spoke about her childhood friend, eleven-year-old Denise McNair, who was one of the little girls killed in the bombing of the Sixteenth Street Baptist Church in Birmingham. Rice said, "The bombing was meant to instill fear." She added, "Those terrorists failed because of the poverty of their visions—a vision of hate and inequality. . . . And they failed because of the courage and sacrifice of all who suffered and struggled for civil rights."

On all of this I believe Mr. Jordan and I would agree. However, I still question the context of Jordan's tossing Birmingham into discussions of 9/11. Is the terrorism visited upon black citizens of Birmingham forty years ago supposed to give black Americans pause as we mourn the murder of three thousand of our countrymen? Or is he suggesting that America's lack of virtue somehow absolves the Muslim terrorists who used high-jacked jet planes as cruise missiles? The fact is, as reprehensible as the violence in Birmingham was, it was not sponsored by the federal government or morally endorsed by the populace. White America did not dance in the streets at the report of the murder of innocent children. On the contrary, the culprits have been hunted for decades and have finally been brought to justice. The same cannot be said of Islam and the Islamic fanatics who seek to destroy all of Western culture. Perhaps Jordan feels the grip on the victim bar slipping and thus seeks to co-opt a portion of the sympathy and benevolence that have poured out for the victims of that horrible attack.

Jordan continued, "War, hunger, disease, unemployment, deprivation, dehumanization, and terrorism define our existence. They are not new to us." Nor are they exclusive to us. I dare say there is not a people on the planet that could not describe some portion of their history in those terms. Were they so inclined, they might also describe their history as one filled with peace, compassion, spiritual communion, and great humanity. Rather than describe our history as defined by what we have accomplished, Jordan chose to reduce our history to what has been done to us. Dehumanization defines our existence? Are we not more than the sum total of our victimization?

In his litany of "terrorist" acts committed against black people, why would

Jordan conveniently neglect to mention self-inflicted ills such as the black on black crime rate. According to crime statistics, fifty-four percent of forcible rape victims are black women who describe ninety-eight percent of their attackers as black men. All told, forty percent of all violent street crime—murder, rape, robbery, assault—is committed by young black men and their victims are overwhelmingly other black people. What about the high illegitimacy rate and the low priority to academics that have proven more devastating to our community than Jim Crow ever was?

The answer is that acknowledging complicity in some of the ills that affect our community would demand that he cede the hallowed ground of victimhood and the political power that goes with it. Hence Jordan's description of black people as "paragons for Americans."

Unfortunately, while there is much to be said for holding the moral high ground, there are also a couple disadvantages to this rather romantic notion of victimhood. First, being a victim implies helplessness. Second, maintaining the role of paragon requires a fidelity to the quality that earned the distinction; in this case, persecution. Third, it seduces one into the misguided belief that there is truly something ennobling in being a victim.

If there is one thing black people have never been, it is helpless. In his book, *The Fire Next Time*, James Baldwin writes: "One is after all, emboldened by the spectacle of human history and Negro history in particular, for it testifies to nothing less than the perpetual achievement of the impossible." If Jordan had chosen to view our history under the light of accomplishment rather than subjugation he would see this. In the span of one generation after slavery, black Americans lifted themselves from almost complete illiteracy to becoming doctors, lawyers, and educators. They built universities and centers of business and commerce. Today, 150 years removed from subjugation, we are the best-educated, wealthiest, healthiest people of African decent on the planet.

It is a shame that a man of Jordan's stature could offer these students nothing but the same old testimony of abuse at the hand of a racist America and encouragement to wear their victim status as a badge of honor. The cruel irony is that he was not speaking to single mothers on welfare, but to future doctors, lawyers, Ph.Ds, city planners, and the like.

When Esther was holding court, it was rare that anyone contradicted her. At twenty-four years old, I certainly wasn't going to open my mouth. But that was years ago. If we were to have that same conversation today, I would tell her the same thing I'd say to Vernon Jordan: Picking at scabs can lead to infection.

Visions of the Motherland

My friend, Hope Sullivan, asked if I would like to be in attendance as President Bush gave an address at the Sixth Annual Leon H. Sullivan Summit in Abuja, Nigeria. "Sure," I said, thinking she was teasing. "I'll just drop everything and fly to Africa." I should begin taking Hope more seriously. It turns out she had some extra tickets. I spent the next three days getting shots, packing, and rearranging commitments. I was even able to convince three friends to go with me. And so my first trip to Africa began with frenzy and a true sense of mission. Dropping everything and flying to Africa is precisely what happened.

The Leon H. Sullivan Summit (formerly The African, African-American Summit) was the brainchild of the late Reverend Leon H. Sullivan, who is perhaps best known as the architect of "The Sullivan Principles," a moral guideline that steered American corporations doing business in apartheid South Africa. Reverend Sullivan dreamed that the summits would transform a part of the globe that has, for years, been a hotbed of civil war, poverty, illiteracy, and disease. A positive change was needed.

To Sullivan, the summits would be a bridge between Sub-Saharan Africa and the Diaspora that would facilitate the transfer of knowledge, healthcare, and commerce. When he established the conference, Sullivan envisioned that the linking of Africa with the Diaspora would help solve the issues of hunger, famine, and HIV, thus initiating an African renaissance.

Armed with a heightened sense of mission, I couldn't wait to arrive and to participate in a forum designed to have such a positive impact on the lives of people around the world. During the entire flight, I was filled with restless anticipation. This was my first trip to Africa and I had no idea what to expect. As the plane touched down in Abuja, my heart began to beat into my throat. Imagine my surprise when I stepped off the plane in the "Motherland" and the first thing I saw was the proud visage of Air Force One. President Bush had arrived to speak at the summit as part of his historic five-day trip through Africa.

To paraphrase Rev. Sullivan, Africa's preservation and development will require education, business development, investments, and technical assistance from America. The presence of President Bush at the summit was therefore not only welcome, it was essential.

Consequently, it was disheartening to hear some of the cynicism that greeted and followed the President's African journey. There are those who suggested his five-day trek was little more than "photo-op" diplomacy. Some have accused the President of using the trip to deflect attention from questions surrounding his administration's Iraqi policy. It should come as no surprise that I believe the President when he says his administration is a true friend of Africa.

A few months prior to my journey, I had the opportunity to attend a briefing at the White House. At the briefing, Special Assistant to the President on African Affairs (now Ambassador to South Africa) Jendayi Frazer presented the President's Africa initiative to an enthusiastic audience. Then National Security Advisor (current Secretary of State) Condoleezza Rice made a surprise appearance, as did President Bush himself, who announced that he would be visiting Africa in the summer. He kept his promise.

It's a good bet Dr. Rice and Secretary of State Colin Powell have both—from the very beginning—been influential in directing the President's attention towards Africa. Both were on the dais in Abuja as well. That afternoon, as I listened to the President speak about promoting commerce and education in Africa, it occurred to me that between Secretary Powell, Drs. Rice and Frazer, and throwing in Deputy Assistant Anna Perez for good measure, black people are perhaps wielding more power internationally under this President than under any previous administration.

The President further demonstrated his sincerity in a radio address following his visit, during which he said: "Progress in Africa depends on peace and stability, so America is standing with friends and allies to help end regional wars. And against the murderous ambitions of terrorists, the United States and African countries are working in common purpose. We will not permit terrorists to threaten African peoples, or to use Africa as a base to threaten the world."

These are the words of a true friend. Terrorists thrive on desperation, fear, and despair. Explicit in the promise to deny terrorists a base of support in Africa is the pledge to rid Africa of misery and bring hope to regions where hope is frequently all too scarce.

The President also spoke of his commitment to fighting the spread of one of the gravest dangers Africa and the world have ever faced, the spread of HIV/AIDS. And the need is urgent. "Across the continent today, nearly thirty million people are living with HIV/AIDS, including three million children under the age of fifteen. In Botswana alone, nearly forty percent of the adult population has HIV."

The President continued: "Over the next five years, the United States Congress has authorized $15 billion to fight AIDS around the world, with a special focus on fourteen nations in Africa and the Caribbean. Working with governments and private groups and faith-based organizations, we will build on the progress in Uganda by establishing a comprehensive system to prevent, diagnose and treat AIDS."

Contrary to the contentions of his critics, this President has done far more than pose for pictures with the natives. He has in fact shown a compassion and commitment to Africa that is unparalleled. George Bush was the first Republican president to visit Africa and he didn't show up on the continent empty-handed. In addition to the Global AIDS initiative that provided $15 billion to help turn the tide of HIV/AIDS in Africa, he introduced the Africa Growth and Opportunity Act, which allows African businesses access to the American market. According to Harry Alford, president and CEO of the National Black Chamber of Commerce, the Bush administration has helped to create more than "150,000 new jobs in Africa and at least $437 million in business growth will be realized this year (2004) alone." Further, the administration is committed to a fifty percent increase in African business and industry development assistance through 2008.

There is alas a limit to how much the President can do. Without an equally committed congress, the President's sincerity isn't worth much. My suggestion to naysayers is rather than criticize the President, help make his commitment a reality by insisting that congress make the Africa initiative more than empty talk. The people's representatives must extend the African Growth and Opportunity Act (AGOA) so that African nations can continue to gain access to American markets. The President's Millennium Challenge Accounts—which tie financial aid to political reforms that expand individual liberty—must be fully funded.

If we are to be true friends of Africa, Congress must continue to fund the $15 billion the President has proposed to fight HIV/AIDS and the $100 million he pledged to East Africa to fight terrorism. The promise of a $15 million grant to train fourteen thousand teachers who will begin the work of educating the children of Sub-Saharan Africa must be kept.

During a speech, former United Nations Ambassador Andrew Young, who is the current chairman of the summit, drove home the importance of the gathering when he said, "A world economy that works must include Africa." I am enthused to see that this administration acknowledges the veracity of Ambassador Young's words and honors the work of the late Reverend Sullivan. With the guidance and friendship of the United States, Africa can lift herself up and take her rightful place in the sun.

Impact the World Through Play!

On the Universal Studios lot there is a street named Spielberg Drive. If you turn left off of Spielberg onto Colonial, you will be transported to a truly magical place. Colonial Drive is a block of attractive homes with flower gardens and beautifully manicured lawns. The street includes famous houses featured in *The Hardy Boys*, *Nancy Drew*, *The New Munsters*, *Animal House*, *Bedtime for Bonzo*, and countless music videos. In fact, the block is currently used as Wisteria Lane where the *Desperate Housewives* currently dwell. If you didn't know any better, you might think you were standing on a suburban street in anywhere USA. Of course, the houses on Colonial drive are all fake. A few of them have real rooms on the inside, but most are just shells waiting to be filled by imagination.

I stepped into that historic place of make-believe one damp day while filming an episode of the CBS series *The District*. I stood there, the rain coming down in buckets on my cold, damp feet, my nose was running like a spigot, and I thought, "Show business is fun!" Of course it is. I wasn't doing anything I didn't do regularly (and for free) as a child. I was being paid to play.

I roll my eyes every time I hear television stars whine about how hard they work. Digging ditches is hard work! Being in television and movies is skate duty. It is to enter into a world of fantasy, discovery, and play. In what other profession can you be paid handsomely for someone to dress you up, put on your make-up, feed you, and generally pamper and fuss over you? And infancy doesn't count. You won't get that kind of treatment at the postal service. At bottom, show business is still just big kids getting together to play.

Not very long ago someone asked me, "What do you do for fun?" I had to pause before answering. I don't play golf or tennis. I don't bowl and I gave up gardening. None of the typical responses came to mind. Then it hit me: I act. That is what I do for fun. I work. I love being on a stage, film, or television set. There is a buzz and an excitement that energizes me like nothing else. I love the smell of the rehearsal hall and coffee brewing in the costume shop. I get off on the hustle and bustle of production assistants and stage managers. I always have. Very little has changed since my days in high school drama club. While my friends smoked dope and drank beer, I got high off being on stage. The men and women scrambling around the set hanging lights and lugging cable remind me of the kids who ran the spotlight in high school. The carpenters working in the shop are the same kids who loved the smell of saw dust and built the sets as teenagers. Running to and fro with safety pins dangling from their hips are the ladies who, as girls, spent rainy afternoons in the costume shop. And, of course, lounging in director's chairs or standing on a camera mark in wet shoes are those like myself who have always loved the warmth of the limelight.

Studios can hire all the business school graduates they want and hire divisions of accountants, but that will not change the fact that from the script supervisor to the first assistant director, from the background actor to the star, all of us gathered on the lot that morning shared a desire to have an impact on the world through play. This is perhaps the true magic of movie making: it elevates the games we played as children to commerce.

The public is fascinated by the lives of television actors. Much of that has to do with the perception of a glamorous lifestyle filled with parties and grand living, however, a large part of that attraction stems from an understanding that play provides a way to bring a sense of harmony to otherwise disorderly worlds. It might seem odd that I would say that in light of the seeming mess that so many television and movie stars make of their personal lives, but stay with me.

I watch my wife go off to work every day and do very practical things. She has important meetings, writes business plans, and sits at her desk making long distance phone calls. She never knows from day to day how office politics will transform her role at the company or when her supervisor will arbitrarily change the rules. When we play, everyone knows his role and we make up the rules, as we need them.

Play is also a form of escapism. Some folks fix old cars or tend their backyard gardens in order to escape. The difference is that cars and vegetable gardens are sensible. The fantastic worlds created in Hollywood are not. A car will drive and you can eat the vegetables from the garden. Play liberates in a way gardening cannot because play demands you step outside of yourself. The houses on Colonial Drive are uninhabitable shells—empty inside, available for new worlds to be created in them every day. That rainy morning, I was able to step away from the confusions of marriage and child rearing and be transported to an upscale neighborhood in Northern Virginia where I was the mayor of Washington D.C. You can't beat that with a stick!

The love of make-believe is perhaps why show people are often the grandest folks you would ever want to meet. We are compassionate, sensitive, inventive, and great at parties. We are big kids who love playing dress up. You might argue that we are also big kids who like attention. But more than anything I think we are simply looking for freedom.

When I am on stage I feel truly free. I am happy. There is nothing in my life that can compare to the adrenalin rush of the curtain going up or the beauty of the overture playing. There is no place in my life where I feel as secure, as beautiful, and as powerful as when I am on stage. Most performers would agree. The stage is where they feel unburdened, at home—liberated.

I recall years ago taking a course in college entitled "psychoanalysis and the performer." My eyes were glazed over during most of the class, but the one thing that stuck with me was the notion that the artist gene is a mutant gene. I was always intrigued by the idea that being an artist (I am using this to include acting as well) meant something had gone terribly wrong with my DNA. But the idea does seem to be more than just a notion. You can teach technique, but you can't teach the feel, the vision, or the love. In this sense, I perform because it is who I am. I did not choose this career, it chose me. And I accepted Hollywood's invitation because this seductress promised me unlimited opportunity to be content, to be loved, to be powerful, to be all the things I was not as a boy.

A pretty tall order. I am not certain any professional endeavor can fill such lofty promises, however, that doesn't stop show business from making them and, for the vast majority of us, leaving them largely unfulfilled.

When I graduated college and entered the industry, the only "Alcoholics" I knew were actors. So many of the older performers I met and worked with spent a great deal of time nursing on rum and coke. I struggled to make sense of it. Twenty years and more than a few heartaches later, I now understand.

Joe, a character in the William Saroyan play *The Time of Your Life* ponders his drinking by proclaiming, "I drink because I don't like to be gypped. I don't like to be dead most of the time and just a little alive every once in a long while." Joe is looking to take the edge off the boredom of waiting. He despises the empty time doing mundane chores and being consumed with ordinary things. Joe wants to play. Saroyan doesn't say it, but I am certain Joe is an actor at heart. As a fresh-faced youngster, the actors I met were like Joe, drinking to get drunk, to take the edge off while they wait to be alive once again, walking the boards under the bright lights. The elevation of play to business is the bargain we make with the devil. The need to dull the ache of broken promises is the cost we bear to play.

Happily, I have not become an alcoholic. My narcotic of choice is food and I can trace the fifty pounds I gained over the years to the fast food I sucked down in order to pay the devil's price.

Clearly, there are quite a few detours on Spielberg Drive. You've got to navigate carefully lest you end up in *Hollywood*. Hollywood is a fantastic place peopled by some of the best people you will ever meet. *Hollywood* is a state of mind, a place where play is corrupted by business. The ethereal *Hollywood* is a pretentious, insincere, counterfeit cesspool where bullies roam the playground in search of deals and performers dull their aches with booze, drugs, and sex. It is a place made base by a culture that extends the reach of make believe into personal relationships, eschewing things like honesty and integrity in favor of ego. It is a place where the grand show folk I love turn to creeps.

Entire rituals have sprung up in this industry simply because *Hollywood* types who never miss an opportunity to preach the virtues of art and creativity cannot figure out how to speak honestly to one another. For instance, the word "no" does not exist in the *Hollywood* vocabulary. Instead, executives in *Hollywood* play a little game called the schedule shuffle. A pitch meeting is a brief meeting an aspiring writer or producer can schedule to "pitch" or sell an executive on a script idea. A common practice among these "very important people" is to have their assistant put you on the schedule leading you to believe that you will be sitting down for a few moments to play. The day before your meeting, the executive's assistant will call you and move your appointment to the following week. No problem. Stuff happens. The following week, however, your appointment will be moved again. This little ritual will be repeated until you finally stop calling back. The executive, who never had any intention of meeting with you in the first place, can always claim at a later date (when they want something from you) that they were just *so* busy and if you had demonstrated a tad more patience. . . .

I have danced that dance on more than one occasion.

There are those folks who will return your calls. I am not sure why, but in my experience the higher up you go, the more likely you are to have your phone call returned. It may be that the folks at the top are not as busy as the folks at the bottom. My sense, however, is that those at the top (in addition to perhaps being decent folk) have realized that there is not much to lose by having a phone conversation. Those at the bottom don't return calls because it is the way they show you they are superior. They have the power to acknowledge you . . . or not.

The first lady of television, Marcy Carsey, is one of those people who always returns phone calls. It may not be right away, but eventually I will hear her sweet voice on the other end of the line. Why then does some Joe Schmo barely out of his twenties and who has not produced anything figure he doesn't need to dial my number even if it is to tell me they need to reschedule?

Not too long ago, I was trying to sell an idea to Bunim/Murray, the folks who created *The Real World* (of which I am a big fan). They passed on my proposal, but after the meeting suggested that if I had any other ideas I should certainly give them a call. "Think of yourself as one of the family," they said. Hey! That's what aspiring producers like to hear. I was one of the family. I didn't realize they meant the cousin who always manages to get left off the invite list. I sent a script to one of their producers (who was five years out of college—tops, and who had not been in my original meeting). After months of unreturned calls and his assistant telling me he was busy, I left a message on his voice mail telling him I wasn't certain whether he truly was the busiest little producer in Hollywood or just a jerk. Lo and behold, he called me back that day just to tell me he had never before been called a jerk. Well, there is a first time for everything.

Oh yes. He passed on my idea.

For actors who face a life of rejection, the level of dishonesty extends to absurd heights. A few years ago, I auditioned for a film starring Denzel Washington. I had a terrific audition and had high hopes of getting the job. The following day I saw my manager who told me that the director loved me. There was just the slightest pause, which told me there was a "but" getting ready to squeeze itself into the conversation. It turned out to be a very big "butt" indeed. It seems that while the director loved me, he felt I looked too much like Denzel. My manager told me this with a straight face. I just laughed. She looked at me with a puzzled expression and I explained: "I have got to be the only actor in Hollywood who looks like Denzel Washington and *can't* get hired!" Who knows the real reason and it doesn't really matter. My point is there is a need in *Hollywood* to seed every relationship with bullshit as if it will grow roses instead of distrust.

I am reminded of the poem "The Mask" by Paul Lawrence Dunbar.

> *"We wear the mask that grins and lies,*
> *It hides our cheeks and shades our eyes,*
> *This debt we pay to human guile;*
> *With torn and bleeding hearts we smile,*
> *And mouth with myriad subtleties. . . ."*

Dunbar was not speaking of *Hollywood* when he wrote those words, but he very well could have been. The mask is a ready attire for all of us living in Hollywood/*Hollywood*, but none rely on it so much as those outside the mainstream.

Hollywood is a tough place for everyone. Even blonds with big boobs get a tough row to hoe. But there is little doubt that it is particularly difficult on minorities. And blacks have it better than some. I am asked all the time if it is difficult to be a black actor in Hollywood. I always respond, "It could be worse. I could be an Indian." Hollywood makes a big show out of being past race. Everyone in Hollywood is so liberal and together and "with it." Bullshit! Hollywood is liberal from here to the bank. Race is never absent and the same racial games played in politics are in the "play" that parades as art in *Hollywood*.

The lovefest that is supposed to be liberal Hollywood simply doesn't exist! All of the super "liberal" celebrities, who love to tell the rest of us how to live our lives, do not practice what they preach. You need look no further than their companies, their staffs, and their productions, which all show a surprising lack of diversity.

If you ever get an opportunity, walk through the offices at the Disney Company and count the number of minority faces who are not answering phones. You will need one hand. As of this writing, I know of no black executive at any major film studio who can actually green light a picture. Look through the trades and see how many blacks are actually running a show. As I write this, there are two.

When I was on *General Hospital*, I had white writers (We did have a black writer—one of two in the entire world of daytime television) tell me that they just didn't know how to write for black characters. The production staffs of most television programs are white unless, of course, it is a black show, in which case, it is exactly the opposite. Most of the film sets I have been around have similar makeups: precious few black production staff unless it is a black film. Of course, rather than simply opening the hiring to all different kinds of folk, the liberals at the networks create diversity programs that simply ghettoize minority writers and directors. The white writers and directors are not forced into "diversity programs," but suddenly black writers and directors do not get a break *unless* they come through these programs. And I have read too many scripts with an amazing lack of creativity when it comes to black characters.

I can't tell you how many times in my twenty-year career I've read a break down for a role and it says something like, "He is an attractive African-American neurosurgeon who is street smart. . . ." I am not making this up. Producers have actually refused to see me for the role of a doctor because I wasn't "street" enough. Only in oh-so-liberal *Hollywood* are black doctors supposed to sound like they didn't spend eight years studying Latin. The descriptions may have changed over the years. Now the breakdown may read "urban," or the director might say that the character "has edge," but the meaning is the same. And the black characters on television are almost always the least developed characters on the program. Black as aesthetic—a seasoning to pepper into a story for "flava." Instead of black "people" what *Hollywood* so often wants is a black attitude and a black sound. (Amazingly enough, no one ever asks if Hollywood is difficult for those of us who are black by ethnicity, but talk like white boys.)

I tell you this black and not black enough stuff haunts me. *Hollywood* is my constant straight man in a perpetual vaudeville act. Pass the seltzer bottle. "Slowly I turned. Step by step, inch by inch."

Some of this is attributable to racism. Hollywood is not immune. Like any other industry in America, show business has its share. I am convinced, however, that the real culprit is superficiality. In *Hollywood,* art and relationships are not viewed as the goal, but a means to an end. Friendships are not easily formed because the first question on everyone's mind is: "What can you do for me?" There is simply no desire to connect. Relationships are there for conducting business, making deals. People in *Hollywood* do not want to play, but to become players. With so little interest in human connections, it is no wonder a writer can look me in the eye and with no sense of shame tell me he is unable to write for a black character. It is no wonder nighttime television is filled with clichés and two-dimensional characters, it is no wonder Hollywood is ghettoized. Complexity simply mucks up the works. Despite living in a world filled with people of different types and attitudes, authenticity in this nether world is to be found only in the familiar.

Whether it is navigating the hallways during junior high school, trying to get a date as a nineteen-year-old, becoming a Republican at age thirty, or trying to get a job as an actor, my authenticity is constantly at issue. "That is not how black people sound." "This is not how black people think." "Black people like this do not exist."

I have struggled for a way to write about this without sounding bitter. Mmmn. Nope. I can't do it. I am not proud of it, but I *am* bitter or at least extremely cynical.

I am forty years old. I look back on my life and, well, in comparison to where I thought I might be at this age, to all my wide-eyed ideals, well, I come up a little short. This is life. In this profession, rejection is part of the game, and while I don't enjoy the rejection, I am not complaining about rejection *per se.* My issue is that while actors are encouraged not to take this rejection personally, the fact is that in Hollywood, people are often hired precisely because of who they are. In other words, while I may be able to put on the mask and *play* "street" there are guys who *are* street and are hired because that is who they are. In a very real way, each rejection is a way of telling me again that I talk like a white boy! That I am not black enough! Slowly I turned! See? I am caught in a macabre replaying of this vaudeville routine! And often times, *Negro Hollywood*—in blackface and spats—is the worst offender.

To this day I have not seen the film *Soul Food.* I refuse! For three weeks, the producers of that project had me on hold: I was being considered, just give us more time, we love him, and all of that. I lobbied every way I knew how, even inviting the director out for drinks. Alas, I could not overcome the perception of me as being too corny to play Vivica Fox's husband. I did some investigating and the trail ended with Robi Reed, a casting director, manager, and one of the producers of *Soul Food.* For years, I had tried to get auditions for films she was casting but had no luck. I heard through the grapevine that it was because she didn't like me. Not black enough for her tastes. Now in all fairness to Robi, I do not know for certain that she felt that way about me or that she actually ever said anything of the sort. It was only hearsay. It just seemed awfully coincidental that I would be on hold for three weeks and suddenly one of the producers—who as a casting director had refused to read me for roles for ten years, who I hear doesn't like me because I am "too corny," makes a decision not to hire me and the L-7 factor (square) is cited. Sadly, it is another small, but tragic example of black people constricting rather than expanding the definition of ourselves. It will be a cold day in Hell before I watch that film. (I have since auditioned for Robi Reed's casting office several times and have heard through reliable sources that she, in fact, thinks I am a fine actor. She has even hired me for a job I was unable to perform due to conflicts. I have still not seen *Soul Food*.)

It is too bad really because Hollywood is at its best when the bullies in *Hollywood* step out of the way and let folks play. Admittedly, my complaints aside, I have been extremely fortunate. I have performed on stage, television, and in film. I have had a career, which is more than a whole lot of folk regardless of race can say. Sure, I have often been hired to play corny black guys, but I have also been able to play some just plain guys. Without a doubt, Hollywood has been the best for me when I have been allowed to step outside of the constraints of race and indulge my imagination.

Acting has, for me, been a way of expressing my uniqueness. That is the kind of individualism our culture celebrates. There is power in the ability to say I am whoever and whatever I say I am at any particular time, I am creating myself as we speak. Liberty in America is about empowering individuals to go as far as their dreams, talent, and hard work can carry them. Play liberates by having an impact on the world through the power of individualism.

Of all the fan mail I received while working on *General Hospital*, the letters I remember most were the ones that described my character of Justus Ward as being "so cool!" I was delighted. There have been so few times in my life that I have been described as cool. Now I have on my resume a character that was genuinely seen not just as cool, but as *so* cool. That is part of what keeps me in show business: Every once in a while I am allowed to become J.C. You don't know J.C.? J.C. is my alter ego. We all have one—the guy or gal we wish we were, the character that is as sexy, smart, or as tough as we fantasize ourselves as being.

Mine is named J.C. and J.C. is Black. I mean dark like Wesley Snipes with his smoldering sexuality! With the swagger and defiance of Laurence Fishburn! The good looks of Denzel, the humor of Eddie Murphy, and the voice of Ving

Rhames. "I'm about to get medieval on yo ass!" This is actually how I see myself. I explain it this way: As a result of my being so "square," I have had a chance to work with some beautiful women, including Halle Berry, Jasmine Guy, Lisa Bonet, Troy Beyer, Angelle Brooks, Vivica Fox, and Angela Bassett! So what on earth do I have to complain about? It's not me! It's Joseph but it isn't J.C. Understand? I don't see myself as the corny straight guy! Yes, I have been able to have love scenes with beautiful women, but they have been rather benign love scenes. I want to be like Wesley in *New Jack City* and pour champagne on Michael Michele or just toss her off me while making love 'cause I am just disgusted or distracted. I'm a black man with things on my mind! I want to be the MAN! The dangerous, cool, rebellious, jive talking man that whitey can't control. I WANT TO BE SHAFT! (Not Sam Jackson's Shaft, but Richard Roundtree's Shaft!)

Shaft was the ultimate individualist hero! He hung out at Café Reggio for God's sake! Think about it. He lived in Greenwich Village, but worked uptown. He dated white women, black women . . . it didn't matter. He had no allegiance to any group but was respected by all of them. I want to be "the cat who won't cop out!" I want to be so complicated that only my woman understands me! I want to be a bad mutha . . . shut yo mouth!

Strangers have welcomed me into their hearts and confidence because they identify with the cool of Justus Ward. Others tell me how they love the film *Strictly Business* and watch it whenever it comes on television. Everywhere I go in the country, people stop me and tell me how important *The Cosby Show* was to their lives growing up. They glow as they tell me how their families still watch the program in reruns and how their children now imitate the stiff dancing I did on the opening credits. Clearly, I am not responsible for the success of *The Cosby Show*. Bill Cosby's brilliance is solely responsible. That combined with the warmth and generosity of Phylicia Rashad and the talents of the core family members is what made the show so delightful. But for three brief years, I got to play with some terrific folks and was part of the magic. That is almost as cool as playing the mayor of our nation's capital.

We are all called to minister to our fellow man in different ways and I have long felt that my calling was through performance. It gives me a great sense of accomplishment whenever someone stops me on the street and tells me that my play has touched their life. The realization that what I do has an impact on the lives of people somehow makes it all seem worthwhile.

Years ago, I appeared on the television program *A Man Called Hawk*. One particularly cold afternoon in Washington D.C., we were shooting in a cemetery. The extras who were to play funeral mourners showed up dressed in Sunday attire—the men in suits, the women in knee-length skirts. Clearly, someone had forgotten to tell them that they would be standing in twelve-degree weather for hours. As a guest star, I was not only making substantially more than the $50 the extras were being paid, I was also given long underwear and a heated van to sit in between takes. It was a brutal test of the actors' dedication. In a rather chivalrous moment, Avery Brooks, the star of the show, gave one of the women mourners his gloves. Even as one poor woman's legs began to turn red from the windburn, not one of the extras left the set. They all stood dutifully by the makeshift gravesite, pretending they were mourning the loss of some fictitious soul. As I made my way to the comfort and heat of the van, I thought I heard one of the extras respond to someone, stuttering through chattering teeth, "Wwhat? And give up sh-show business?" I couldn't have put it better myself.

IDENTITY

Doobie In the Funk

During my junior year in high school, seating assignments put me next to a really pretty girl in biology class. She was a white girl and she was fine! She looked like a model. I won't describe her, mainly because I don't really remember what she looked like in detail, just that she looked good. One day in class, we did an experiment during which we had to put our hand over our partner's chest and count the number of heartbeats. With this girl as my partner, I almost passed out! That's how fine she was. At any rate, I'll let you personalize her image. Whatever a fine, eleventh-grade white girl looks like to you, that's how she looked.

Across the aisle from us sat two guys who, well, let's just say weren't particularly friendly. We were the only three black students in the class and while that alone didn't demand camaraderie, I thought we should at least be polite to one another. Instead, they always seemed to look at me as if I had stolen something of theirs. It was a look that suggested they were deciding whether or not to kick a little tail. Oh, my butt was going to get kicked; they just hadn't decided *when.* I imagine they also wondered why the chip on my shoulder wasn't as big as the ones on theirs. They talked back to the teacher, didn't pay attention in class, didn't do class work . . . you know, punishing the white man by flunking biology.

One day, it all made sense. The class broke up into groups of four and five to work on a project. I partnered up with the pretty girl who sat next to me and the girls who sat behind me (Stacey Friedman and her desk partner). After a time, the guys called me over to their table. I was hesitant, but hopeful. I thought perhaps they finally saw I wasn't such a bad guy. Maybe they wanted my help. Instead, they asked me if I was blind. I didn't understand the question, so they asked me again and nodded in the direction of my lab partners, all of whom were white. These guys wanted to know why had I chosen to team with them. I looked around the room and thought, "Am I supposed to team up with you two guys? You guys who have never said anything nice to me the entire semester? You guys

209

who don't do your work and fail tests?" Mind you, I only thought this. I figured getting my butt whooped in third-period biology class wasn't the brightest idea. I simply said that Stacey lived around the corner from me and had been a friend since third grade. Feeling that a butt kicking was still a distinct possibility, I scurried back to my chair with no further conversation.

Later that year, there was some trouble in class. One of these guys got into a fight with a white guy. Actually, *fight* isn't quite the right word. The white guy was doing his best demonstration of the old civil-defense drill: duck and cover. *Beat down* would be a more appropriate term!

The teacher, Mr. Bollicker, was about an hour away from retirement so he wasn't about to step in between and break it up. Instead, he stood, watching the action with the rest of us. The action moved over right in front of my desk.

I remember watching the brother pound away, thinking, "Yep, I am pretty certain I don't want to be *your* lab partner," when suddenly I hear the beautiful white girl say, "Stop! Stop it! Why don't you just leave him alone, you stupid nigger!"

Silence. The fight stopped. The class was stunned. *I* was stunned. Mr. Bollicker was having a heart attack. The black guy gave her one of those looks he used to give me. Suddenly, she found religion. "I-I'm s-sorry. I j-just wanted you t-to stop."

The bell rang and with an I'ma-getchu-after-school look, the two black students left. Stacey and the other girls told Fine White Girl not to go to her next class, but to go to the office instead. Fine White Girl turned to me and asked me to escort her to the office. Stupid Black Guy said, "Sure."

Science classes were on the opposite side of the building from the office. We walked from one end of the school to the other, her arm locked in mine like we were going to the prom. She was shaking like a leaf, rattling on and on about how sorry she was, how she hadn't really meant it, how I was different. And me? I stood there with a stupid grin on my face thinking, "What the hell am I doing? Didn't she just call somebody a *nigger?* Surely she has to know that if she gets jumped I am not going to fight for her. I'm just as scared of those guys as she is! It's not like I'm going to be her boyfriend—not that I would mind."

I hated myself. For the first time in my life I thought, "Maybe the ugly things those guys thought about me were justified. Maybe I am a Tom. Maybe I *don't* know the deal and *have* fooled myself into believing that I am different or better because I have white friends." Of course, nothing could have been further from the truth. My walking her to the office that day had nothing to do with tomming. At its core, it was as simple as a guy having a crush on a pretty girl and who saw no reason for her to get the snot beat out of her because she'd said something stupid.

But of course, when it comes to race, not to mention racial name-calling, nothing is that simple. After that day, I never saw her with the same eyes. Our relationship changed. Somehow, we managed to get through our biology work together, but the humor and friendship with which we had done our work was gone. From that moment forward, we were merely civil. I hated that that word suddenly made me comrade-in-arms with people who didn't like me, who I didn't like, and, as far as I could tell, with whom I had little in common. This experience was my baptism into the consciousness divide of the Good Negro.

A number of black authors have written about this duality of consciousness held by black Americans. In his landmark book, *The Souls of Black Folk*, W.E.B. Du Bois wrote, "The Negro ever feels his two-ness—an American, a Negro, two souls, two thoughts, two unreconciled strivings . . . two warring ideals in one dark body, whose dogged strength alone keeps it from being torn asunder."

A hundred years later, in his book *Authentically Black*, John McWhorter took this thought another step when he wrote, "A tacit sense reigns among a great many black Americans today that the 'authentic' black person stresses personal initiative and strength in private, but dutifully takes on the mantle of victimhood as a public face."

In my forty-plus years, I am certainly familiar with all of the mental gymnastics involved in the attempts at self-definition both Du Bois and McWhorter describe. I have equally intimate knowledge of the tightrope walk experienced by so many black people, of being circumspect around white people, ingratiating oneself—making them feel safe?—and being less so around black people. It is not a desire not to be perceived as black, we simply don't want to be identified as *that* kind of black.

I remember hearing of a dance club in Washington D.C. that got in a lot of hot water for having an unspoken "No Nigger" policy at the door. They argued that their policy was not anti-black at all. They allowed black people in the club regularly. The clientele they turned away—the people the policy was designed to discourage—was a particular *type* of person distinguished by their dress and behavior.

There exists among many black folk a need to distance oneself from the clowning, the shuffling, the ignorance and unsophistication of a certain number of our brethren. My buddy's parents, two educated and proud black people, used the N-word around his home all the time. "We are black and consciously so," went their refrain, "but we are not like those niggers over there!" There are few black people who do not know the experience of hearing some tragic report on the radio or television news, quickly offer the small prayer: "Dear Lord, please don't let them be black." And of course the deep, sad sigh when the newscaster discloses that alas, one more ignorant Negro has set the entire race back twenty years. On more than one occasion I have been in the company of whites and have felt the twinge of embarrassment at the sight of some loud or unruly behavior by blacks.

Yet, quiet as it's kept, we are not above embracing that very same negritude when it suits our purposes. Black people learn from an early age that no matter how humble we may actually be, putting our better natures to the side and allowing our race to speak for us often has its benefits. Namely we often have our way with white folks. And if you act your color often enough, even black folks will be scared of you.

Recently at the grocery store, I stepped out of line to grab a soda. When I turned back, a white woman had pushed my cart to the side and taken my place in line. As I stepped back to my cart, her eyes grew wide and she sheepishly stepped aside taking her rightful place at the end of the line. There is not a doubt in my mind that she was intimidated not by anything I said—I didn't utter a word—but by my size and color.

I have a sense that this divide exists at all economic levels. No matter how little you have, there is a desire to somehow separate yourself from *those* other folks. I do think, though, that this split becomes more acute as one achieves greater economic and professional success. The Good Negro thus becomes a middle-class phenomenon. A certain level of professional or financial achievement sets him apart, gives him distance from the masses and allows him room to look on and offer indignant criticism or shake his head and suck his teeth in embarrassment and consternation. "You will never get ahead behaving like that!" "Why can't you get your act together?" "Follow my example." And, of course, "They are going to ruin it for the rest of us."

A scene from *Strictly Business,* a film I did years ago, comes to mind. My character, a successful commercial real-estate broker named Waymon Tinsdale, walks into his office to find his friend Bobby (the mailroom clerk played by Tommy Davidson) sitting at his desk eating Chinese takeout and talking on the phone. At one point, Bobby asks Waymon why he hasn't entered him into the executive training program. Waymon suggests that Bobby is too rough around the edges. He speaks slang and dresses sloppily. Bobby replies, "Am I supposed to wear Armani?" At that Waymon says, "No, but you don't have to dress and act so, so. . . ." "Black?" Bobby asks. To which Waymon answers, "Well, yes, black."

I hated that scene! It was manipulative and unfair! Bobby's dress was inappropriate for work. His behavior was equally unprofessional. He came to work late, goofed off, and talked back to his supervisors. But what the writers were getting at in their clumsy way was this duality that exists among middle-class blacks. Essentially, Waymon was asking Bobby to be a Good Negro and to stop acting like a Nigger.

I did not dislike those boys in my high school biology class so much for their bad black behavior as I did for their nastiness toward me. Nevertheless, there was an element of this Waymon/Bobby exchange in my interaction with those boys. Why couldn't they just act right? I was as shocked as everyone else in the class at the pejorative slam that came from my lab partner. At the same time, my indignation was somewhat lessened because on some level, I agreed with her. He *was* a nigger! And I was not.

This, however, is the world as seen through black eyes. The focus on race was a means to separate what was white from what was not. Things were good by virtue of their whiteness. Integration has somewhat broadened this definition to now include that which is not black. But in the eyes of Fine White Girl, I was not a good black. I am betting she didn't even see me as black at all.

She certainly would not have been the first, nor was she the last. I have heard many white friends say that they have never seen me as black. This is meant as a compliment. I am fairly certain they mean that I like the things they do and laugh at the jokes they do and am not given to derailing conversations with a petulant black perspective, during which they must nod and feel my pain. My response to these compliments is that while I am appreciative of their acceptance, I *am* black. So, here is yet another pose in the mental yoga that black people practice: Striving to realize our individual humanity while still holding tight to some portion of our racial identity. (I am quite certain my white friends and neighbors do not put themselves through these mental acrobatics. However, every black person I know is constantly involved in this type of intricate analysis.)

A friend's co-worker once shared a funny anecdote tied to Princeton, her alma mater. Apparently during her school years, Princeton students would wear the sweatshirts of different colleges and universities from around the country. The co-worker happened upon a sweatshirt bearing the crest of Howard University. She knew nothing about Howard but wanted to join in the fun so she put on the sweatshirt. When her black doorman—the Good Negro—saw her in the sweatshirt, he took her aside, and informed her that Howard was a historically black university. He suggested that she might want to change sweatshirts, which she quickly did. As the co-worker told the tale, she laughed at her naiveté and was genuinely embarrassed at her haste to remove the shirt. My friend laughed along, in part, she later said, because she felt happy that her co-worker felt comfortable enough with her to share this story. Freedom was never so sweet as finally being accepted as a total being. Sweet that is until she remembered that SHE had attended Howard. She suddenly didn't see what so &*%$ funny!

Like my friend, I agreed to walk that white girl to the office in reciprocation for what I saw as her acknowledgement of my humanity. It was freedom. Some will argue that her request was simply a matter of expediency, that I was a good black boy and she would be safer with me—certainly safer than with the white boy who just got beat down. If the chips were down, perhaps I too would become a *nigger* in her eyes. I am more inclined, however, to believe that she felt comfortable making such a request of me not because I was one of the good black people, but because I was her lab partner and friend. I would also argue that in this respect, she is the only one who saw me as a whole person. At least more whole than the two other black boys in class who were never able to see beyond my race and never bothered to try. For them, the color of my skin demanded fidelity, no matter their character, no matter their behavior and, oddly enough, no matter how they treated me as a person.

It is refreshing to be viewed in one's humanity, to experience the world as a full being, *sans* hyphen. And yet in the context of this situation, it was also utterly inappropriate. The interjection of race—her calling the boy a nigger—made it impossible for her then to truly acknowledge my individuality, no matter how badly I required or longed for it. There could be no true reconciliation of my two selves because there was no real embrace of my full humanity. Black is not the sum of who I am, but it is a part of who I am. To not see my blackness is to not see the whole of me; indeed, it is to ignore an essential part of me. The fact was that whether I liked it or not, those boys *were* a part of me and when that girl sullied them she sullied me as well.

If this is a black burden, it is also white folk's confusion. There exists in white America a misguided notion that we are somehow striving to be released from our blackness. The truth is, we are striving to be released from *race*. We are, as Du Bois said, "longing to attain self-conscious manhood." Rendering us colorless does not liberate us individually. In many ways, it makes us less human than the nigger no one wants to let in the club. We are determined to walk the land as fully realized human beings, to be in harmony with color and humanity. White people cannot pick and choose when to see race and when to ignore it. So long as the racial construct remains, full realization of black individuality will be impossible. The best for which we may be able to hope is some easy balance between our human and racial selves, a constant adjusting and readjusting lest the tension between the two tear us asunder.

It may finally be that we must forget about reconciliation of these two selves altogether and instead adopt what James Baldwin calls the recreation of self. In the end, we may be forced to dig deep within ourselves and recreate an identity out of "no image that yet exists in America." And once you have decided who you are, once you have been set free with keys which you fashion, you must "force the world to deal with you, not with its idea of you."

Of course nothing is that simple for me. It was just my luck that my situation was made more complicated by my growing up in a Jewish neighborhood. Some years ago, I was on my way home from shooting a commercial when I struck up a conversation with one of the other actors. He guessed that I wasn't from New York. Somehow it came to light that I grew up in a Jewish neighborhood in Denver, Colorado. At that revelation, the production assistant who was driving the van turned around and snapped, "I knew it! All day I have been telling myself there is some Jew in that guy!"

So now what? Which am I? Maybe neither. Maybe both? I mean, it would be cool, "but can you imagine some Doobie in your funk?"

Beneficial Exposure

I was halfway through the film *Deacons for Defense* when my eldest son plopped down on the sofa to watch the movie with his old man. The film is a dramatization of the formation of the civil rights group, "The Deacons for Defense and Justice." The DFD was a group of black veterans living in Louisiana who, in 1964, organized themselves to protect civil rights workers and protestors from the Ku Klux Klan. Admittedly the film was not age appropriate for my young son. The events depicted occurred nearly four decades ago so I could honestly say my son did not relate to the drama. However, there were images of violence and a rather liberal use of the N-word. Seeing us on the couch, my wife cringed and gave me a sharp look that told me I should change the channel. I agreed, but as I reached for the remote, I stopped short. I turned to her and said, "Our son has to know."

Ideally, little boys should be playing with trucks, not learning that there are people who despise them simply because of the color of their skin. As I sat watching the movie, I secretly hoped he would get bored and go off to play with his brothers. I feared destroying his innocence with the answers to the questions the movie might create in his mind.

Later, I spoke to an educator about my concerns and she admonished me to be more conscientious in the future. "He's not ready for this," she said. "It will scare him." She suggested that I give him time to go to school where teachers can lay the foundation and the context for the behavior depicted in the film. The educator was right, but not because my son is too young to process racism without the benefit of public school curriculum. If we lived in a world where people openly showed the type of hate depicted in *Deacons*, that, in my mind, would be context enough. Waiting for the school system to lay a foundation could cost him his life. The educator was correct because my son is growing up in a world where people view each other very differently than they did in the world of my youth.

In 1967, when I was my son's age, the Deacons for Defense and Justice were still active. The water hoses and bombs of Birmingham were vivid pictures in the nation's consciousness. There were calls for black power and we were only a matter of months away from chants of "Burn, Baby, Burn." My parents didn't have the luxury to wait for the public school to lay a foundation and put racism into context—it was something we all dealt with daily.

In my hometown, it was not unusual for white salespeople to pass over black customers who had been waiting in line. I remember my mother clearly instructing us to speak up and say, "Excuse me, I believe I was next." I heard the N-word all the time in those days. We kids anticipated it. We even practiced a rhyme to say in response, just in case: "I'm not a nigger; I'm a niggero. When I become a nigger, I will let you know."

It has been more than fifteen years since a white person has called me that name. I was walking down the street with a lady friend when a car full of teenagers passed by and they hollered out the window. We were so surprised, we turned to each other and wondered aloud, "Did they say what I think they said?" We were so incredulous that we actually burst out laughing.

It is clear that the urgency with which my mother and father talked with me about prejudice isn't necessary today. In the world in which my son is growing up, no one thinks twice about the presence of a precocious little black boy. The school he has been attending is racially mixed, as are the junior and senior high schools in our neighborhood. The children with whom he plays are of every color in the human spectrum and their parents are wedded in every possible racial combination. Today, the only people using the N-word in public are black.

Still, there is a voice that whispers to me, "He has to know."

But as my educator friend said: "everything in its time." Unfortunately, I cannot undo what has been done. My son's curiosity has been sparked. He has recently begun looking around in our neighborhood, his school, and the stores we shop and cannot fathom that there was a time when the color of his skin meant there were places he could not go and things he could not do. He is filled with questions, which he sometimes asks in unusual places—like the middle of the grocery store, at the top of his lungs.

I can't honestly say that I am disappointed. His questions fill me with a sense of mission and I launch into stories of my childhood, stories of being denied service and of being called names. His questions allow me to remove the veil covering the ugly side of our American heritage. Perhaps, I am motivated by an atavistic need to protect my son, a primal desire to ensure that my sons enter the world armed and prepared to battle the evils of white racism or whatever dragons may cross their paths. That is certainly a part of it. I also don't want to lie to my sons. I don't want to hide the truth of the world from them. Although our nation has moved beyond those days of hatred, it remains a part of our nation's legacy. My sons should know about America, warts and all. But I think the reality is this-I believe in heroes. I believe because of heroes, hope and inspiration can be found in the most horrid of circumstances. Rather than frighten him, seeing this side of our nation's past could inspire him to aspire to greatness. This was a story about ordinary men who behaved heroically. I want him to know on whose shoulders he stands.

The DFD were not alone. There are other names—many familiar to us, others less well known—that also belong in the pantheon of heroes. During the summer of 1964, James Chaney, Andrew Goodman, and Michael Schwerner, three civil rights workers who were organizing voter education/registration in Meridian, Mississippi were murdered and found buried in an earthen dam.

There were men like Herbert Lee, who was killed in 1961. Jim Reeb, who along with two co-workers, made the mistake of taking a short cut to an evening meeting in Selma and was attacked by racists. Reeb later died from his injuries. Jimmy Lee Jackson was beaten and shot by Alabama state troopers during a protest march in 1965. There are others—names we will never know—who also paid the ultimate sacrifice.

Educating my sons on this part of their history helps them know the price of their liberty has been steep and knowing helps them understand why so much is demanded of them, why excuses will not be tolerated, and why they are expected to imbue their lives with purpose. Excellence honors the memory of those who walked the path before them with worn out shoes.

My son recently asked me if he could watch *Ruby Bridges*, the true story of a little black girl who integrated the schools in New Orleans, Louisiana, in 1960. My wife shrugged, "It's up to you." I recalled the words of the educator and put the video into the player.

If he's asking, he's decided that he has to know.

Mancala In the Promised Land

My wife and I took a tour of the elementary school our son would be attending the next year. Amidst the penmanship guides and poems about spring that lined the walls of the classrooms, we noticed the Heritage Board. Decorated with photos of each child, along with a brief description of where that child was from, the Heritage Board allowed the children to trace their heritage. My wife and I looked at one another and wondered aloud, "What will our son put down?"

Later, the principal revealed that the Heritage Board was just one part of the first-grade social studies curriculum. The board enabled students to tell the stories of the journeys their parents and ancestors took to come to America. The children then contrasted and compared the beliefs and customs of various cultures, thereby learning the ways in which immigrants helped to define Californian and American culture.

Once again I wondered, "What story will my son tell?" With few exceptions, American blacks cannot trace their ancestry beyond the shores of North America. I wanted to know what children put on the Heritage Board when they could not point to an actual country from which their ancestors originated. The principal suggested that our son might consider listing his heritage as simply African.

While the designers of the curriculum may not have intended it, ultimately this portion of study was about identity. The assignment asked the children to answer the questions: "where do I come from?" and "who am I?" I suppose there would be no harm in taking the principal's suggestion and dressing my son in Kente cloth, teaching him a few words of Swahili, and having him present a sculpture from Benin for show and tell. There is certainly value in learning about African art and culture. Unfortunately, in the context of the social studies project, none of these affects accurately answers the questions posed by the project.

Africa is home to 3,000 different ethnic groups, which speak over 1,000 different languages. To which of these does my son belong? Swahili was not a language spoken in West Africa, the region from which most African slaves were taken, and I am not sure my son should wear the dress of Ashanti kings when the Ashanti probably sold his ancestors into slavery. This tincture of Africa is more representative of Pan-Africanism than it is a true reflection of my son's West African heritage. His first grade teacher will be hard pressed to pinpoint on a map the exact location of Pan-Africa.

It is not that I don't want my son to know or value the African part of him. My son is an American, however. Pretending otherwise simply reinforces the notion that the only portion of his African-American heritage in which he can feel pride is the African part. I do not accept as truth that our history in this country boils down to slavery and degradation, nor will I allow my son to assimilate the lie that his cultural pride must be rooted in a land thousands of miles away, in a people with whom he does not share language, values, or customs.

My American son can feel proud of the incredible strength and resilience demonstrated by those early African captives. The generations of craftsmen, artists, scholars, and statesmen, to whom they gave birth helped shape the culture of the greatest nation on earth. My son can look with dignity to the millions of anonymous American blacks who, despite being a generation removed from slavery, built banks and insurance companies, founded universities and thriving business districts. Black Americans were leaders of the civil rights movement, a movement that not only forced America to live up to its ideal but also influenced the struggle for human rights in every corner of the globe, including Africa.

My son doesn't need to reach back to the "motherland" for self-esteem. He can look to his own American family and find examples of courage and excellence in the persons of his parents, grandparents, aunts, and uncles. The story my son should tell is the one that begins on these shores.

Happily, the principal emphasized to me that the school was going to reinforce what the children learn in the home. Armed with this news, I started planning for the time when for the Heritage Board rolls around. My son will be dressed in cowboy boots and hat to reflect his father's Colorado upbringing and wearing a red, white, and blue bandanna around his neck. When the teacher calls on him to proclaim his heritage he can stand proudly and say, "I'm an American."

Defining Humanity

During a trip to Africa, I had the honor of being present as President Abdoulaye Wade of Senegal broke ground for the Museum of Black Civilizations. The museum forms one part of a triptych of major cultural projects being built in Senegal. The other elements are Remembrance Square and the Monument of African Renaissance. Together, the monuments envision an "Africa springing from the bowels of the earth to mark its presence in the face of the West." During the ceremony, President Wade spoke of the significance of building on African soil, a museum that rivaled those found in Europe and America. He also emphasized the importance of African American visitors to the monuments "coming back to their roots."

On that day, former Ambassador Andrew Young was also on the dais. Speaking extemporaneously, he stressed the bond between Africans and African Americans and then, calling forth the spirits of our slave ancestors, asked the American delegation to join him in singing two Negro spirituals. The sound of his voice rose above the hum of the crowd as he sang, "Freedom. Free-e-dom." While many members of our contingent joined in, I did not.

This, to me, was one of the fantastic ironies I witnessed during my trip. Despite being firmly in the Third World—economically and technologically—the Africans I encountered thought of themselves as being very much in the First World. In contrast, American blacks firmly ensconced in the First World tended to view themselves through a nineteenth-century lens. While President Wade spoke of an Africa springing forth and facing the West with power and majesty, Ambassador Young sang slave songs.

We seemed to be engaged in a curious dance in Africa. Every African speaker referred to the Americans as lost brothers and the Americans played the role of lost children come home to Africa. To my knowledge, the delicate subject of African complicity in the slave trade raised its ugly head only once and that was briefly. During one of the small discussion sessions in Nigeria, an American panelist made a reference to the sons and daughters of slaves. An African gentleman stood up and took exception to the imagery. "Others are free to call my parents what they wish," he stressed. "However, I would never refer to my own parents as 'slaves.'"

Americans in the audience raised their voices and pointed out that this was most likely because his ancestors were not slaves. One American educator even stood up and gave an impassioned speech about his slave grandmother.

While I have my doubts as to the veracity of his tale, it made for good theatre.

It was also wholly beside the point. The African gentleman was not disputing historical accuracy; he was suggesting that we begin to define ourselves in terms of our own humanity instead of by the inhumanity of others. Indeed, he was asking: How many generations must pass before we begin to see ourselves as free men?

My analysis generated some discussion among the other travelers. "This is part of our history," I was told over and over again. "We must embrace it in order to find ourselves." Fine. But if we are going to embrace it, let's embrace all of it. We can begin by admitting African complicity in the slave trade. Our captive ancestors were not enslaved in the Americas; they were enslaved in Africa. They were not *stolen* from Africa; they were *sold* from Africa. I am aware of no African ships sent searching for her lost children or any African delegations dispatched to ask for us back. I think there is a difference between recognizing what is historical fact and trading in the currency of victimization.

Don't misunderstand me. My journey to Africa was a poignant and extraordinary experience that I would not trade for the entire world. What I do suggest, however, is that we readjust our general vision of ourselves, especially as it relates to our relationship with Africa. It is, after all, not Africans who are building schools in American neighborhoods or sending doctors, educators and, more importantly, money to America.

When our plane landed in Abuja, Nigeria, we were greeted with the sight of Air Force One—a symbol of American power, prestige, and goodwill. As black Americans standing on African soil, we were similarly endowed. We were not Africans come home, but Americans come with commerce, technology, and benevolence. We journey to Africa not only with liberty; we come with power! Our vision of black America must begin to reflect that powerful self. Like the monuments President Wade is building in Senegal, our comportment as free men will bid us to sing songs of glory and limitless possibilities.

Roots, Rhythm, and Rocks

When I mentioned I was going to Africa at the barbershop, the entire shop fell silent. I felt as if I was in one of those old E.F. Hutton commercials: "When E.F. Hutton talks, everybody listens." All eyes were upon me. Smiles and nods of affirmation came my way, as if I was about to experience a right of passage reserved for a lucky minority of American blacks: I was visiting the Motherland and everyone in the shop was damn proud of me.

One patron exclaimed, "I just want to go once in my lifetime, just to smell the air and to smell the soil." He was not alone in this wish. Renee, one of my traveling companions, had promised to bring back some soil for her older sister. She waited to collect her souvenir until she got to Gorée Island, the port through which hundreds of thousands of African slaves departed the continent on their way to the new world. Unfortunately, she neglected to bring anything in which to carry the soil, so at the last moment she reached down and picked up a handful of rocks.

There is a romanticism associated with Africa that runs deep in the black community. I must confess, I have not been unaffected by it. I too have wondered about Africa, and my trip filled me with expectation. Like the barbershop customer who just wanted to smell the air, I wondered if my first breath in Africa would trigger some genetic memory. Would I be transported back to a time before the Middle Passage, my identity unalterably changed as a result of the trek?

For me, the bloom fell off the African rose fairly early. Maybe it was when a soldier armed with an AK-47 boarded our bus on the way to the hotel. Or maybe it was when I realized that Nigeria was so rife with corruption that cashing a traveler's check was a major ordeal. The romance was certainly gone once we drove through the countryside and witnessed poverty like I have never seen before. Even through rose-tinted glasses, there is an unavoidable ugliness in mud huts and shantytowns that have no running water, electricity, or indoor plumbing. There is nothing sentimental in children playing in the garbage and filth-covered streets.

Alas, my visit to Africa proved less of a homecoming than an affirmation of my Americanness. Sadly, this revelation will not elicit handshakes of approval from the guys at the barbershop.

On my trip, I accompanied a small delegation from Philadelphia's Zion Baptist Church to an elementary school in the heart of Abuja. The group was donating a computer to the school. As we exited the bus, we were escorted to the library by drums, dancing, singing, and lots of smiling children. The library was a cinderblock building with a dirt floor, no windows and, no shelves or books. I was humbled in the face of so much need. The public school my son attends not only has an extensive library of books, but also a full computer lab with enough brand new computers that no child has to share. This is in addition to the computer that sits in each and every classroom. Seeing the small amount others had made me realize how well off we are here in the States. I felt proud of American accomplishments. I felt blessed and lucky.

Later in the trip, I had an opportunity to meet socially with several Nigerians. Among my fellow travelers there was a tendency to speak of American blacks as if we were Africans living abroad, everyday Africans did not share this view. They saw us as Americans, first and always. Even to the Nigerians I met who, by and large, were educated in the West we were as American as, well, George Bush. On balance, I happened to agree with them.

That's not to say I did not feel the tug of Africa at all. I discovered that it is very difficult to be a black American and experience Africa purely as an American. Everywhere I looked, there were bits and pieces of myself. Sometimes, discovery was in something as subtle as a facial expression. Other times, there was recognition in more substantial gestures. Everywhere we went, we were greeted with singing, dancing, and drums. The young girls' movements brought to mind the black girls I went to high school with who always seemed to be snapping, popping, and bouncing down the hallways to some unheard music inside their heads. I saw myself in silly things like the Africans' rather elastic notion of time. Here in America, when someone is late, we say they are running on CPT or "Colored People's Time." I have little doubt this is a direct descendant of "African time," which seems to run about half an hour behind CPT.

But the pull was never so strong as when the delegation arrived in Dakar, Senegal. Due to time, only a handful of our party was able to make the trip to Gorée Island. I was one of the unlucky ones who stayed behind. Renee, however, shared her experience with me, describing the fortress in detail: "There is a doorway behind the steps that led outside to the cargo hold of the ships," she said. "The guide, speaking through an interpreter, told us that this was the 'door of no return.' Then he stopped himself and in a moment that seemed completely unscripted said, 'No, that's not right because YOU have come back.' That is when I got emotional."

As we sat on the plane waiting to return to America—to return home—Renee turned to me and placed one of the small rocks from Gorée Island in my hand. I felt its weight and my eyes filled with tears.

Black and White

In 1969, my family moved from the all black enclave of northeast Denver, Colorado, to an all white and predominately Jewish section in the southeast part of the city. If we were not the first black family in the area, we were certainly the second, and it was several years before there was a third. I imagine that like so many other adults pursuing the American dream, my parents moved seeking better and healthier opportunities for my three sisters and me. Our new house was bigger, the schools were better, and the nights were quiet—filled with the peace of falling snow in the winter and the whisper of water sprinklers and crickets in summer.

Of course, as the saying goes, "nothing in life is free." Growing up in southeast Denver meant I spent more time around white families and white children than I did with black. If someone were to describe my youth as growing up in a white world, they wouldn't be too far off. My parents attempted to keep us connected to the black community. We maintained old friendships with other black families and spent time in various organizations like Jack and Jill (begun as a black cultural and family organization in 1938, Jack and Jill developed a reputation of discrimination based on class and skin color). At best, my youth was integrated; at worst, I was the lone black spot in a sea of whiteness.

A photograph from my youth league football days sits on my mantle. The 1972 Holly Ridge Eagles were undefeated that year, 12-0. I played center on offense and on defense anchored a defensive line that gave up very few points. (Those were the days real boys played football! Youth league players were expected to play *both* ways!) The first time my son Connor saw the photo, he announced excitedly, "I know which boy is Daddy!" It wasn't difficult—I was the only black kid on the team. As a Cub Scout, I was the only black kid in my den, and quite honestly I don't remember any other black kids in my entire pack.

With few exceptions, my elementary school years were rather uncomplicated. One of the beautiful things about kids is that they are very accepting. I had lots of friends, went to birthday parties, played ball, learned to dance the hora and was relatively happy.

Many years later, my wife and I moved to our current neighborhood because it offered us a decent lifestyle. The public schools in the neighborhood are some of the best in the city and property values in the area are rising fast. I see the same happy-go-lucky attitude in my sons as I had as a boy and, like me they are being raised in an integrated environment. The children on our block are black, white, and Asian, plus several who are delightful interracial mixtures. The boys they play with at school are of similarly diverse backgrounds. The people who frequent our home are of varied races, economic, and educational backgrounds. My sons are very infrequently in an all-black environment.

As parents, our quandary is perhaps best summed up by a conversation I had with my wife one evening. She was concerned that her racial authenticity and the identities of our children might be compromised if we didn't *seek* out more black people to include in our circle of friends. I huffed and puffed and launched into a speech about true diversity and colorblind societies. Her confession, by the way, came as quite a shock, given the fact that we have many black friends. What I didn't tell her was that in spite of all my bluster, deep down I shared her concern even if for very different reasons.

One of the differences between my parents' move to southeast Denver and our move to West Hills, California, is that I don't believe my parents ever had a notion about giving their children a taste of their roots, so to speak. Coming of age in the 1940s and '50s, they were no doubt more focused on the awakening opportunity for them and their children. It probably never occurred to them that there might be a cost and that that duty might be demanded in the form of their children's racial identity. Balancing individualism while staying grounded in "black culture" in ever-increasing integrated environments is an issue many black families face as they gain economic affluence and political and cultural clout.

It would be terrific if the innocence of children lasted forever; if they never had to worry about being called names or fitting in; if they could go on about the business of growing into themselves and exploring the world without worry that they would be discriminated against because they are black or even worse, because they are not black enough.

I know, however, that the incorruptibility children enjoy will one day give way to the cruel realities of race, which hides like a viper beneath every innocent rock. For me, the last vestige of childhood innocence fell from my eyes when I entered junior high school. "Individuality" can be a very difficult place to be for a teenager, it is a no man's land, a desert between popularity and acceptance, somewhere off the coast of ostracized and ignored. To say I was "snake bit" would be an understatement.

I spent my seventh grade year in a private school—again, one of only a handful of black students. The next year, I returned to public school and for the first couple of days, I was in culture shock. Something had happened while I was away in private school. The kids with whom I had gone to elementary school, attended birthday parties, participated in cub scouts, and played in youth league sports had suddenly become "white." What's more, the kids I didn't know—the ones bussed in from across town—were "black," and there was no two ways about it.

A very clear and deep line had been drawn. For instance, every afternoon at lunch there was a football game played on the dirt field outside the lunchroom. The black boys were on one team and the white boys were on the other. The games were intense and serious business! I still remember the dust flying, the grunting, and the fierce looks on every face. These were not games during which the score was not kept because kids just want to have fun. You had better believe they kept score! Some days the black team would win and some days the white team would win, but always the next day they would rush through lunch to continue the battle. I found myself betwixt and between—my old friends suddenly distant because I was black, and the new kids antagonistic because I lived in "Honkyville" (as they called it) and talked like a white boy. I didn't play. I watched. But I wanted so badly to play. I had played youth league with or against almost all the guys on the white team. I knew I was as good as those boys, even better than some on both sides. But if I played, whose side would I be on?

It will come as no surprise that I hated junior high school. Thirty years after the fact, I can still feel the dull ache of waking up every morning knowing that in addition to my school work, I would spend the day having to defend myself against the verbal, emotional, and sometimes physical attacks from white kids who rejected me merely because of the color of my skin, and black kids who rejected me because my parents had not had the foresight to seek their approval before buying a house in a white neighborhood.

My wife and I are not the only parents trying to address the issue of identity for our children. My best friend keeps his rather high falutin' daughter grounded by taking her across town to his parents' Baptist church so she can be exposed to some black kids from "the 'hood."

Moreover, this concern doesn't apply to only black families. My son Connor's Korean friends go to Korean school on the weekends. There are Greek, Jewish, and Afro-centric schools as well. I am sure they all have weekend programs. For us, an Afro-centric school might be an option were it not for the rather sticky fact that we are not African. We are of African descent. Connor's friends have relatives in Korea and Korean is spoken in their home. Our children are several generations removed from Africa so the black church route seems a better option than Afro-centric school, though the church idea also seems to fall a bit short of a true cultural immersion.

Accept for the moment that there is something called African-American Culture. Taking into account the history of the black church and its impact on that culture, the fact remains that a black church in the San Fernando Valley was not good enough for my friend's daughter; he chooses to go across town for a particular "flavor" of blackness. So unlike our neighbors who go to Korean school, there is nothing particularly "cultural" about my buddy taking his daughter across town to church. He is simply choosing people for what they represent rather than for who they are. And let's be honest—when we segment by race, it is difficult not to begin segmenting by class. When we seek "black" friends, just any ol' black folk won't do. Whether upscale or down, it has to be the "right" kind of black folk. This is especially true in Hollywood.

I had this debate with the husband of a very successful black couple we know. He chastised me for not being proactive enough in pursuing black cultural enrichment for my children. He complained that his children didn't have any black friends to play with in their private schools and gated community. This of course left my wife and me a bit speechless since their kids played with our children and our children are black. He and his wife decided one solution was to join Jack and Jill.

While this seemed a dedicated effort, at best, I saw it as a rather halfhearted commitment. Rather like the story about the farm animals who decide to make a ham and egg sandwich, the chicken is dedicated while the pig is committed. If immersion in blackness was truly the necessity he claimed it to be, why not move out of their exclusive San Fernando Valley neighborhood to south central Los Angeles where their children would find more than enough black faces to play with? Of course the reason they play the role of the hen and not the pig is that he and his wife are as conscious about class as they are concerned about their children's cultural upbringing. In fact, after joining Jack and Jill, these friends grumbled that the working and middle-class members were taking over the local chapter so they transferred their membership to the Beverly Hills chapter. It just wouldn't do to have their children play with just "any" black child. How different is this from our friends who have determined that their daughter needs exposure to kids from the "hood" to keep her real?

The premeditation with regards to race is what disturbs me. As parents, my wife and I try to make certain our children are exposed to museums, the library, art, music, and of course, the theatre. We take special pains to open up their worlds, because we believe such exposure will lead to them being well-rounded, curious adults. One of our duties is also to try and make certain they are engaged with people with whom we share values, beliefs, and traditions. In fact, by this definition of cultural enrichment, we are on track and should relax. People who share our culture can be of any race or ethnicity. It is only when we deliberately add the specter of race that it becomes unseemly. When we begin to emphasize our racial identity (as opposed to our humanity), the people with whom we surround ourselves become the sum of their collective ethnic makeup. The lesson our children learn from this behavior is that the friendship of the Korean boy next door or the white boy down the block is of lesser value than the friendship with the black kid from across town solely because of the color of his skin. How often do we black folks accuse whites of doing a very similar thing?

I continue to ask myself if my wife's worry is necessary. She and I have a home adorned with African artifacts, paintings by black artists, and a library filled with books—many by and about black people. These pursuits are not calculated. We include them as a part of our daily lives without thinking about it. Without question, part of the reason we do so is because no matter how successful, educated, or integrated we become, we still seek out images and stories that reflect some sense of who we see when we look in the mirror. It is possible we also naturally gravitate towards those who reflect our notions of who we are not only in terms of what we see, but in what we believe. As our children's view of themselves sharpens and they discover the differences that exist between them and their friends, we will try to answer any questions they may have as honestly as we can. Beyond that, I am not certain how much more we can do.

The argument is really theoretical anyway, isn't it? I mean, for better or worse, we live in a society that is preoccupied with race. This nation began a love affair with race the moment the first black African slaves stepped onto the shores of the New World. This dalliance has since developed into a full-blown obsession and led to all sorts of creative ways to subjugate people's humanity in favor of their race. We check boxes on government forms, create social policy based on ratios of black and white, and hire diversity specialists to tell us what it all means. No matter how badly we want to define ourselves separately from the color of our skins, there is no place to hide from race (and race experts), no respite for those weary of carrying its weight. I truly hope that I live to see the day we defeat this obsession, when we will look beyond skin color and begin to view one another as the sum total of our hearts, minds, and characters.

So you see, I do not worry that by not submerging my children in black life they will miss out on some crucial element of themselves. I am not even fearful of white racism. I have every confidence that my sons can handle that. During my childhood, what white people thought of me was usually the least of my problems. What I fret over is my sons being rejected by other black people. I dread them feeling the loneliness of being on the outside. If at all possible, I would like to protect them from the inevitable shock of meeting people who look like them, but with whom they may have little in common other than the expectation that they share a common bond because of race.

There is little parents can do to prevent their children from being touched by the cruelty in this world. Just as they will scrape their knees or bump their heads, they will have their feelings hurt and their hearts broken. Quite frankly, if they are to grow into mature human beings, perhaps that is best. We can only hope we equip them with tough skins and barring that, the ability to get jobs with good mental health benefits. I have a sense that what my parents believed when they packed up our station wagon and moved me and my sisters to Southeast Denver was that if they succeeded in keeping us healthy, gave us values, morals, and the ability to think critically, they would have accomplished quite a bit. From there it would be a relatively short bridge to being honorable, compassionate, and contributing members of society—not black society, but the much broader society of man.